T0247582

THE PROOF

The
Proof

*Uses of Evidence in Law,
Politics, and Everything Else*

Frederick Schauer

THE BELKNAP PRESS OF
HARVARD UNIVERSITY PRESS

Cambridge, Massachusetts
London, England

2022

Library of Congress Cataloging-in-Publication Data

Names: Schauer, Frederick F., author.
Title: The proof : uses of evidence in law, politics, and everything else /
Frederick Schauer.
Description: Cambridge, Massachusetts : The Belknap Press of
Harvard University Press, 2022. | Includes index.
Identifiers: LCCN 2021044207 | ISBN 9780674251373 (cloth)
Subjects: LCSH: Evidence. | Evidence (Law) | Empiricism.
Classification: LCC BC173 .S33 2022 | DDC 121/.65—dc23/eng/20211102
LC record available at https://lccn.loc.gov/2021044207

For Quila, who makes me laugh,
and Bobbie, who makes me think

Contents

Preface

Recent developments give new urgency to questions about evidence. The rise of the internet, the widespread use of social media, the Covid-19 pandemic, the accelerating concern about climate change, the 2020 US presidential election, the assault on the United States Capitol on January 6, 2021, and the Trump administration generally are obvious examples of contemporary events in which controversies about facts and the evidence offered to prove them have taken center stage. More and more, the use and misuse of evidence has a prominence that would surprise anyone who thinks of evidence as a collection of often-silly lawyers' rules governing the conduct of trials. But evidence is not only about trials and not only about law. It is about science; it is about history; it is about psychology; and it is, above all, about human rationality. What do we know, and how do we know it? More specifically, what do we know about the facts of the world, and how do we know them?

No one book can hope to deal with the subject of evidence in its full depth and complexity. But we cannot ignore the increasing importance of questions of evidence in public policy and personal decision making. And it would be a mistake to neglect what scientists, philosophers, historians, psychologists, and even lawyers can teach us about the questions of evidence that dominate the headlines, pervade public policy, and guide the decisions we make in our everyday lives. In this book I draw on these and other perspectives to make sense of the evidentiary dimensions of human decision making. Although I hope that this book will contribute to academic discussions of evidence by philosophers, lawyers, psychologists, and others, my principal goal is to illuminate for nonacademics as well as academics the role of evidence in politics, policy, and the countless other domains in which facts matter—and where getting the facts right matters even more.

This book was first inspired by news outlets' increasing observations that this or that public official—usually, but not always, ex-president Trump (and his lawyers)—had made some statement or taken some action "without evidence." The phenomenon was highlighted in the aftermath of the 2020 presidential election, when, in a televised speech on November 5, 2020, Trump claimed to have won the election. Only because of widespread fraud, he insisted, could anyone possibly conclude otherwise. Shortly thereafter, Republican senator Pat Toomey of Pennsylvania observed that there was "no evidence anyone has shown me of any widespread corruption or fraud" and that the president had "made very, very serious allegations without any evidence to support it." Republican representative Adam Kinzinger of Illinois echoed that thought, insisting that "[if there are] legitimate concerns about fraud, present evidence and take it to court." And then longtime Trump ally Chris Christie, former Republican governor of New Jersey, complained bluntly, "Show us the evidence." By the eve of the second impeachment trial in February 2021, the question whether the Senate would hear live evidence was prominently discussed and debated, albeit with the expected but perhaps depressing conclusion that the Senate would make its decision without listening to any such evidence at all.

Although some politicians and news outlets are to be commended for noticing the importance of evidence, public and political discussions of evidence tend to employ a loose and superficial view of what evidence is, where it comes from, and how it should be evaluated. All too frequently, for example, commentators on a variety of issues conflate the lack of evidence with falsity—taking the absence of evidence as being equivalent to evidence that the statement is false. That looseness needs to be inspected. Similarly, public discourse often couples the idea of evidence with any of numerous qualifying and annoyingly confusing adjectives. Phrases such as "hard evidence," "direct evidence," "concrete evidence," "conclusive proof," and many others all suggest, misleadingly, that the lack of overwhelming proof beyond a reasonable doubt for some conclusion is sufficient to reject a conclusion for which there actually is at least some evidence. This common phenomenon also needs more rigorous examination, as does the role of experts—not only in using evidence, but also in reaching conclusions that then serve as evidence for the decisions of those who lack the requisite expertise. In response to current events, we often see officials and others display a dangerous lack of respect for the evidentiary conclusions of genuine experts, but these events also sometimes endow professionals, experts, and expert institutions with an authority that extends well beyond the scope of their expertise.

A further inspiration for this book is my own experience decades ago as a trial lawyer dealing with the law of evidence on a daily basis, followed by more than forty years of teaching, studying, and writing about the law of evidence. This book is not about law, but it draws on the law as a source of occasional wisdom and more than occasional illuminating examples.

It would be ironic if a book on evidence were to underestimate the importance of providing evidence for its assertions. Consequently I have made every effort to provide references for the analysis and arguments that follow. Extensive notes not only provide support for what is claimed in the text. They can also be useful for the reader who would like to go further or deeper than the flow of the text permits. And, most importantly, what will appear to some as excessive referencing is my way of recognizing that whatever insight may be found here builds on the previous insights of others. For this purpose, even if for no other, too many references are far preferable to too few.

The good news for most readers is that the notes providing these references and the occasional marginally useful digressions are endnotes and not footnotes. The text is designed to be read without referring to the notes—which spares the reader the distraction of going back and forth between text and notes, like watching a tennis match from midcourt—but a quick scan of the notes after reading each chapter may allow the interested reader to see if anything in the notes provides useful elaboration.

This book, like my previous books, has been written as a book, and not as a loosely stitched together and only lightly revised collection of previously published articles. Writing a book from scratch requires time and resources. I am grateful to the University of Virginia School of Law, and more specifically the University of Virginia School of Law Foundation and the generous alumni and friends who fund its efforts, for providing the support that has made this possible. And although this book does not collect previous publications, some of the ideas and topics examined here have emerged in my earlier writings and presentations. Accordingly, I am happy to express my gratitude for audience comments at Dartmouth College, Harvard University, the University of Chicago, Rutgers University, the University of Surrey, the University of California at Los Angeles, the University of Texas, the University of Virginia, Universidad Autónoma de México, the Max Planck Institute for Research on Collective Goods (Bonn), the Duck Conference on Social Cognition, the MacArthur Foundation Project on Law and Neuroscience, the Jurisprudence Discussion Group at the University of Oxford, the World Congress on Evidential Reasoning at Girona University, and the 28th (Lisbon) and 29th (Lucerne) World Congresses of the International Association for Philosophy of Law and Social Philosophy. Comments on these papers and presentations by Ron Allen,

Amalia Amaya, David Bernstein, Ruth Chang, Damiano Canale, David Enoch, Valentin Hartmann, Sarah Moss, Michael Pardo, Martin Rechenauer, and Levi Spectre have been particularly helpful. So too have less formal but just as valuable conversations with numerous colleagues at the University of Virginia School of Law, especially my colleague, friend, and office neighbor John Harrison. His repository of knowledge about what seems like everything is matched only by his genuine curiosity about the few things he does not know. Impressively detailed constructive comments from two anonymous reviewers for Harvard University Press have also been of great assistance in producing the final draft. And Barbara Spellman, herself a prominent teacher and scholar of the psychology and law of evidence, has saved me from numerous substantive errors as well as from my unfortunate tendency to think that no sentence has ever been hurt by making it longer.

THE PROOF

Chapter 1

As a Matter of Fact

ELVIS IS DEAD. Tabloid headlines to the contrary, Elvis Presley really did die on August 16, 1977, and he has remained dead ever since.

For purposes of this book, the importance of Elvis's death is that it is a fact. And as a fact, its existence is distinct from people's personal or policy preferences. As we will see, even issues as seemingly straightforward as the death of Elvis are not nearly so simple, but it is still crucial at the outset to distinguish the fact of Elvis's death from the preferences of many people that he be alive and perhaps even the preferences of some people that he be dead. Such preferences exist apart from the fact that Elvis is dead.[1]

For all its triviality, the Elvis example highlights three important distinctions about the place of facts both in public policy and in personal decision making. First is this distinction between the empirical reality and what some or many people prefer or wish that empirical reality to be. Disliking anchovies is a preference. Believing that anchovies do not exist is an empirical mistake. And taking a dislike for anchovies as a reason for denying their empirical existence is a fallacy.

The second important distinction is between actual empirical reality and what some or many people believe that empirical reality to be. It is a fact that vaccination does not cause autism, even though many people believe otherwise.[2] It is a fact that the earth is warming, although some people and political parties are committed to denying that fact. And recently, and to some extent still, major government policies regarding public expenditures, regulation of businesses, and personal freedom have turned on whether the rates of incidence, hospitalization, and death from Covid-19 are rising, falling, or disappearing. But these rates, whatever they are, are facts. So are conclusions about whether these rates are higher than, lower than, or the same as they were a month ago, at least assuming a common scale of measurement. Accordingly, when a president or anyone else asserts that the rate is lower than it was at some time in the past, we can check the assertion against the facts. And we can also investigate whether some drug—such as hydroxychloroquine, whose effectiveness was often and erroneously touted in the early days of the Covid-19 pandemic—is or is not effective against Covid-19 and whether it does or does not cause side effects of a certain type.[3] These are facts, and they exist apart from whatever may be asserted by a president, the Centers for Disease Control and Prevention, or anyone else.

The Covid-19 pandemic highlights the third important distinction—the distinction between (a) what the facts are and (b) what ought to be done about them. Describing the world and prescribing policy are two different things. The fact that the rate of Covid-19 infection is falling, whenever it is in fact falling, does not itself tell government whether to relax restrictions that are in place, nor does that fact tell people whether to start eating in restaurants, participating in live political rallies, or attending church services. And the fact that rates of infection are rising, whenever that is the fact, does not itself tell universities to cease holding in-person classes or advise individuals to stop taking public transportation. All these decisions about what to do are based on facts, but they require something more than facts alone. It is wise—indeed essential—to follow the science, and thus to follow the facts, in making policy and personal decisions. But following the facts and following the science means basing policies on actual facts—and not incorrect factual beliefs or "alternative facts." It means using rather than contradicting what the science tells us. But following the facts and following the science does not, and cannot, mean—despite occasional pronouncements by scientists and government officials to the contrary—that science and facts alone can determine what some policy ought to be. Making policy decisions requires using the facts to reach what are irreducibly normative and value-laden conclusions. And these policy decisions usually require trade-offs whose resolution cannot be determined solely by the facts. What to *do* about the facts is not solely a factual inquiry, just as what to do with science is not solely a scientific task. However important it is to follow the science and follow the facts, it is also important to recognize that science, and the facts, can only take us so far.

Facts alone cannot indicate what people or governments should do, but facts remain the foundation for sound public and personal decision making. In memorably remarking that people are entitled to their own opinions but not their own facts, the late senator Daniel Patrick Moynihan reminded us that making correct decisions depends on getting the facts right.[4] As he put it on the same occasion, "First, get your facts straight." And although Moynihan was talking largely about governmental policy decisions, questions of fact provide the basis for many of the more personal decisions we make on a daily basis. Some people, for example, refuse to patronize establishments owned by members of the Ku Klux Klan or by others who hold racist or other opinions that the potential customers abhor. But the initial question facing the potential customer is whether the proprietor is or is not a Klan member, or does or does not harbor racist views. These are questions of fact, and they are part of our everyday lives. It may (or may not) be a morally good thing to refuse to patronize a shop whose owner is a member of the Klan, but it is plainly not a morally good thing to refuse to patronize a shop on the belief that the owner is a Klan member if in fact he is not. Our lives and our decisions involve numerous choices that are driven by values—normative political or moral or personal preferences. But acting on those preferences requires making an initial judgment that is factual and not normative. Doing the right thing matters, but getting the facts right is the first step.

The forgoing is obvious to the point of banality, but highlighting the increasingly common questions about what *is*—and not just about what we or some government ought to *do*—is the appropriate entry into what this book is all about. More than two centuries ago the philosopher David Hume warned against the fallacy of deriving "ought" from "is"—of moving from the descriptive to the normative, or from what is to what ought to be—without recognizing that the move requires judgments that cannot be based on facts alone.[5] But it is no less a fallacy to attempt to derive "is" from "ought." It would be nice if there were world peace and nonfat bacon, but wishing won't make it so. This book is based on the premise that controversies about facts are important in their own right, but even more so because they provide the foundations for questions of personal choice and public policy. Leaving to others questions about how we or government ought to act, this book is an attempt to provide some insight into how we do—and, yes, *should*—confront the factual questions and controversies that are all around us.

The Idea of Evidence

It is one thing to say that there are facts; it is quite another to determine what those facts are. And once we shift from the idea of a fact to questions about figuring out what those facts are—to deciding which claims about the facts are true and which are false—we enter the realm of *evidence,* the subject of this book. Evidence is what provides the justification, or warrant, as philosophers are prone to put it, for believing that something is true—or false. Pieces of evidence are facts, but they are the facts that lead us to the conclusion that other facts do or do not exist. The fact that the skin tone and whites of someone's eyes appear yellowish is evidence for the further fact that the person has hepatitis.[6] The fact that the engine on my car is making a pinging sound is evidence for the fact that the gasoline in the tank is of too-low octane. The fact that Herman's fingerprints are on the door handle of Susan's stolen car is evidence for the fact that Herman was the thief. And the fact that then-nominee and now Supreme Court Justice Amy Coney Barrett signed an anti-abortion advertisement some years ago is evidence for what she then believed, which is in turn evidence for what she now believes, which is in turn evidence for how she might now decide.[7]

This book deals only indirectly with what makes a fact a fact, and with what makes a true statement true and a false one false. But it deals directly with how we *know* that statements or conclusions are true or false. In philosophical terminology, the focus of this book is on epistemology and not ontology (or metaphysics). In everyday language, the book is not about what is or what is not. It is about how we determine what is, and how we know what is not. It is about the assessment of factual truth and falsity in public policy, in public deliberation, and in personal decision making.

The Demand for Truth

Evidence is the prerequisite for judgments of truth (and falsity). But as we will see in Chapter 13, what psychologists call "motivated reasoning" is a large part of the evidentiary terrain. Unfortunately, how people perceive the facts of the world is often substantially influenced by their normative preferences about how they would like the world to be. It is a question of fact—in theory verifiable—whether the soccer ball crossed the line into the goal, but supporters of the team that kicked the ball will almost invariably believe in close cases that the ball crossed the line, just as supporters of the defending team will equally invariably believe that it did not. Although the location of President Barack Obama's birth is a question of fact, it comes as no surprise that his supporters believed (correctly) that he was born in Hawaii, just as many of his political opponents believed (falsely) that he was born in Kenya. And when asked who "won" a debate between candidates for president, a question whose answer is admittedly far less factual and far less verifiable, it is still noteworthy that both prospective voters and pundits reach conclusions that are expectedly and tediously consistent with their political preferences.[8] So too, as in recent events, with a closely contested election, where again many people's assessments of the facts align all too conveniently with their political and outcome preferences.[9]

Even more fundamentally, however, evidence matters only to those for whom truth matters. And it is not clear that truth matters to everyone, in the same contexts, and to the same degree. If we think of truth as something that can be preferred (or not), we can then understand a preference for truth as competing with preferences for happiness, affection, friendship, ambition, wealth, health, lack of stress, and a myriad of other emotions and conditions that may at times conflict with and be more important to some people than truth. Although Henry Clay was talking more about policy than fact when he observed in 1839 that he would rather be right than president, his observation has endured precisely because we recognize that many (most?) politicians would rather be president than right.[10] Being right is a preference for the truth, but not everyone has that preference, or has it in the same amount, or has it all the time.

If truth is a preference, then we should recognize that there can be a market for truth. Suppliers of truth, and thus suppliers of evidence, will understand that not everyone wants evidence, or wants it to the same degree. And if this conclusion seems uncomfortable, it is not uncomfortable for the publishers of supermarket tabloids. Many people enjoy reading about the travails of the rich and the famous, producing a demand for information—the more detailed the better—about these travails. And the suppliers of information about such travails, the supermarket tabloids prominently among them, seek to satisfy the demand, whether the travails actually exist or not. Obviously at some point stories about the misfortunes and missteps of the rich and famous will be so untethered from reality—from the evidence—that the demand will contract. And equally obviously, at some point the reality will be sufficiently uninteresting that the demand will again contract. The successful publishers of sensationalist supermarket tabloids are those who can best assess this relationship between the demand for sensationalism and the demand for truth. These financially successful tabloid publishers have located the optimal equilibrium—the point beyond which more truth (and thus more evidence) will decrease demand for the information, and the point beyond which less sensationalism will also decrease the demand for the information. Success in the tabloid business depends on discovering whatever balance between sensation and truth maximizes readership (and thus sales and advertising revenue).

This is not a book about the publishing industry, whether tabloid publishing or academic publishing or anything in between. But this detour into tabloid publishing illustrates that it is hardly obvious—as if recent events were not enough to make the point—that more truth (or more knowledge) is equally important for all people (or institutions) at all times and for all subjects. And it is equally not obvious that evidence, the basis for our knowledge and the basis for our judgments of truth and falsity, is equally important for all people at all times and for all subjects. This book is about evidence, and is premised on the idea that evidence is often important because truth is often important. But understanding the place of evidence in the world, in public policy, and in personal decision making requires understanding that evidence and truth are not the only values there are.

Of Facts and Opinions

It is a fact that Adolph Hitler had a mustache, and it is a fact that he was born in Braunau am Inn, Austria, on April 20, 1889. It is also a fact that he was evil, but this latter fact, unlike the others, is evaluative. It involves a judgment, or what some would call an "opinion." In this case the judgment is easy, and few people, or at least few with whom I associate, would dissent from characterizing Hitler as evil. Frequently, however, the evaluation is less obvious and more contested. And often, and even more of a problem, the evaluation hides within a seemingly factual statement. The philosopher Philippa Foot gave us the idea of a "thick ethical concept," labeled as such by the philosopher Bernard Williams.[11] A thick ethical concept is a description combining the factual with the evaluative, as we see in adjectives such as "rude" and "generous," nouns like "coward" and "hero," adverbs like "carelessly" and "carefully," and even verbs such as "hurry" and "loiter."

Offering thick descriptions, as with stating bald facts, requires evidence. And in that sense this book applies as much to evidence for (or against) the conclusion that Francesco Schettino, the captain of the ill-fated *Costa Concordia* who in 2012 abandoned ship, leaving thirty-two crew and passengers to die, was a "coward" as it does to the conclusion that the *Costa Concordia* sank.[12] But what counts as evidence for describing some behavior as "cowardly" requires reference to criteria for cowardice that are neither as obvious nor as uncontested as the criteria for describing an event as a "sinking."

Looking at some recent political events and controversies, for example, we can say that to accuse someone of being a member of the Communist Party USA, an actual organization with actual members, is to make an accusation that is, in most cases, either true or false. But accusing someone of being a small-c communist, or, more frequently these days, a socialist, is to make an accusation that presupposes a contested definition.[13] Much the same applies to asking someone if she believes that there is systemic racism in the United States, as Justice Barrett was asked in her confirmation hearings. The question presupposes a definition of the value-laden and contested idea of systemic racism, and as such is a question about a contested political issue masquerading as a purely factual question with a nonevaluative answer.[14]

This book is not about rhetorical or political strategy, nor is it a book of normative political or moral argument. It is a book about evidence and thus about how we know whether something or someone qualifies as a something under specified criteria or a specified definition. Was that a bird or a bat that was flying around the house at dusk? Is that 1930s car a Dodge or an Oldsmobile, and how do we know? But the focus of this book is not on what the definition of (or criteria for) some evaluative attribute—rudeness, cowardice, bravery, systemic racism—should be. Or, to put it another way, not all questions are questions about evidence, despite how common it is to try to make questions about values look as if they are questions only about bald facts and thus only about evidence.

A Few Words about the Law

This book is not about the law of evidence that governs trials in courts of law. Nor is the book about the law of evidence as it is portrayed on television and in the movies, which is emphatically not the same thing. Still, it would be a mistake to ignore the law in examining the way in which evidence is and should be treated in public policy and in everyday life. Although the law of evidence occasionally affects our nonlegal evidentiary determinations, that is rare. The greater importance for the law of evidence in nonlegal contexts comes from the fact that the legal system has been thinking about evidence somewhat systematically and often carefully for almost three centuries.[15] This is especially true of legal systems in common-law countries.[16] Sometimes the result of this process—the legal system being what it is—is that bad ideas become entrenched over time because of the legal system's occasional (or frequent) preference for long-standing poor ideas over novel good ones. Indeed, Justice Oliver Wendell Holmes once observed that it was "revolting" to be required to follow earlier conclusions—precedents—that "persist . . . for no better reasons than . . . so it was laid down in the time of Henry IV."[17] Nevertheless, sometimes a few hundred years of thinking by mostly intelligent and mostly thoughtful judges can generate sound ideas and valuable perspectives, especially when that thinking has taken place in the context of concrete cases involving real people with real problems. It would be a mistake to ignore this repository of accumulated wisdom, and I have no intention of doing that here, any more than I wish to ignore the accumulated, even if less systematic, wisdom about the nature and use of evidence that has been produced by natural and social scientists, historians, and philosophers, among others, as they wrestle with the problems of evidence.

A Preview

The organization of what follows is topical rather than strictly logical or serial. Each of the chapters deals with a particular topic within the broad subject of evidence, but the arrangement of the chapters does not follow a systematic progression of argument from beginning to end. Instead, the arguments within the chapters are somewhat independent of each other, making each chapter at least slightly self-standing. Occasional references back to earlier chapters—or announcements of what is to come in subsequent ones—will help tie things together, but the reader seeking an unwavering march from premises to conclusion will be disappointed. When Justice Holmes observed that he "care[d] nothing for the systems—only the insights," he made clear that, for him at least, interstitial and incremental observations and analyses may often be more valuable than grand comprehensive theories.[18] The topic of evidence is especially amenable to Holmes's approach, and the organization of this book is premised on the belief that there are interesting and important things to say about evidence, even if not everything that is interesting and important about evidence will fit together neatly, systematically, or logically.

That said, the chapters that follow can be divided into four main groups. Chapters 2, 3, and 4 are largely about the concept of evidence itself. Here we focus on questions of inference and relevance, examining evidence through the lens of the idea of probability, with particular attention to the way in which the burden of proof is an idea of pervasive importance and common confusion. Specifically, Chapter 2 deals with the basics of inference and relevance, looking at how evidence bears (or does not bear) on the conclusions of fact that interest us. Chapter 3 focuses on the idea of the burden of proof, exploring how, in a world of uncertainty, we determine whether and when the inconclusive indications of the evidence are or are not good enough for one or another purposes. And Chapter 4 aims to connect these notions of inference and burden of proof to ideas of probability and statistics, recognizing that questions of "how much," even if not expressed in numbers, lie at the heart of many important questions about evidence.

Much that we know, we learn from what others tell us. The image of Sherlock Holmes in his deerstalker hat searching with an outsized magnifying class for physical clues is endearing and enduring, but much of the evidence we use comes not from what we see or find but from the statements—the *testimony*—of others. Chapters 5, 6, 7, and 8 focus on testimony in this broad sense. Chapter 5, making some use of philosophers' recent interest in testimony, will explore the very idea of testimony, and look at when and why we should reach a conclusion just because of what someone has told us. But not everything that people say is accurate. Chapter 6 focuses on the devices lawyers and others have long used to attempt to assess the accuracy of what others say. Does it help that someone has sworn to something, whether in court or elsewhere? Does cross-examination help in testing testimony, whether eyewitness or otherwise, for truthfulness or accuracy? And how can we *calibrate* testimony once we recognize that knowing something about the testifier will help to assess the evidentiary value of the testifier's testimony? Indeed, as we increasingly confront a world in which political figures and others say things—often intentionally—that are untrue, we often wish we had a good way of separating liars from truth-tellers. Chapter 7 looks specifically at lie detection, tracing both the development of lie-detection technology and the legal system's persistent skepticism about the value of such technology—and its surprising lack of skepticism about the ability of judges and jurors to determine who is telling the truth and who is not. Not all sources of error, however, are the product of lies. Honest people make mistakes, even mistakes about things they believe they have seen with their own eyes and heard with their own ears. And they even make mistakes about things they themselves have experienced. Chapter 8 takes up the problem of honest mistakes in perception and recall, a problem that lies at the heart of our ability to treat the statements of others as evidence for what they have reported.

As recent controversies have prominently and often tragically demonstrated, expertise matters. It is sometimes said that we live in an "age of experts."[19] We live also, however, in an age of dueling experts, in which the conclusions of experts are marshaled on multiple sides, and in which the notion of "expert opinion" as a collective consensus judgment of multiple experts is elusive. Chapters 9, 10, and 11 explore the world of experts and expertise, concentrating on the ways in which expertise can be used, evaluated, and, at times, challenged. Chapter 9 examines the conclusions of science and scientists as evidence, using recent controversies about vaccination, climate change, Covid-19, and genetically modified organisms (GMOs) to probe the role of scientific experts in the evidentiary determinations that are increasingly central to public policy. Chapter 10, the chapter that is connected most explicitly with law and the courts, deals with current debates over the forensic techniques that have long dominated police-focused television as much as they have the activities of real courts and real detectives. But are these techniques—fingerprints, voiceprints, tire marks, ballistic tests, handwriting identification, and much more—as reliable as they are purported to be? And how do we know? Chapter 11 then leaves the world of science but not the world of expertise, looking at many of the factual conclusions—in realms as diverse as wine-tasting, art authentication, and the writing of history—that rely heavily, often for better but sometimes for worse, on the conclusions of experts, even though the methods that produce those conclusions are distant from anything that looks like science.

Chapters 12 and 13 deal with topics not so neatly grouped together but connected with what we can learn from contemporary research in cognitive and social psychology. Chapter 12 takes up the question of character and the related question of the relevance of past acts to current determinations. Does character matter? Does what people are like help us to determine what they have done? Can knowing what people have done in the past tell us what they might do in the future or what they might have done in the present? And Chapter 13 addresses the phenomenon of motivated reasoning. In evaluating evidence, do evaluators see what they want to see? How much of what we *want* to be the case influences—or distorts—our judgments of what *is* the case?

As the foregoing should make clear, the topic of evidence implicates a wide variety of only loosely connected subtopics. But there is nothing wrong with that. Sometimes, even if not always, the whole really is greater than the sum of its parts, and perhaps the vast subject of evidence is good evidence of that phenomenon. Still, there are a few themes that run erratically through what is to follow. First is that probabilities matter. A lot. The very idea of evidence is about inductive reasoning and thus about probability, even if not necessarily with numbers attached; and the probabilistic nature of evidence will be a recurring focus. Second, evidence comes in degrees. Sometimes, and seemingly more often recently than in the past, people reach conclusions and make statements for which there is, literally, no evidence. But although "no evidence" really is no evidence, weak evidence is still evidence. And weak evidence often has its uses. Repeatedly, the question of how much evidence there is will be as important as the question whether there is any evidence at all. The third running theme follows from the second. Whether what evidence we have, or how much evidence we have, is good enough depends on what we are to do with it, and on the consequences of the evidence we have being sufficient or insufficient to support some conclusion. In other words, questions of "Compared to what?" and "For what?" will be a recurring motif. All of this, I hope, will become much clearer as the book proceeds.

Chapter 2

Zebras, Horses, and the Nature of Inference

ACCORDING TO A WELL-KNOWN adage attributed to Dr. Theodore Woodward of the University of Maryland School of Medicine in the 1940s, "When you hear hoofbeats, think horses, not zebras." The point is that horses are far more common than zebras, at least if we are not in a zoo or on the African savanna. And although it is remotely possible that the sound of hoofbeats was created by a thundering herd of zebras escaping from a nearby animal sanctuary, the more likely explanation is that the sound of hoofbeats was created by horses. Probabilities matter. And because probabilities matter, the most likely explanation of some phenomenon is, tautologically, most likely correct.

Of course, going with the most likely explanation doesn't get you a Nobel Prize, or even a minute on the evening news.[1] And that is why "man bites dog" persists as a hackneyed staple of the world of journalism. Dog bites man is common, expected, and hardly newsworthy. Man bites dog, being unexpected, makes news.

And it is not just daily journalism. A popular book of a few years ago—*The Black Swan*—celebrated the identification and investigation of unusual and unexpected events.[2] And properly so, at least for some purposes. After all, no one would remember the Wright brothers if Wilbur had said, "Orville, why don't we just take the train?" And when George and Ira Gershwin's hit song from *Porgy and Bess* in 1935 observed that "it ain't necessarily so," it reminded us that probabilities are just that—probabilities—and that sometimes the less probable is more significant though less likely.

Recognizing and pursuing the unusual and unexpected is indeed valuable for discovery, creativity, and innovation.[3] But it is also often valuable to expect the expected—to recognize that probabilities are important, and to rely on them. Absent further information, horses and not zebras is the winning bet.

The relevance of "horses, not zebras" for evidence is that evidence is about inference, and inference is about probability. Deductive inference (All birds have backbones; this parrot is a bird; therefore, this parrot has a backbone) is central to rational thinking. But so too is inductive inference, where the conclusion does not necessarily follow from the premises. For example, "Most Italian citizens speak Italian; this woman is an Italian citizen; therefore, she *probably* speaks Italian." Such inductive inference, where the conclusion might not hold in some particular instance—is at the core of the idea of evidence. Someone being an Italian citizen is very strong evidence that they speak Italian, but this inductive inference might turn out to be mistaken in a particular case. Some Italian citizens do not speak Italian. They might come from the German-speaking region in northern Italy, or they might speak only the local dialect of Sicily or Venice, or they might be in a family of relatively recent immigrants whose family language is the language of their country of origin. This possibility of error, however, does not mean that someone's Italian citizenship is not evidence that they speak Italian. Believing that someone who is an Italian citizen speaks Italian is a very good inductive inference, and what makes it a good inference is not that the inference is a logical necessity, as it would be in the case of deduction, but instead that it is based on evidence.

Consider the process of medical diagnosis, the domain in which "horses, not zebras" was developed and is often still used to help educate medical students about diagnostic techniques. The physician sees a symptom, or collection of symptoms, and infers (or hypothesizes) from her knowledge the likely cause of those symptoms. More precisely, she might not only see symptoms, but also learn various aspects of her patient's lifestyle and medical history, which, when combined with symptoms, we can call "indications." The physician might, for example, know that a patient who is displaying a ring-shaped redness on his skin and complaining of chills and headaches happens to enjoy hiking in short pants and camping in the wilderness. Based on these indications, the physician infers that the patient has Lyme disease, and she does so because these indications have previously usually been associated with Lyme disease.[4] It is possible, of course, that these indications—these pieces of evidence—were caused by something other than Lyme disease. Some bruises might produce ring-shaped redness, and so might ringworm, and there are many possible causes of headaches and chills, even for hikers and campers who wear short pants. Such a confluence of indications being caused by something other than Lyme disease is hardly impossible, but it would be rare—and thus, given these indications, inferring ringworm as the cause of the circular redness, say, would be analogous to inferring zebras, with the role of horses being played by Lyme disease. Faced with the indications just described, a competent physician will ordinarily, in the absence of contrary evidence, diagnose and treat for Lyme disease. And she does so not because it is certain that Lyme disease is the correct diagnosis, but, instead, on the basis of probabilities.[5] Ian Hacking describes inductive inferences, such as this one, as necessarily "risky," because, unlike logical deduction, they could be wrong in a particular case.[6] There is a chance, even if small, that the sounds are coming from zebras, no matter how strong the probabilistic inference in favor of horses, and thus inferring that the sound of hoofbeats is coming from horses involves some risk of error. But that risk is inherent in inductive reasoning, and thus inherent in reaching conclusions on the basis of evidence.

The example of Lyme disease calls to mind the relatively recent movement in health care going by the name "evidence-based medicine." The label is initially alarming. Is there really some other kind of medicine, as the label suggests? And are there are real doctors who practice something other than evidence-based medicine? Evidence-free medicine, perhaps? That would be disturbing. Who would want a doctor who didn't care about evidence?

But let us look closely at the evidence-based medicine movement. It originated at McMaster University in Canada, took hold with gusto in the United Kingdom, and now has a worldwide presence.[7] And a movement it is, attracting a coterie of devoted adherents and occasionally provoking angry objectors.[8] At the heart of the movement is the claim, as influentially put, that evidence-based medicine is the "conscientious, explicit, and judicious use of current best evidence in making decisions about the care of individual patients."[9] By itself, it is hard to see what could be controversial about that. But as we dig deeper into the debates that evidence-based medicine has inspired, it becomes clear that the controversy stems from evidence-based medicine's originally explicit and still implicit claim that the evidence that comes from randomized clinical trials is at the top of an evidentiary hierarchy. For true believers in evidence-based medicine, the more qualitative and sometimes impressionistic evidence that comes from the knowledge, skills, and experiences of actual patient-treating physicians ranks lower on the evidentiary hierarchy and is therefore less valuable. But if you were one of these experienced physicians, having long based your diagnoses and treatments largely on the lessons you had gleaned from years of practice and hundreds or thousands of patients, you would take the evidential hierarchy of the evidence-based medicine movement as threatening. Or insulting. Or both.

This is hardly the place to referee the dispute between the enthusiasts of evidence-based medicine and their detractors. But the dispute highlights the idea that there can be better and worse evidence, with the measure of better or worse being the strength of the inference to some conclusion that comes from the evidence, and the measure of that strength being the probability that the conclusion is correct. As the evidence-based medicine movement reminds us, that probability is typically greatest when the evidence comes from carefully designed and conducted controlled experiments or other methods of equivalent rigor. A good example comes from the research on the effectiveness of the various Covid-19 vaccines. Prominently, the initial tests of the Moderna mRNA-1273 Covid-19 vaccine employed a study using more than thirty thousand subjects, half of whom were given the vaccine and the otherwise identical other half being given a placebo. It turned out that there were ninety-five infections in the placebo group and five in the treatment group, the differential producing the widely publicized conclusion of a 94.5 percent effectiveness rate.[10] And this is just the kind of study that the evidence-based medicine movement puts on the top rung of its evidentiary ladder.

But now consider a hypothetical clinician who has treated thirty-eight unvaccinated patients who have already tested positive for Covid-19. She gives all of them the standard treatment for conventional influenza—Tamiflu, for example—and almost all of them suffer no further progression of the disease and need no hospitalization, although two of them do get worse and must be hospitalized. When she then sees her thirty-ninth unvaccinated Covid-19 patient, she infers from these past experiences that Tamiflu is effective in alleviating Covid-19 symptoms and prescribes and treats accordingly.

It is possible that the same percentage of patients that this clinician has treated would have gotten better even without the Tamiflu, and nothing in this experience-based inference about Tamiflu's effectiveness definitively rules out this possibility. It is also possible that a different treatment would have produced an even higher recovery rate, whether measured by speed of recovery or percentage of those treated who recover. And because a well-designed and well-executed controlled trial would have been configured for the very purpose of ruling out these and other non-Tamiflu causes of the patients' recovery, the probability of the conclusion drawn from the controlled trial being correct can be expected to be higher than the probability of the conclusion drawn from the experience-based inference being correct. Because reasoning from evidence is inductive, and because inductive reasoning is probabilistic, evidential reasoning is necessarily probabilistic, and higher probabilities are the measure of better evidence.

It is important to acknowledge, however, that there is nothing about an experiment or a laboratory that makes experiment-based evidence *necessarily* stronger than other types of evidence. The probability of a conclusion that comes from a controlled experiment is often but not invariably higher than the probability of conclusions derived from other types of evidence. There are badly designed experiments and sloppy laboratories. There are also experience-based qualitative inferences that come from a very large number of instances—data points—over a long period of time, and that qualitatively attempt to isolate causes and exclude alternatives in a manner that is less precise but theoretically similar to what scientists do with controlled laboratory experiments.[11] And so although the disputes about evidence-based medicine teach us that there can better or worse evidence, and remind us that the probability of some conclusion being correct is the measure of the strength of the evidence, the disputes also remind us that qualitative or experience-based evidence is still evidence. By using the phrase "evidence-based," the evidence-based medicine movement implicitly wants us to believe that medicine that does not rely heavily on published and peer-reviewed laboratory or other experimental evidence is not using evidence at all.[12]

But that is a mistake. There are other kinds of evidence, and sometimes those other kinds of evidence will produce inferences with a high probability of being correct. The question is not one of evidence versus no evidence, but of better versus worse evidence. The controlled experiment or randomized clinical trial evaluated in a peer-review process is the gold standard of scientific inference.[13] But other forms of information and the inferences flowing from them can often be probably correct, even highly so. And thus these other forms of information can count as evidence, and frequently as very good evidence.

To observe that weaker evidence is still evidence is not to deny that there are people, far too often political and public figures, who make assertions that really are supported by no evidence at all. There is, for example, no evidence whatsoever that a mysterious figure called "Q" has infiltrated the Democratic Party with his brigade of Satanist pedophiles.[14] To describe the claims that such a conspiracy exists as being made "without evidence" is entirely correct. And so is the conclusion that the charges of electoral fraud in the 2020 presidential election were made without evidence, as United States federal district judge Matthew W. Brann angrily concluded on November 21, 2020.[15] But these are extreme cases. Far more commonly, accusations that some statement has been made, or conclusion reached, without evidence are accusations that the available evidence is not the right kind of evidence or is not enough evidence to satisfy the accuser. Sometimes the available evidence for some conclusion is so flimsy that it ought to be treated as completely nonexistent, even if that is not technically correct. But often the charge of "no evidence" reflects the mistaken belief that anything other than concrete physical or documentary evidence, or perhaps the testimony of eyewitnesses, does not count as evidence at all. The lesson of this section, one to which we will repeatedly return, is that this is simply not true. All sorts of things are evidence, including physical objects—prototypically the murder weapon or the body— written documents, personal observation, past experience, and what others have told us. And although so-called circumstantial evidence is commonly dismissed or denigrated on television or by lawyers for guilty defendants, the legal system properly recognizes that circumstantial evidence can be very good evidence, and so do the rest of us in countless ways and on countless occasions.[16] Indeed, even the lack of evidence can be evidence.[17] So although we should interrogate the conclusions of officials and others about the evidence supporting their conclusions, we should also interrogate those who desire a different kind of evidence than has been provided for some conclusion, with the aim of trying to determine exactly what kind of evidence would satisfy them.

Complaints about the absence of evidence are as often a mask for complaints about the quantity of evidence as they are about the type of evidence. We will return in Chapter 3 to quasi-quantitative issues of just how much evidence, and of what strength, we need for some conclusion or some action. Now, however, it is important to highlight the significant differences, not only between "no evidence" and "not the *kind* of evidence that will satisfy me," but also between "no evidence" and "not *enough* evidence to satisfy me." And just as the former complaint is often couched—and clouded—in phrases such as "no hard evidence," "no concrete evidence," and "no direct evidence," the latter is often expressed as "no conclusive evidence," "no definitive evidence," or even "no proof."[18] In slightly different ways, each of these contains the (perhaps unintended) negative inference that the complainer wishes to denigrate at least some evidence in support of the conclusion. Sometimes the denigration is justified, and sometimes not, but such phrases should put the listener or reader on alert that there is indeed some evidence, rather than there being no evidence at all.

What Is Evidence For?

Now let us step back. What is the *point* of evidence? When put that way, it becomes clear that we do not value evidence for its own sake. Evidence is not like happiness, pleasure, or dignity, which are plausibly considered ends and not means. Rather, evidence is a means to some end, and the end is some factual conclusion of interest to us. And embedded in the factual conclusions that interest us is the assumption that those conclusions are valuable because and when they are *true*. So we can say, conventionally, that evidence is valuable insofar as it leads to truth—or, more precisely, to a belief in things that are true.

With respect to any piece of alleged evidence, therefore, we need to ask two questions. The second is what the evidence is trying to establish, but the first is whether the alleged evidence is itself true. If yellowish-appearing skin is evidence of hepatitis, the first question is whether the skin is actually yellowish. If automobile engine "pinging" is evidence of too-low-octane fuel, first we must determine whether there is in fact a pinging sound. Similarly, and where the truth of the evidence is less obvious, if we are to count as evidence a witness's observation of the defendant lingering in the vicinity of the bank shortly before the bank that the defendant is charged with robbing was robbed, we first need to know whether it really was the defendant that the witness saw. And if in an election it is evidence of voter suppression that the percentage of voter turnout in a largely African American neighborhood is much lower than the percentage in a largely white neighborhood, we must determine initially whether the percentage of voter turnout in the African American neighborhood actually is lower than in the white neighborhood.

Obviously, these "first step" foundations are themselves the product of evidence. That the defendant was lingering near the bank at a certain time is a conclusion from the evidence supplied by a witness's perception, and the perception is evidence of what the witness claims to have observed. But although the witness lingering near the bank is a conclusion *from* evidence, it is also evidence *for* some other conclusion—that the defendant robbed the bank. Leaving the courtroom aside, we can say, for example, that a decrease in the size of the Arctic ice cap is evidence of global warming, but believing that the Arctic ice cap is shrinking is itself based on evidence. And voter turnout being lower in the African American neighborhood than in the white neighborhood is both evidence for the conclusion of voter suppression and itself a conclusion based on the evidence that tells us about voter turnout. All evidence, or at least almost all evidence, has this double aspect. It is typically based on other evidence, and it is also evidence of something else. When we say that an item of evidence is evidence of something, therefore, we need to bear in mind that the item of evidence is also the something that another piece of evidence is the evidence of.

Evidence is thus typically based on other evidence.[19] More importantly, something is evidence insofar as it leads to some conclusion or leads to confirming or disconfirming some hypothesis. But "leads to" is too vague. What precisely is the relationship between some fact and some conclusion that makes the fact evidence, rather than just a free-floating piece of data? What does it mean to say that evidence *supports* some conclusion? Or that it is evidence *against* some conclusion? Exploring these questions is our next task.

The Preachings of Reverend Bayes

The Reverend Thomas Bayes (1702–1761) was a Presbyterian minister who, we presume, spent part of his Sundays preaching the Gospel. But no one remembers him for his sermons. Reverend Bayes is remembered instead for his contributions to the theory of probability and statistics, one of which was Bayes' theorem, whose formal symbolic version need not detain us here. But nonformally, Bayes' theorem is about the way in which additional evidence incrementally (or serially) contributes to some conclusion. Under a Bayesian approach to inference, people start with some estimate of the probability of some conclusion. This, in Bayesian terminology, is the *prior probability*—or simply, as often expressed these days by those who employ Bayesian methods, the *prior*.

And then when people are given additional evidence, they consider each new piece of evidence and readjust the probability of their earlier conclusion upward or downward to produce the *posterior probability.*

Consider the prominent and occasionally still-contested example of Thomas Jefferson and Sally Hemings. If we were to have asked, some decades ago, what the probability was that Thomas Jefferson impregnated an enslaved person in his household named Sally Hemings, we would have produced or assumed a probability, not zero, based on the facts that Sally Hemings was an enslaved person in Jefferson's household, that male slave owners in Virginia and elsewhere often had (almost always coercive) sexual relations with their slaves, and that sexual relations sometimes produce pregnancy. These background facts would have produced a prior probability that Jefferson impregnated Hemings and was the father of one or more of her children. And when evidence of various writings of Hemings's children describing Jefferson as their father came to light, this evidence raised the probability that Jefferson had impregnated Hemings. A number of census records consistent with Jefferson being the father of Hemings's children then raised the probability even further. And then DNA testing confirmed that some of Jefferson's descendants had some of the same DNA as some of Hemings's descendants, which raised the probability even more. What started out as a low-probability possibility ended up as a high-probability conclusion with the successive addition of subsequent incremental items of evidence. And, indeed, the Thomas Jefferson Foundation, devoted to studying and preserving all things Jefferson, explicitly relied on Bayes' Theorem in explaining how they reached the conclusion that Jefferson was the father of Hemings's children.[20]

Under a Bayesian approach, the test of whether some fact is evidence of some other fact, or of some conclusion, is incremental. If a fact increases the likelihood of some conclusion above what it would be without that fact, then that fact is evidence for the conclusion. And if a fact decreases the likelihood of some conclusion, then it is evidence against the conclusion. But if the fact neither increases nor decreases what we believed before—the prior probability—than the fact is simply not evidence at all, or at least not evidence for or against the conclusion in question, although it might be evidence for or against some other conclusion.[21]

This incremental definition of evidence is widely accepted by many of those who practice or philosophize about science.[22] Unfortunately, this sound conception of evidence is occasionally replaced by a less-sound conception of evidence sometimes found in the philosophical literature—that evidence is only *potential evidence* unless the conclusion it supports is true.[23] But this is a mistake, or, more charitably, an odd and nonstandard understanding of the definitions of evidence and of the word "evidence." Take the example (the basis of the 2020 movie *The Last Vermeer*) of the famous art forger Han van Meegeren.[24] In 1937 the Boijmans Museum in Rotterdam purchased through multiple highly respected art dealers a painting alleged to be a Vermeer entitled *Christ at Emmaus*. The painting not only was alleged to be a genuine Vermeer but also appeared to be such to the highly knowledgeable dealers and to the equally highly knowledgeable experts at the museum. The museum arranged to have the authentication tests available at the time conducted, and discovered that the kind of paint appeared authentic for the time and for Vermeer, that the canvas was correct for the dates and the artist, that the wood on which the canvas was stretched was similarly correct, that the brush strokes on the painting appeared to be Vermeer's style and could only have been created by the kind of brush that Vermeer used, and that the widely respected Vermeer expert Abraham Bredius had declared the painting to be an authentic Vermeer. Ten years later it was discovered that the painting was a forgery, which we know because the forger confessed.[25] The question then is whether, knowing now that the painting is a forgery, we should consider the paint, the canvas, the wood, the brushstrokes, and the expert opinion as having been evidence, or instead as mere potential evidence whose status as evidence disappeared upon discovery of the forgery.

It may seem as if the question whether these various bits and pieces of information are evidence or only potential evidence is a mere definitional dispute, but it is more than that. The view that these items of information are only potential evidence assumes that we finally evaluate the status of some fact as evidence—or not—only after having discovered the fact of the matter. But that is not how we evaluate evidence, and it is not why we use or care about evidence. We care about evidence because of what it can tell us about some aspect of the world about which we are uncertain. Questions of religious faith aside, when we are certain of some feature of the world, we do not need evidence for it, although we might have *had* evidence for it. Only when we are uncertain do we need and use evidence, and that is the point at which we must determine whether something is or is not evidence. Determining whether something is evidence occurs during and part of the process of discovering the truth, and not after we know what the truth is. And that is why it is important to understand evidence as that which makes some uncertain conclusion more (or less) certain as a result of having the evidence, a status that does not evaporate after we have determined the truth.

The foregoing "anti-potential" account, which accepts that there can be actual evidence in favor of a hypothesis that turns out to be false, parallels the legal system, which also treats as relevant evidence, and therefore as evidence, any fact that makes some conclusion more or less probable than it was before considering that fact. As put in Rule 401 of *Federal Rules of Evidence,* replicated almost verbatim in the state evidence law of most states, "Evidence is relevant if . . . it has any tendency to make a [material] fact more or less probable than it would be without the evidence." And it is hardly surprising that the law would see things this way. In a trial, rulings about the admissibility of evidence take place individually and incrementally, and obviously prior to a final verdict. The judge must therefore decide whether something counts as evidence under circumstances of uncertainty about the truth of what the evidence is presented as evidence for, and uncertainty about what the other items of evidence will be. Accordingly, the law has little use for the idea of potential evidence. And outside the courtroom, neither do we.

In the broadest sense, therefore, the very idea of evidence is compatible with the teachings of Reverend Bayes. Although there are debates about whether people are good or bad at probabilistic reasoning, we should not impose too stringent a test on the very idea of Bayesianism.[26] In this book I sample only selectively from the Bayesian buffet, and thus focus only on the way in which the valuable core of a Bayesian approach lies in its incrementalism—the way in which Reverend Bayes counsels us to think of evidence as making some conclusion, or some other fact, more probable than we thought it was prior to learning of this evidence. Perhaps this approach would work best if people could assign numerical probabilities to their prior and posterior probabilities, but whether people can or should is a side issue. As long as we can accept that "beliefs come in degrees"—and thus, as long as we can accept that "more than," "less than," "stronger than," and "weaker than," for example, are sensible and realistic ways of thinking, including ways of thinking about evidence—questions about whether we can accurately quantify such ideas are peripheral.[27] When we ask if something is evidence for some conclusion, or when we criticize someone for not offering evidence, all we are doing is seeing if something "moves the needle." In the context of the debates about evidence that followed former president Trump's November 5 post-election speech alleging widespread electoral fraud, for example, we should ask ourselves what we estimated the likelihood of such fraud to be prior to that speech. And those from both parties who criticized the president for offering no evidence are best understood as saying that nothing the president said caused them to adjust what their previous (and probably very small) assessment of the likelihood of fraud had been.

We can imagine, counterfactually, a speech that would indeed have provided such evidence. Suppose Trump had said, "I have been informed by four state attorneys general, three of them Democrats, that they are now investigating allegations of electoral fraud." Even though such an assertion might have been made with no further information, and even though the assertion is based on the assertions of others—hearsay—the assertion itself might still have counted as evidence, assuming (again, possibly counterfactually) that the president would not have said it had he not been prepared to provide more detail. But with this and no other assumption in place, the very statement would plausibly have counted as evidence, even absent any documents, even absent more detail, and even absent any results of the alleged investigations. We will explore further in Chapter 5 the ways in which simple unverified statements—as with the hypothetical presidential statement just described—can be evidence, but for now the point is only that something being evidence is compatible with it being weak evidence, and compatible as well with there being other evidence inclining in the opposite direction.

And Back to the Zebras

The "horses, not zebras" adage emphasizes the fundamentally probabilistic nature of inferences about evidence. Even when people say they saw something with their own eyes—zebras, for example—what they are really saying is that they have had these perceptual experiences in the past, and that they have been reinforced in the belief that those perceptual experiences have a particular origin. When people first see something with a certain size and shape and pattern of stripes, they are told that these perceptions indicate zebras. And every time they again have these perceptions, they are reinforced in the belief that the perceptions are perceptions of zebras. So the next time they have the same perceptions, they identify the source as a zebra, even though it remains (remotely) possible that what they think they are perceiving as a zebra is actually two boys together wearing a zebra suit.

This may be too philosophically abstruse, but common inferences display the same pattern. I wake up in the morning, see a wet street outside, and infer that it has been raining. Although it is possible that the wet street has been produced by a street cleaning vehicle, my neighbor's malfunctioning sprinkler system, or a truck with a leaking load of fuel oil, I infer that it rained because rain is what usually produces wet streets. This inference is based on a generalization, the kind of generalization that is an essential feature of our reasoning processes.[28]

Generalizations are typically—maybe necessarily—what makes an item of alleged evidence *relevant*.[29] What makes a car being a Volvo relevant to its reliability is the generalization that Volvos are more reliable than cars in general. If the rate of reliability for Volvos were the same as that for all cars, the proper response to the fact that a car is a Volvo, if reliability is the question, is "So what?" Similarly, the Internal Revenue Service uses something called the Discriminant Income Function to determine whether a taxpayer's return should be audited. And the characteristics that the IRS considers "relevant"—those that make it more likely than otherwise that an audit will change the return—are, in the words of the IRS, based on "past experience with similar returns."[30] Thus, the IRS's alleged conclusion (the Discriminant Income Function being, not surprisingly, highly secret) that being a drywall contractor is evidence, even if slight by itself, of under-reported income is based on the experience-based generalization that drywall contractors are more likely than all taxpayers in general to under-report income, and more likely even than the category of all self-employed taxpayers.[31]

Thus, an alleged piece of evidence becomes *relevant* by being a member of a class of pieces of evidence whose presence makes it more likely than it would be without the evidence that some conclusion is either true or false. "Volvos are reliable" is a generalization. This car being a Volvo is relevant to its reliability precisely and only because of that generalization.

Is Evidence Holistic?

The focus of this chapter has been on what might count as evidence. But there is a difference between what counts as evidence and what we do with the evidence that counts. Under a pure Bayesian approach, what we do when it is time to reach a conclusion is to see where we are at that stage in the process of Bayesian updating. Each incremental item of evidence adjusts the probabilities, and at the moment of decision— whether a decision about facts or a decision about what to do—we make a decision based on the probabilities at that point.

This seems straightforward, but this Bayesian understanding of how to reach a decision based on multiple items of evidence has long been subject to what appears to be a challenge. One version of the challenge is based on an idea, attributed initially to the philosopher Gilbert Harman and developed most influentially by the late philosopher Peter Lipton, that goes by the name of "inference to the best explanation."[32] According to this approach, the evidence for (or against) some conclusion is not evaluated incrementally. Instead, all of the evidence is evaluated holistically, with the aim of seeing which explanation best explains all of the evidence that we have to that point obtained.[33]

Philosophers have vigorously debated the relative virtues of Bayesianism versus inference to the best explanation.[34] And so have those who study how judges and jurors evaluate evidence in courts of law.[35] But rather than wade into those debates, I want to suggest that determining which of these allegedly competing accounts of our evidentiary practices is more descriptively accurate or normatively desirable is a function not only of what we want to know, and not only of why we want to know it, but also, most importantly, of *when* we want to know it.

One question with which we are frequently confronted is whether some fact is or is not evidence at all. We are not, or at least not yet, seeking to explain a phenomenon, but merely trying to identify which facts will help us find some explanation. At this stage we do need a hypothesis, or a question to which we seek an answer, even if only tentatively. Observation—fact-finding—is necessarily theory-laden. To make relevant observations regarding a hypothesis, we cannot just go out into the world and accumulate random facts. We need some reason for accumulating these facts rather than those, a reason that will guide us in deciding which facts we care about and which are irrelevant—or, in legal terminology, which are immaterial. If we are seeking an explanation of why the Arctic ice cap is shrinking, the fact that Alicante is a Spanish city on the Mediterranean Sea—and that is certainly a fact—is of no interest. But once we have some question we wish to answer or a hypothesis we wish to test, we then look for those facts that seem useful in answering the question or testing the hypothesis. And for this task—the task of determining if something is evidence at all—the incremental approach commonly associated with a Bayesian perspective seems most helpful. If we already have a hypothesis and are interested in whether that hypothesis is true or false, then a Bayesian evaluation of whether some fact makes that hypothesis more likely true (or more likely false) than we thought it was prior to considering this fact seems most consistent with both how we do, and how we should, approach the issue. When we are evaluating facts to see, initially, whether they will count as evidence at all, we typically look at those facts one at a time, and thus evaluate those facts individually and incrementally to see if they make the hypothesis more or less likely, or if they help us answer the question at hand.

Once we have all of the evidence in hand, however, it would seem odd to then make an incremental evaluation of all of it. Yes, we could pick apart each of the items in our basket of evidentiary facts and evaluate them incrementally in good Bayesian fashion. But doing so seems both artificial as well as being unfaithful, as an empirical matter, to our actual reasoning methods. Instead, at the point of decision, when all of the evidence is in, we do look at all of the evidence more holistically. In doing so, we often simply recognize that various individual pieces of evidence may, as Susan Haack argues, combine to produce a conclusion that is greater than the mere sum of its parts.[36] Looking at pieces of evidence in this mutually reinforcing way is not necessarily a search for an overarching explanation or story, but it is compatible with attempting to determine, on the basis of all of the evidence, which conclusion, or which hypothesis, best explains all of this evidence. This latter version of evidentiary holism is inference to the best explanation, and it may capture most faithfully how people actually do reason about hypotheses once all of the evidence is in, and how people ought to reason most rationally at this stage of the process. Indeed, Lipton frames his defense of inference to the best explanation by emphasizing that we start "with the evidence available to us."[37] In doing so, he makes it clear that his account is a post-collection explanation of what we do with the evidence we have collected, and neither a pre-collection account of how we collected that evidence in the first place nor a pre-decision account of how we sorted the evidence we have collected into the relevant and the nonrelevant.

Inference to the best explanation not only is compatible with Bayesian incrementalism in this way but also is compatible with a probabilistic approach. And here the key word is not so much "explanation" as it is "best." If our goal is to evaluate competing plausible explanations to see which is more likely true, and thus to see which among the accounts before us best fits the evidence we have, then probabilities, even if not numerical, remain strongly in the picture. One explanation may be almost certainly true based on what we know about the world, whereas another may be possible but less likely. Escaping zebras is one explanation for the sound of hoofbeats, and my neighbor's horses is another. But when we say that the former is more likely than the latter, we are engaging in a probabilistic assessment, a probabilistic assessment that is implicit in most searches for the "best" explanation. The idea of inference to the best explanation is often a sound way of understanding what we do with the evidence we have in hand. But what we do with that evidence remains irreducibly probabilistic, at least if our principal goal is the discovery of truth and the rejection of error.

Chapter 3

The Burden of Proof

IT WOULD BE NICE if our evidence-based conclusions were as airtight as our mathematical ones. Two plus two equals four. The square root of 81 is 9. Period. But in the world of fact, and thus in the world of evidence, things are never so clear. Like it or not, uncertainty in factual judgments is an inevitable aspect of the human condition. Did Lee Harvey Oswald act alone in killing President Kennedy? Did Jack Ruby act alone in killing Lee Harvey Oswald? Do any ivory-billed woodpeckers still exist? Did the abominable snowman (Bigfoot, or Yeti) ever exist? What about the Loch Ness Monster? Did William Shakespeare write the plays now attributed to William Shakespeare? Was Thomas Jefferson the father of Sally Hemings's children? Did former President Clinton sexually assault Juanita Broadrick, which she alleges and he denies? Did former President Trump sexually assault E. Jean Carroll, which she alleges and he denies?

When faced with such factual uncertainty, we typically have at least some evidence for one conclusion or the other, and maybe for both, but rarely do we have no evidence at all. And so we should not confuse uncertainty with *ignorance*.[1] Webster's Dictionary tells us that to be ignorant is to be "destitute of knowledge," but we are rarely destitute when it comes to reaching conclusions about facts. Typically we have evidence—even if that evidence is weak, and even if there is some evidence both for and against some conclusion. Which is to say that having evidence is entirely compatible with being uncertain. Moreover, to know something is compatible with the possibility that what we know, or at least what we think we know, might be wrong. Philosophers typically equate knowledge with a degree of certainty that excludes the possibility of error, but ordinary people and even ordinary academics recognize that it is no mistake to believe that what we think of as knowledge may exist short of no-doubt-about-it absolute certainty.[2] And what is important here is that below some level of complete certainty and above the level of complete ignorance we find most of the important issues of evidence. The question then is how much certainty is enough, and how much uncertainty we can tolerate. And this leads, naturally, to the question of how much evidence is enough, and for what.

The legal system's approach to factual uncertainty is familiar. In a criminal case, the prosecution will prevail, and the defendant will be convicted, if the jury (or judge, if there is no jury) finds the defendant guilty "beyond a reasonable doubt." Defendants will often be acquitted, and properly so, even when there is evidence against them, sometimes considerable evidence, as long as the strength of that evidence does not clear the "beyond a reasonable doubt" threshold.

There are debates about whether belief beyond a reasonable doubt, or any degree of belief, can (or should) be translated into numerical probabilities. In the context of actual trials, some number of courts, judges, and commentators argue that providing a numerical probabilistic equivalent to "belief beyond a reasonable doubt" would add a needed degree of clarification to an otherwise intolerably vague idea. Other courts, judges, and commentators, however, take the opposite view, insisting that adding numbers would lend an aura of false precision to an inevitably (and perhaps desirably) imprecise concept.[3] For now, and consistent with the probabilist sympathies that pervade this book, let us assume that attaching rough percentages to the various burdens of proof can add useful refinement.[4] When those who share this view assess, whether experimentally or otherwise, what "beyond a reasonable doubt" means in numbers, they widely conclude that to believe something beyond a reasonable doubt is to have a degree of belief (philosophers call it a "credence") that is equivalent to between 90 percent and 99 percent certainty.[5] "Beyond a reasonable doubt" does not mean convinced to an absolute certainty, as with my absolute certainty that I now have five fingers on my right hand, and judges commonly instruct jurors about the difference. But most analyses conclude that beyond a reasonable doubt means at least 90 percent certain.[6]

By contrast, the typical standard of proof in a civil—not criminal—case is the "preponderance of the evidence," or, as often put in British Commonwealth countries, the "balance of probabilities." So when Jack sues Jill for negligently causing him to fall and injure his head, he needs only prove his case by a preponderance of the evidence—that it is more likely than not, even if only barely more likely than not, that Jill was negligent and that her negligence caused the damage and the injuries.[7]

The difference in practice between proof beyond a reasonable doubt and proof by a preponderance of the evidence was vividly illustrated two and a half decades ago in the legal proceedings against former football star O. J. Simpson. Simpson was charged with having murdered his wife, Nicole Brown Simpson, as well as a waiter named Ron Goldman, who had dropped off at Brown Simpson's house a pair of sunglasses she had forgotten at the restaurant where Goldman worked. The 1995 California criminal trial was front-page worldwide news for months.[8] And at the conclusion of the trial, the jury decided that the prosecution had not proved beyond a reasonable doubt that Simpson was the murderer, and he was acquitted. But shortly thereafter, several members of Goldman's and Brown Simpson's families sued Simpson in a civil action for the tort of wrongful death. That being a civil case, the plaintiffs needed to prove their case only by a preponderance of the evidence. And in 1997 the jury so found, concluding that Simpson was civilly liable to Goldman's family for the amount, including punitive damages, of $33.5 million dollars.[9] To be sure, the first trial (criminal) and second trial (civil) took place in different courts with different judges and different juries, and neither the evidence nor the trial strategy was precisely the same in both trials. Still, both cases were based on much the same evidence of the same acts.[10] That being so, the divergent results of the two trials illuminate the fact that evidence sufficient to prove something by a preponderance of the evidence might be insufficient to prove the very same thing beyond a reasonable doubt. And thus a failure to convict under a beyond a reasonable doubt standard is often far from a vindication, the claims of acquitted celebrity defendants notwithstanding. The Scottish verdict of "not proven" makes this non-vindication clear, and thus ameliorates some of the problem, but that is a verdict not generally available outside of Scotland.[11]

Jumping from past to present, we see a similar scenario play out in the controversy about the standard of proof to be applied in college and university disciplinary proceedings against students and faculty accused of sexual assault and faculty and administrators accused of sexual harassment. Under Title IX of the Civil Rights Act of 1964, as repeatedly amended, sex discrimination in colleges and universities, typically but not necessarily discrimination against women, is declared unlawful and thus a violation of federal law.[12] Moreover, colleges and universities are considered in violation of Title IX if they do not provide adequate procedures by which students who are victims of sexual assault can obtain redress and initiate procedures leading to punishment of the perpetrators by the college or university. That is all familiar, and in many respects straightforward. But now things get more complicated.

In 2011 the Office for Civil Rights for the US Department of Education sent out a "Dear Colleague" letter informing colleges and universities that they would be considered in violation of Title IX if they employed a standard of proof any higher than preponderance of the evidence in disciplinary proceedings against those accused of sexual violence.[13] In other words, it was more or less a federal requirement that educational institutions covered by Title IX initiate disciplinary proceedings against those accused of sexual violence—typically students accused by other students—and that in those proceedings the accused student must be found guilty if it was determined more likely than not (the preponderance of the evidence) that the accused student committed the acts with which he (typically) was charged.

In 2017, however, with the Trump administration having succeeded the Obama administration, the same office rescinded its 2011 letter and replaced it with an interim guide instructing colleges and universities that they were free to use either preponderance of the evidence or a higher "clear and convincing" standard. And many colleges and universities accepted this invitation to raise the burden of proof necessary for a finding of culpability from preponderance of the evidence to a more demanding "clear and convincing" standard.

The standard of proof by clear and convincing evidence does not exist in the criminal law but is found in various other parts of the law. It is, for example, the standard of proof commonly applicable to involuntary civil commitment of mentally ill individuals who are thought to be dangerous to themselves or others.[14] It is also the standard prescribed by the US Supreme Court for libel actions brought by public officials or public figures, who can recover against a publication for libel only if they can prove by clear and convincing evidence not only that what was said about them was false, but also that the publisher knew it was false at the time of publication.[15] And although attaching a numerical probability to "clear and convincing" might be especially difficult, the "clear and convincing" standard plainly establishes a heavier burden than "preponderance of the evidence" and a lighter one than "proof beyond a reasonable doubt." We might imagine "clear and convincing" as something in the vicinity of a .75 likelihood.

The difference between the two standards of proof may seem minor. And the whole issue may seem even more minor still. Major policy disputes are rarely about competing conceptions of the burden of proof. But this controversy was an exception. Fearing that the revised policy would encourage colleges and universities to use the higher "clear and convincing" standard, victim advocacy groups objected, arguing that the higher standard would allow some actual perpetrators to escape punishment—perpetrators who could be found responsible by a preponderance of the evidence, but not by clear and convincing evidence, especially given the frequency with which there is no physical evidence and no witnesses other than the accuser and the accused.

In response, others were worried about fairness to the accused and the "due process" rights of those charged with very serious offenses. These individuals and groups argued that under a mere preponderance of the evidence standard, a large number of accused students and faculty would be found culpable even though they had not done what they were accused of doing. A preponderance of the evidence standard is, after all, compatible with a 49 percent chance of mistake.

Both groups were right. Compared to a "preponderance of the evidence" standard, the higher "clear and convincing" standard increases the number of likely guilty individuals who are likely to escape punishment. And compared to a "clear and convincing" standard, the lower "preponderance of the evidence" standard increases the likely number of individuals who are not guilty but who will nevertheless wind up being punished for something that they probably did not do.

In the context of the criminal law, this trade-off has been known for centuries. Famously, William Blackstone observed in the eighteenth century that "it is better that ten guilty persons escape, than that one innocent suffer."[16] Others have used various other ratios to make much the same point.[17] And that point is that any imperfect decision procedure will make mistakes. By traditional stipulation, statisticians often label the error considered to be more serious the Type I error and the less serious one the Type II error. More commonly, people talk about false positives and false negatives. In the context of punishment, the false positive is punishing the person who should not be punished—typically someone who is innocent. And the false negative is not punishing someone who should be punished—the guilty. As Blackstone recognized, the traditional view under the common law is that personal liberty (or life) is so important that we should treat the false positives as more serious errors than the false negatives, and design our procedures, systems, and institutions accordingly.

Even in the criminal law, however, this preference for avoiding the false positive is not absolute. If it were, we could minimize the incidence of false positives—false punishments—by punishing no one. But we do not do that, and thus we accept that the system will make mistakes of both kinds. Accordingly, society recognizes that even a Blackstone-type skewed ratio will accept some false positives—mistaken convictions—as the price to be paid for punishing many who are in fact guilty.[18]

In the criminal law, numerous procedural mechanisms and protections embody the Blackstonian perspective. Most relevant here is the requirement that the prosecution prove its case beyond a reasonable doubt—meaning that, as the Simpson scenario illustrates, some number of actually guilty people will likely escape the grasp of the criminal law. Other aspects of American criminal procedure similarly embody the preference for false acquittals over false convictions, if false verdicts there must be. The prohibition on double jeopardy in the Fifth Amendment and the requirement of a unanimous jury verdict to convict are among the most prominent examples.[19]

So let us return to college and university disciplinary proceedings based on allegations of rape or other forms of sexual assault. Advocates for the "clear and convincing" standard, some of whom we suspect would prefer a "beyond a reasonable doubt" standard, insist that a judgment of guilt in a campus disciplinary proceeding on a charge of sexual assault, even though it might not produce imprisonment, has such disastrous future consequences for anyone found guilty that a finding of guilt in a campus disciplinary proceeding ought to be treated as equivalent to a criminal conviction, and thus subject to the same burden of proof as that of the criminal law. And advocates for the lower "preponderance of the evidence" approach emphasize the difference between university sanctions, even expulsion, and actual criminal penalties. The sanctions available to the criminal law, after all, include imprisonment, which universities cannot impose, loss of the right to vote, which still exists in some states for those convicted of felonies but is again beyond the power of a college or university to prescribe, and an official criminal record, which is more difficult to conceal than a university disciplinary sanction.

The case for the lower standard, akin to that of a civil lawsuit, is typically supported by one of two arguments, one not very good and the other somewhat stronger. The weaker argument is that a preponderance of the evidence standard minimizes the number of errors—that is, maximizes accuracy. That is true, but the reason the maximizing-accuracy argument did not persuade Blackstone and countless others is that in most contexts we are interested not only in the raw numbers of mistakes or non-mistakes. We know, and Blackstone knew, that some mistakes are different from others, and any rational decision theory will take this into account in settling on the appropriate procedures.

The stronger argument acknowledges that not all errors are equivalent, and that the goal cannot simply be minimizing the number of errors. Nonetheless, especially in the context of disciplinary proceedings at educational institutions, this argument insists that the consequences—the costs—of an erroneous acquittal may be even greater than in the criminal law. For Blackstone and others of his time, the consequence of an error of letting a guilty person escape punishment was primarily the absence of deserved retribution. It is possible that Blackstone was not especially worried about the further crimes a wrongfully acquitted person would commit, or about the people who would be injured by those further crimes, even though there is an argument that he should have been, and that those who adopt the Blackstonian perspective should be now.[20] But if we return to the present and to the university campus, those who advocate a lower burden of proof argue that students and faculty who are erroneously acquitted in a nonpublic proceeding, especially of sexual assault, will continue to be a danger to others in the same closed and relatively small community. As a result, so the argument goes, the harms of erroneous acquittal include not only the harms of failing to punish but also the actual or potential harms to other members of the very community that the university is committed to protecting. And this, it is said, is as much of a harm as a false conviction, meaning that we should treat the false negatives as being as problematic as the false positives, with the implication that the "balanced" preponderance of the evidence standard should be employed.

This is not the place to resolve this debate, especially because it will likely turn out that the debate will be "resolved" for the time being in favor the lower burden of proof as a result of the 2020 presidential election and the change in staffing of the Department of Education that the change of administration has produced.[21] This political reality does not resolve the underlying normative issue, but that is not the goal here. Rather, the point is to illustrate that the normative issue is not only about evidence. It is about a conflict of substantive values, a conflict being played out on the field of evidence and procedure. Setting a burden of proof is inescapably an exercise in determining what, substantively, is at stake—and this determination is not based on principles of evidence alone.

Understanding the relationship between burdens of proof and substantive values also helps us avoid the common error of assuming that the legal system's burden-of-proof standards should be used by other fact-determining or adjudicative systems. The Title IX controversy is one example, but there are many others. Consider the question of the burden of proof in the US Senate when it conducts an impeachment trial.[22] The prevailing view is that the senators should each determine their own burden of proof, but this hardly answers the question of how those senators, individually, should make that decision. And that requires consideration of the purposes of an impeachment trial, the consequences of the different verdicts, and the consequences should those verdicts be mistaken—purposes and consequences that are different from those in an ordinary criminal trial. In the most recent trial of an impeachment, however, the February 2021 trial of the second impeachment of Donald Trump, the proceedings conjoined the issue of the factual burden of proof with the constitutional question whether a president (or other official) could be impeached and tried after leaving office, with the conjunction of the two issues making it especially difficult to discern what burden of proof the individual senators actually employed.

Determining the burden of proof is pervasive even beyond these prominent instances. What burden of proof, for example, should be used by an adjudicative body dealing with accusations such as cheating in an international bridge tournament. In a case well known to bridge players, visual evidence supporting the accusation was inconclusive, and an analysis of the bids and plays made by the accused players, and offered in opposing the accusation, also was inconclusive. What standard should the adjudicative body then use?[23] Moving even further away from anything resembling a trial in a courtroom, what burden of proof should teachers apply when determining a question of classroom misconduct that was not observed by the teacher? What of the professor who suspects a student of plagiarism? What of the purchaser of a used car who suspects that the dealer rolled back the odometer? And what of the baseball umpire or basketball referee who is simply unsure of the right call, but nevertheless must decide at that very moment?

Or, these days, what of the official who views the video and is empowered to reverse the call of the on-field or on-court umpire or referee?[24] In these instances, and countless more, a burden of proof is at work, even if it is not made explicit. And setting the burden of proof, even if not done explicitly or deliberately, will unavoidably be based on an assessment of the purpose of the decision, the deeper values implicated, and the consequences that flow from mistakes. And for this, more than two hundred years later, Blackstone is still our guide.

Slightly Guilty?

In the 1967 movie *The Producers*, a satirical comedy directed by Mel Brooks about a theatrical scam, the criminal trial of the scammers is punctuated by a jury verdict of "incredibly guilty." As should be obvious, "incredibly guilty" is not one of the options given to real jurors in real trials. Still, the idea of being "incredibly guilty" suggests that there can be degrees of guilt. And if there can be degrees of guilt, and if someone can be incredibly guilty, or very guilty, or really, really guilty, then what lies at the opposite end of the spectrum? One possibility is that perhaps there are people who are only slightly guilty.

The Producers is not clear about whether "incredibly guilty" is a reference to the measure of the wrongness of the act for which the defendants were convicted, or instead to the strength of the evidence of their guilt. The two are different. There can be overwhelming evidence of minor offenses such as littering and jaywalking and weak evidence of major crimes such as serial murder and rape. But here I focus on the latter—the weight or strength of the evidence—in thinking about the possibility of being slightly guilty.

In the previous section we contrasted the legal system's idea of proof by a preponderance of the evidence with its higher standards of proof, in particular proof by clear and convincing evidence and proof beyond a reasonable doubt. But that is only half the story. Literally. If these standards describe a range of something like 50.1 percent to 99.9 percent, then, putting aside an exact 50-50 probability, what about the range from zero (or perhaps 1 percent) to something like 49.9 percent? If we are thinking about punishment in the strict sense, then ignoring the lower range makes perfect sense. After all, if there is a 40 percent chance that someone committed some crime, then there is a 60 percent chance that they did not, and we should not imprison someone who more likely than not did not do what we would be sending them to prison for.

But not so fast. What if we are 40 percent sure that the babysitter is a pedophile? Or 20 percent. Or 10 percent? What if the evidence shows that there is a 10 percent chance that the heart surgeon who is to operate on me tomorrow cheated in medical school, perhaps by having someone take their surgery exam for them? And should observant Jews patronize the kosher butcher when they believe there is a 20 percent probability that the butcher uses pork in the allegedly kosher frankfurters?

All these possibilities follow naturally from recognizing the uncertainty of evidence and the variability of burdens of proof. And these possibilities follow as well from the way in which, as Blackstone stressed, allocating the burden of proof, and by how much, flows from an assessment of the comparative harm and frequency of the errors of false positives and false negatives. So suppose we flip the Blackstonian ratio. What if we were to believe that letting guilty people go free is really horrible or extremely dangerous, and thus that it is better that ten innocents be punished than that one guilty person escape? This scenario seems bizarre, but it turns out to represent a plausible approach in various non-courtroom contexts. Consider the physician deciding whether to prescribe antibiotics for the patient who, to reprise an earlier example, has a ring-shaped redness on his arm and reports that he has been raking leaves. The patient displays no other indications—evidence—of Lyme disease. On this evidence, it is possible that the patient has Lyme disease, but it is probable that he does not. Still, failure to treat for Lyme disease at an early stage can have serious consequences. True, overprescribing antibiotics is, over time, good for neither the patient nor society, because overprescribing can foster the emergence of antibiotic-resistant strains of bacteria. Also, some people have allergic reactions to antibiotics. Nevertheless, the negative consequences of prescribing unneeded antibiotics in the normal case are minimal, whereas the consequences of not prescribing needed antibiotics are potentially catastrophic. Under such circumstances, it may be better that ten "innocent" cases (no Lyme disease) be "punished" (treated) than that one guilty case (actual Lyme disease) "escape" treatment. Accordingly, it may be wise to treat for a disease even when the evidence suggests that its likelihood is far below 50 percent.

The same holds true when the idea of punishment is less metaphorical than in the Lyme disease example. For instance, under what circumstances should we deprive people of their liberty—a serious consequence, even if it is not described as punishment—because of a risk that those people will endanger the health and safety of others? The obvious example in the era of Covid-19 is a quarantine for people with contagious conditions. Under English law, for instance, it is permissible to restrict the liberty of people with cholera, leprosy, malaria, meningitis, tuberculosis, and typhoid fever.[25] The practice of quarantining people with contagious conditions raises the issue of when, if ever, it is justifiable to deprive people of their liberty when their probability of having a disease or condition that can cause great harm is less than .50. Blackstone is relevant but tells only part of the story. Is it better that ten people with a highly contagious serious disease—meningitis, for example—be allowed to mingle in the population of a large city than that one person without the disease be restricted? The answer is not so clear.[26]

There are similar issues with whether and when to release on parole persons whose risk of recidivism is small but still greater than that for the population at large. If an adult male has been convicted of a sexual offense against a child, incarcerated, and then released, the likelihood of a further sexual offense, depending on the nature of the offense and the relevant time period, is somewhere between 6 and 35 percent.[27] And although these and other data are contested, it is clear that the recidivism rate is well below .50 and well above the rate of offending for a randomly selected adult male member of the population. The question, therefore, is what burden of proof should be used in assessing the evidence that someone is likely to reoffend.

Far more controversial and far less defensible are questions such as how much evidence is necessary to impose restrictions on the unconvicted members of a class whose occupation or avocation—priest, scout leader, Little League coach—statistically indicates a likelihood of offending greater than for the population at large, but far less than .50? This is not the place to answer that question, for it will depend on the degree of the danger, the probability of the danger, the stringency of the restriction, and the moral issues surrounding questions of when people must be treated as individuals and when they can be treated as members of a class.[28] But although class-based detention is plainly unacceptable on moral and legal grounds, other forms of restriction present the same question. Being watched carefully, for example, is far less restrictive than being incarcerated, but it is not nothing. And because even being watched carefully is not nothing, a potential "watcher" is implicitly adopting a burden of proof in evaluating the strength of the class-based evidence in determining whether to treat a member of that class differently from how any other person would be treated. Of course this example presents a situation in which the moral stakes are very high. But consider the opposite end of the moral scale: Should the purchaser of a notoriously unreliable make of car—a Yugo, for example, or a Trabant—engage in more careful inspection of that car than for an equivalently aged Volvo or Subaru? If the answer is yes, then the history of the make of car has influenced the burden of proof, with a twelve-year-old Yugo being presumed unreliable and a twelve-year-old Subaru being presumed reliable.

The tendentious example of child molestation is merely one aspect of a large and rich literature on preventive justice and preventive detention.[29] Depending on the consequences of non-prevention, and thus on the costs of mistaken non-preventions, and also of course depending on the costs of mistaken preventions, there may be circumstances in which the burden of proof to justify an act of prevention may differ from the burdens of proof normally applied in both criminal and civil trials. This is not the place to describe the literature on preventive justice and what that literature says about burdens of proof, and it is certainly not the place to take a position in the debates about preventive justice. But even the lower-temperature issue of whether to buy a used Yugo or a used Subaru suggests that supposing that the range of burdens of proof has a lower bound of preponderance of the evidence—.51—may be too quick. At least in some contexts, slightly guilty may be guilty enough.

Better to Be Safe than Sorry?
The Precautionary Principle

We often use evidence to reach a conclusion about a specific fact or specific act. Did Susan rob the First National Bank on September 30? Was Thomas Jefferson the biological father of Sally Hemings's son Eston Hemings? How many votes for president did Donald Trump and Joe Biden each receive in the state of Michigan in November 2020? But just as often we use evidence to support or challenge a general hypothesis about a category of acts or events, or about some larger phenomenon. What do we (or scientists) mean when we or they say that cigarette smoking causes cancer? And what is the evidence for that conclusion? Are Volvos reliable? How do we know? Does the use of aerosol cans damage the ozone layer? Does damage to the ozone layer cause climate change? Does the increased legal availability of guns increase the incidence of unlawful gun-produced harm?[30] Does playing violent interactive video games cause an increase in the aggressive tendencies of teenage males who play those games? Does an increase in aggressive tendencies among teenage males cause teenage males to commit actual acts of violence?[31] Does the amount of alcohol consumption that would ordinarily have no detrimental effects create problems when consumed by pregnant women?

In seeking to answer such questions, we typically rely on evidence that leads to probabilistic assessments, including probabilistic assessments of causation. No one claims that every cigarette smoker gets lung cancer, and no one claims that every case of lung cancer is caused by cigarette smoking. And no one who says that Subarus are reliable denies that there are unreliable Subarus, just as there are reliable cars of other makes. Instead, the claim, akin to the understanding of evidence and its relevance discussed in Chapter 2, is that something is the cause of some effect if it raises the probability of the effect, just as smoking raises the probability of lung cancer for the smoker, just as eating spicy Mexican food raises the probability of heartburn, and just as a car being a Subaru raises the probability of its being reliable.[32]

But what is the evidence for these conclusions, and how strong must it be in order to justify a particular conclusion about causation? More importantly, how strong must the evidence of causation be to justify some particular policy intervention based on that conclusion? At this point, questions of burden of proof again become crucial. How strong must the evidence be of a dangerous side effect of a prescription drug before the Food and Drug Administration prohibits its further distribution? How strong must the evidence be that there are sharks in the vicinity before a public beach is closed to swimmers? What strength of evidence is necessary to require people to wear seatbelts or motorcycle helmets? And what about restrictions on the use of recreational drugs?

In the context of many potential but still uncertain dangers to the environment, or potential but uncertain risks to health, a common approach to such questions is what is often, especially in the industrial democracies of western Europe, called the *precautionary principle*.[33] The basic idea is straightforward: When there is evidence that some substance or practice presents a possible and plausible (even if far from certain) risk to the environment or human health, the practice or substance should not be permitted.

The precautionary principle is controversial.[34] And it is controversial because it raises the Blackstonian ratio to what some believe to be unrealistic and dangerous levels. Unrealistic because it strikes some as exaggerating minuscule possibilities beyond reason. And dangerous, to the same critics, because it ignores the benefits that may come from slightly harmful products, substances, and technologies—where "slightly harmful" is a measure of the likelihood, and not the gravity, of a harm. Critics say that the precautionary principle looks at only one side of the cost–benefit equation, and unwisely intensifies and misrepresents low-probability dangers at the expense of higher-probability benefits.

Defenders of the precautionary principle—generally, and also recently in the context of various responses to the Covid-19 pandemic— respond that some of the low-probability possibilities are so catastrophic that the expected harm is still great.[35] Even evidence of a small probability of a great danger may still represent a very large expected danger when we do the calculation of probability multiplied by consequences that any expected value calculation requires. And although the debates about the precautionary principle involve scientific estimates whose accuracy is contested and are beyond the scope of this book, the issue nevertheless stands as an example of how, in some contexts, quite low burdens of proof may well justify actions taken on their basis. The precautionary principle is based on the idea that not very much evidence, or not very strong evidence, might be sufficient to justify restrictions when the improbable but possible consequences of what the evidence indicates are sufficiently grave.

The Tyranny of Adjectives

The claims of former president Trump and his allies that there was widespread fraud in the 2020 presidential election were remarkable for many reasons. One of those reasons is that not only many commentators, and not only many political opponents of the president, but also many state and federal judges and election officials from both political parties concluded that the allegations were made with no evidence at all.[36] Nebraska senator Ben Sasse's December 30, 2020, observation in a long Facebook post—"If you make big claims, you had better have the evidence"—pretty much sums it up.

The rejection of Trump's fraud claims both in courts of law and in the court of public opinion was often justified by the fact the allegations of fraud were based on a complete lack of evidence. But rarely is there so little evidence for a conclusion, and rarely are the objections to the evidentiary support for assertions by public authorities and officials so unqualified. More often, objectors to some conclusion insist that the conclusion has been made without "hard evidence," "concrete evidence," "conclusive evidence," "solid evidence," or "definitive evidence." And the list goes on. Moreover, when the objections are characterized as a failure of "proof," the implication is that "proof" is stronger than mere evidence, and that whatever evidence there might be does not rise to the level of proof.[37]

The claim that there is a lack of "conclusive evidence" or "definitive proof" for some conclusion typically implies—or concedes—that there is at least some evidence supporting the conclusion. You would not object to there being no conclusive evidence if you could object that there was no evidence at all. The objection that the evidence is not conclusive or definitive, and so on, is ordinarily a rhetorical device used to smuggle a high burden of proof into the evaluation of a contested evidentiary claim. And often those contested evidentiary claims are not claims about individual acts that may or may not have occurred, but instead are claims about the state of the evidence (usually scientific) for some general conclusion (often a general conclusion about causation). If we go back several decades, for example, when the debates about smoking causing lung cancer or heart disease were more contested than they are now, the tobacco companies often argued—in the face of *some* evidence that smoking caused lung cancer and heart disease—that the evidence was not conclusive, not definitive, not solid.[38] More recently, the vaping industry has asserted that there is "no conclusive evidence" that vaping leads to smoking.[39] Similarly, the beer, wine, and spirits industry claims there is "no conclusive evidence" of a link between moderate drinking and birth defects or fetal alcohol syndrome.[40] And the website nintendoenthusiast .com insists that there is "no definitive proof" that video game use causes a decrease in time spent on employment-related tasks.[41]

Claims that some evidence is not sufficiently conclusive, definitive, persuasive, hard, concrete, or solid are claims that implicitly call for a specific burden of proof, typically one that is contested. But identifying this rhetorical phenomenon does not resolve what the burden of proof should be for the kinds of issues that arouse this kind of adjectival tyranny. And here again there is no avoiding the question about the relationship between the burden of proof and the consequences of finding that the burden of proof has been satisfied. The Blackstonian ratio supports the requirement of proof beyond a reasonable doubt in the criminal law because being imprisoned (or executed) is a pretty awful thing, making it important to get things right within the limits of reason and practicality. But it is also important to get things right in making policy-relevant attributions of causation, even if the desired ratio of false negatives to false positives need not be the same as it is in the criminal justice system. When Supreme Court Justices Scalia and Breyer argued about whether there was evidence that playing interactive video games with violent content (probabilistically) caused actual violent aggression in teenage males, what was at stake was a California law restricting such games—a law that sought to restrict activity protected by the First

Amendment.[42] And thus the burden of proof to justify the regulation, and therefore the burden of proof for evaluating the causal claims, was heightened in a way that it would not have been had the question been about the weight of the evidence necessary to regulate something like traffic or mining, neither of which is protected by the First Amendment or any other constitutional provision.

The video game example involves constitutional rights, but the same considerations apply whenever there is reason to impose a special burden on one side of an evidentiary dispute about causation or about the magnitude of some danger. But whether it be the degree of causation, the severity of danger, or any other policy-relevant question for which evidence is important, the larger lesson is that the burden of proof depends on what is at stake. Accordingly, the burden of proof is different when the stakes are different, even when the evidentiary question is the same. Parents deciding whether to allow their children to play violent video games need not be bound to the same heightened burden of proof as the state is when it is deciding whether to restrict the same activity, just as the local animal shelter need not be convinced that a suspected animal abuser is guilty beyond a reasonable doubt before refusing to hire that person to take care of the cats and dogs in its care.

It is worthwhile pausing over the previous point. Perhaps because of newspapers and television, which not surprisingly find the criminal law more interesting than civil lawsuits or employment decisions, the standards of the criminal law—particularly the ideas of a presumption of innocence and the necessity of proof beyond a reasonable doubt—are often assumed to apply whenever someone is accused of wrongdoing, even if the accusation takes place outside of the legal system and even if the conclusion that there was wrongdoing produces sanctions typically of lesser consequence than those administered by the legal system. But it should now be clear that the easy transposition of the standards of the criminal justice system to the full range of accusations of misconduct is too easy. This is true even when misconduct or wrongdoing is not the question. Perhaps, as has often been argued, the precautionary principle is misguided, often ignoring the benefits of risky technologies and imposing a conservative (in the nonpolitical sense of that term) bias on innovation. But for our purposes, the basic lesson of the precautionary principle is the lesson about the pervasiveness of questions about the burden of proof, a pervasiveness that makes the burden of proof relevant to any determination of evidence in the uncertain world in which we find ourselves trapped.

Once we understand that different decision-making environments may apply different burdens of proof to the same factual issue, as with the different burdens of proof in O. J. Simpson's civil and criminal trials, we can recognize the common mistake of excess deference to the legal system. To take an unfortunately common example, suppose that some professional athlete has been accused of domestic violence or sexual misconduct. And suppose also that the accusation is taken seriously enough by law enforcement to warrant formal investigation and, sometimes, prosecution. But when the team or its owner or its coach or manager is asked what the team is going to do about the issue, a frequent response is that the team will decide what to do after the legal system has made its decision. Admittedly, there is some risk that early disciplinary action by the team, if sufficiently publicized, will taint a subsequent criminal trial. But there is also the risk that acquittal or nonprosecution in the criminal process will relieve the team of its responsibilities to decide who it wants to have on its team. People only 70 percent likely to have assaulted their spouses should not be imprisoned, but it is far from clear that people 70 percent likely to have assaulted their spouses should be retained as shortstops or quarterbacks.

A Long Footnote on Statistical Significance

Closely related to the question of burden of proof is the question, recently and perhaps surprisingly the subject of controversy, of the *sta-*

tistical significance of experimental or other empirical research.[43] Just as the evidence emerging from various studies is too often described as not being conclusive or definitive, experimental and other scientific conclusions often are discounted as evidence because they lack statistical significance. But statistical significance is just a number—and an artificial threshold. The artificial threshold may serve valuable purposes in holding scientific studies to a high standard of reliability, but it often has the troubling side effect, in the same manner as inconclusive evidence, of discounting as evidence that which has evidentiary value even if it does not meet the high threshold.

In the natural and social sciences, statistical significance is the measure of the probability that some experimental result, or an even more extreme experimental result, would have been produced even if the null hypothesis—the hypothesis that there is actually is no effect—were true. In other words, what is the probability that what appears to be a positive result—*A* causes *B*, for example—would have been produced even if *A* did not cause *B* at all or if there were no relationship between *A* and *B*. And this likelihood is conventionally described in terms of a *p*-value, where the *p*-value is the probability that positive results—rejection of the "null hypothesis" that there is no connection between the examined variables— were produced by chance. Suppose we are examining the hypothesis that an observed ring-shaped mark was caused by Lyme disease. The null hypothesis would be that the cause of the ring-shaped mark was not Lyme disease. A *p*-value for some test of the relationship between an observed ring-shaped mark and actual Lyme disease that showed the existence of that relationship would thus be the probability that the result produced by the test was produced randomly—by chance. In recent years, a *p*-value of .05 or less has conventionally been taken in most experimental disciplines to be the threshold for statistical significance. A *p*-value of greater than .05—a greater than 5 percent probability that the same results would have been the result of chance—has been understood to mean that the results are not statistically significant.

Because the .05 threshold has the effect of branding large numbers of experimental outcomes as "non-significant," which most lay people would interpret as "insignificant," it has recently become controversial. Some researchers, reacting to reports of scientific conclusions that could not be replicated, have urged that the threshold for statistical significance be made even more conservative, perhaps by reducing it even to .005—a 1 in 200 chance of the same results being produced by chance—but much of the recent attention has been produced by claims that .05 is too high. And there have been related pleas simply to abandon the practice of describing results in terms of statistical significance at all.[44]

The impetus for this latter claim parallels the worry about the effects of demanding "conclusive" or "definitive" evidence. Just as inconclusive or even weak evidence may still be evidence, and may still be useful evidence for some purposes, so too might conclusions—rejections of the null hypothesis—that are more than 5 percent likely to have been produced by chance still be valuable, depending on what follows from those conclusions. Suppose that a trial of an experimental drug indicated that it could cure a previous incurable fatal disease, but that the p-value of that trial, given the sample size, was .20. If you suffered from that disease, and if no other treatments were available, and if no other trials were in the offing, would you want to use the drug, even recognizing that there was a 20 percent chance that the rejection of its ineffectiveness was purely a matter of luck? I suspect that most people would say yes, recognizing that an 80 percent likelihood that the rejection of ineffectiveness was still good enough, at least if there were no other alternatives.

Plainly there is a difference between whether you would take the drug and the question whether the study should be published in a reputable journal, be eligible for grant funding, be approved by federal authorities for prescription and sale, or count for tenure for the lead researcher at a university. And that is the point. By setting a statistical significance threshold at what is too often presented as a context-independent .05, the scientific community has presumed that a threshold for evidence being good enough for publication, grant funding, or tenure is the applicable threshold for all purposes. Some of the objectors to the emphasis on statistical significance wisely say that it would be better simply to accompany any experimental finding with a report about the likelihood of the results being produced by chance, and discard the notion—traditionally packaged in the language of statistical *significance*—that what is not good enough for certain undeniably legitimate purposes within the scientific community is not good enough for anything.

The theme that runs through the ideas of being slightly guilty, the precautionary principle, the concern about the misuse and overuse of the term "conclusive," and, now, of statistical significance, is that evidence comes in degrees. Stronger evidence is better than weaker evidence, but weaker evidence is still evidence. And in some contexts, and for some purposes, weaker evidence may be good enough.

Chapter 4

How to Tell the Truth
with Statistics

GENERATIONS OF UNDERGRADUATES have been taught that statistics are something to fear. At least that is the lesson that many have taken away from their statistics classes, though it is hardly what their instructors intended. Ever since it was published in 1954, Darrell Huff's *How to Lie with Statistics,* although offered as an introduction into how to understand and use statistics accurately and effectively, has too often been remembered (and misused) for its title alone.[1] Some people take the title to mean that the most important thing about statistics is that they can be used to deceive. Actually, the book is about the truthful and honest use of statistics, and Huff analyzes the dishonest uses to give us a better understanding of the honest ones.

One important way to use statistics honestly is as evidence. But we need to narrow the focus. In everyday talk, a statistic is a number, or a collection of numbers. It is a statistic that the population of Charlottesville, Virginia, where I live, was 49,181 in 2019; it is a statistic that Babe Ruth hit sixty home runs in 1927; and it is a statistic that so-and-so's grade point average at such-and-such university was 3.87 on a 4-point scale. All of these are just numbers, or—as with the gross national product of the United States in the first quarter of 2020 being $17,442.93 billion—a large aggregation of smaller numbers.

Of course, these numbers can be used as evidence, depending on what we want to know. If we want to know whether Babe Ruth was a good hitter (yes) or whether Charlottesville has more people than Jersey City (no), these numbers are evidence for these conclusions. But in a more important sense, the relevance of statistics to evidence lies in statistics not as pure numbers but as the foundations for *statistical inference.* What can we learn from the numbers, and especially what can we learn from aggregate numbers about particular acts or events? Can we use population-based statistics—statistics about some group of somethings—as evidence about a particular member of that group, or what some particular member might have done?

Suppose you are interested in buying my car, and I am interested in selling it to you. You ask me if it is reliable, and I say that it is. What I have asserted—my *testimony,* a topic that will occupy Chapters 5–8—is evidence of the car's reliability, but not very good evidence. I might not know very much about cars. And I undoubtedly have an incentive to exaggerate or flat-out lie. Still, even people who want to sell cars to others occasionally tell the truth, sometimes even when it is not in their interest to do so. As a result, my statement is some evidence, even if skimpy, of my car's reliability. But it also turns out that my car is a Subaru. *Consumer Reports* tells you not only that most Subarus are reliable, but also that Subarus have a better reliability record than most other makes of cars. Is this evidence that the particular Subaru that I want to sell you is reliable? Needless to say, *Consumer Reports* has never even seen this particular car. The question is whether what *Consumer Reports* says about the class of Subarus—the population of Subarus—is evidence of the reliability of this particular Subaru. The question assumes, obviously, that not every Subaru is reliable, but also that this particular Subaru is a member of the class of Subarus, and that the

Consumer Reports conclusion is an accurate conclusion about the same class of which this particular Subaru is a member.[2] This question—whether the reliability of the class of Subarus is evidence of the reliability of this particular Subaru—is a question of statistical inference, or, as it is put by the people who study such things, a question of using population-level data as evidence for individual (or sample) characteristics.

The Subaru example illustrates the basic issue for us here—whether what we know about some group can be evidence of what we want to know about some individual member of that group. So, to take a standard example from Statistics 101, suppose we have an urn containing 100 wooden balls. We know that 90 of those balls are solid-colored, and 10 are striped. Someone reaches into the urn and picks out a ball, which I cannot see, but I must guess whether it is solid or striped. The question is whether what we know about the distribution of solid and striped balls in the urn is evidence that the single ball that has been picked is solid. There is, after all, a 90 percent chance that any ball picked at random from the urn will be solid. That being so, there appears also to be a 90 percent chance that any particular unknown ball is solid. And if that is so, then the distribution of balls in the urn, which we do know, is evidence for the characteristics of the single ball that has already been picked, which we do not.[3]

Recall from Chapter 2 the way in which *all* evidence involves statistical inference of this sort. The defendant's running out of the bank wearing a ski mask and carrying a bag is evidence, even if not conclusive, that the defendant has just robbed the bank. But that behavior is evidence of robbery only because of the fact, a fact based on other evidence, that the class of people who wear ski masks and run out of banks with bags in their hands consists predominantly of people who have robbed the bank. Or consider Lyme disease once again. What makes ring-shaped redness evidence of Lyme disease is that prior research has shown that Lyme disease generally produces ring-shaped redness, and that ring-shaped redness is rarely caused by anything else. What the physician knows about some larger category provides the evidence in the particular instance.

All relevant evidence is statistical (and probabilistic) in this sense.[4] The focus of this chapter is statistical evidence of a more overt character. When does actual statistical data, especially when presented and understood in explicitly numerical terms, count as evidence of the existence of particular facts? And if the lesson from Chapter 2, as summarized in the previous paragraph, appears to be "always," it turns out that things are not quite so simple.

Gatecrashers, Prison Yards, Blue Buses, and Other Stories

The problem of using group statistics to prove facts in particular cases has intrigued lawyers and philosophers for more than fifty years. The interest was initially prompted by a 1968 decision of the Supreme Court of California dealing with just this kind of explicitly statistical evidence.[5] Malcolm Collins and his wife, Janet Collins, had been charged with robbery, Janet having allegedly assaulted a woman and stolen the victim's purse, after which she allegedly fled the scene with Malcolm, who was waiting in his car nearby. The victim's identification of Janet was uncertain, but the victim was confident that she had been robbed by a Caucasian woman with dark blond hair tied back in a ponytail. And although the victim did not see Malcom, a witness who did not observe the robbery testified that he did see a Caucasian woman with a blond ponytail get into a yellow convertible driven by an African American man with a beard and a mustache shortly after the time of the alleged robbery and less than a block away from the scene of the alleged crime. Malcolm Collins, Janet's husband, was African American, owned a yellow convertible, and frequently wore a beard and a mustache.

At the trial, the prosecuting attorney, sensing a weakness in the identification evidence, called a statistics instructor from a local college to testify. The prosecutor asked him to assume a bunch of statistics about the percentage of women who had blond ponytails, the percentage of marriages that were interracial, the percentage of cars that were yellow convertibles, the percentage of African American men who had beards, and the percentage of African American men who wore mustaches. And then the prosecutor asked the witness to apply the product rule to those numbers and estimate the probability that the defendants, who possessed those characteristics, were the same people as the ones with those characteristics who had robbed the victim. The product rule, as the statistician witness accurately described it, says that the likelihood of multiple independent events occurring together is the product of the likelihood of each of those events. If the question is about the combined likelihood of the nine of hearts being picked from a deck of cards and a fair coin tossed in the air coming up heads, the product rule says to multiply 1 / 52 times 1 / 2, producing a combined likelihood of 1 / 104.

The statistician-witness explained this to the jury, and the prosecutor then asked him to apply this to the statistics about the characteristics of the robber and her accomplice as provided by the prosecutor. That the witness did, producing a vanishingly small likelihood that someone other than the blond pony-tailed defendant and the bearded mustached yellow convertible owning African American defendant who was her husband had committed the crime. The jury was convinced, and the couple was convicted.

The California Supreme Court easily and correctly reversed the conviction. In the first place, the prosecutor had no factual basis for the individual probabilities he had provided to the witness. And, second, the product rule works only when the factors are independent, as with days of the week and tosses of a coin. But if the factors are not independent of each other, multiplying the two probabilities to get a combined probability is fallacious. For example, very few men weigh more than 300 pounds and very few men are sumo wrestlers, but the probability that some man weighs more than 300 pounds and is a sumo wrestler cannot be determined by multiplying the two probabilities; and that is because men who are sumo wrestlers are more likely to weigh more than 300 pounds than are men in general, and men who weigh more than 300 pounds are more likely to be sumo wrestlers than are men in general. Weighing over 300 pounds and being a sumo wrestler are thus *correlated,* and the two probabilities are not independent.

And that, in addition to the lack of any foundation (evidence) for the individual probabilities, was the problem here, because there was no indication that the probability of the attributes multiplied by the statistician, as well as the attributes of Janet, Malcolm, and Janet and Malcolm together, were independent. To give one example, the vast majority of men who have beards also have mustaches (Abraham Lincoln and Amish men being notable exceptions) and treating the two as independent was one of the multiple blunders that led the California Supreme Court to reverse the conviction.

Although the result in the *Collins* case was plainly correct, the case spawned a raft of academic hypothetical cases designed to test whether the use of statistics alone, if actually used properly, can count as evidence sufficient to justify a legal verdict. One of these hypothetical cases, adapted from a real Massachusetts decision in 1945, has come to be known as the Blue Bus problem.[6] Suppose a car is forced off the road by a bus, but it is a dark and rainy night and all the victim can see of the offending vehicle is that it was a blue bus. It turns out that of all the blue buses in town, 80 percent are owned and operated by the Metropolitan Transit Company, and 20 percent by the Public Service Company. Assuming that the bus was driven negligently, and assuming that the negligence caused injury to the driver of the car, can that driver recover against the Metropolitan Transit Company in a civil suit, where the burden of proof is only a preponderance of the evidence? There appears to be an 80 percent chance, after all, that it was the Metropolitan's bus that caused the accident. In a civil suit, with the burden of proof being something like 51 percent, it would seem that the Metropolitan

Transit Company ought to be liable. But most people resist that outcome, insisting, as did the Massachusetts Supreme Judicial Court in the real case, that without some "direct" evidence of Metropolitan Transit's involvement there could no liability. Direct evidence—presumably something like the victim testifying that she saw the words "Metropolitan Transit" written on the side of the bus—would be necessary. Mere statistics pointing to the same conclusion, whether those statistics be numerically quantified or not, cannot suffice. Or at least that was the conclusion of the real court in the real case, and that is the intuition that most commentators on the real case and on the fictional blue bus case have had as well.[7]

A slew of other hypothetical examples has tried to make the same point. The philosopher Jonathan Cohen, not long after *Collins* surfaced in the academic literature, offered what he called the Paradox of the Gatecrasher.[8] Suppose that there is an event—a rodeo, in Cohen's example—for which admission is charged. One thousand spectators are counted in the seats, but there is evidence that only 499 people paid admission. Therefore, 501 people entered fraudulently. And then suppose the rodeo organizer sues—again civilly—one of the 1,000 spectators, alleging that that spectator entered fraudulently. Even with no other evidence, there appears to be a 501 / 1000 probability that this randomly selected spectator entered fraudulently, and thus it would seem, by a (bare) preponderance of the evidence, that this person should be held liable. Cohen, like many others, finds this outcome objectionable, and seeks to explain why what seems statistically impeccable is nevertheless unacceptable.[9]

Or consider an example offered by Charles Nesson, which in simplified and slightly modified form goes as follows:[10] Twenty-five prisoners are in the prison yard. The prisoners crowd around a guard and kill him, but one has run away and hidden before the killing takes place. One of the twenty-five is prosecuted for murder. The prosecutor can prove the events just described but cannot prove that the defendant was not the one who broke away from the group and was thus innocent. The prosecutor can consequently only prove that there is a 24 / 25 chance that the defendant was a murderer. Is this sufficient for a conviction? And, if not, then why not?

These examples have been well massaged in the legal and philosophical literatures for decades.[11] It turns out, however, that some of these examples present an issue extraneous to the statistical evidence problem—although not, as we shall see in the following section, to broader questions about evidence. Consider again Cohen's Paradox of the Gatecrasher and its assumption that a randomly selected spectator can be sued, civilly, for having committed one unspecified instance of the 501 fraudulent entries. But that assumption leads Cohen—and us—astray. There were indeed 501 fraudulent entries, but each is a different act, taking place at a different time, even if distinguishable only by seconds, and taking place at a different location, even if different only by millimeters. These tiny differences among the 501 may seem trivial, but they are not trivial to the law, which operates on the assumption that liability requires specification of the particular act for which someone is to be held liable. "You did one of these, even if we don't know which one" is unacceptable in law. And if our randomly selected entrant is sued for having committed a precisely specified fraudulent entry, the probability is then no longer 501 / 1000, but 1 / 1000, a different matter entirely. Once the defendant is sued for having committed a particular specified act, the statistics no longer justify liability, and the alleged paradox evaporates.

So too, even more obviously, with the Prison Yard hypothetical. Especially in criminal prosecutions, we do not prosecute people for having committed one of a multiple number of unspecified acts. Suppose that location A and location B are two hundred miles apart. A radar device identifies a car as having traveled from A to B in a time that was possible only by either driving in excess of the speed limit or ignoring at least several of twenty stop signs. Can the driver be prosecuted for the crime of having either exceeded the speed limit or failed to stop at the stop signs, but without specification of which of these?[12] And if it seems wrong to prosecute for an unspecified something in this case, then so too in the Prison Yard. A randomly selected prisoner in the prison yard would not be prosecuted for having done just *something* connected with the death of the guard. It would be necessary to allege a particular act, or a particular role in the guard's death, and without that there could be no prosecution. And if a particular act were to be specified, the likelihood that a particular prisoner committed it, with no other evidence, would then be 1 / 25, hardly enough for a conviction.

This issue of specification does not arise in the Blue Bus case, making it a cleaner example for examining the use of explicitly statistical evidence. Here there is a precisely specified basis for liability, and the only question is whether the company that operates 80 percent of the blue buses is liable for the injuries resulting from that specified act. Now, even more clearly, we see the divergence between the common intuitions and the result indicated by the statistics.[13] The statistics provide evidence—a preponderance of it, if there is no evidence inclining in the opposite direction of the bus's ownership.[14] But common intuition wants something allegedly more "individualized," as it is often put.[15] Without some evidence pointing specifically to ownership of this bus, so the argument goes, there can be no liability.

Here it becomes crucial to distinguish between whether something is evidence in the first place from whether that evidence is strong enough to justify a legal verdict. Law enforcement authorities know, for example, that by far the largest percentage of married women killed in their own homes have been murdered by their husbands.[16] Any good police officer, even lacking individualized evidence that this particular husband killed this particular wife, will accordingly investigate the husband carefully, even at the expense of postponing the investigation of other possibilities. This might turn out to be a mistake, especially if it comes at the expense of not investigating something less probable that turns out to be correct. Still, a detective who allocates scarce time and limited investigative resources to investigating the husband hypothesis and not, say, the stranger hypothesis or the burglar hypothesis, is, based on the probabilities, pursuing a wise strategy. Horses and not zebras. Needless to say, we do not imprison husbands solely on the evidence that their wives have been murdered. But being the husband justifies on probabilistic grounds the targeted investigation, even if the lone fact of being the husband is hardly sufficient for conviction. Being the husband is still evidence, based on the probabilities, of the husband's culpability, despite its not being sufficient evidence to convict or even arrest. But as I have repeatedly stressed, and as the law recognizes, something being evidence is different from that something being enough evidence for some type of consequence. Evidence sufficient to justify investigation is usually insufficient by itself to justify conviction or arrest. But evidence insufficient for arrest or conviction can still justify pre-arrest investigation.

Using purely probabilistic (or statistical) evidence to justify an investigation is common and widely accepted—think of Captain Renault in *Casablanca* ordering his officers to "round up the usual suspects." But if using statistical evidence as the basis for an investigation is acceptable, the common intuitive reaction that there must be individualized evidence for anything beyond investigation, whether in the legal system or more broadly, becomes curious.[17] Some of the tension between people's common positive reaction to probabilistic investigation, on the one hand, and their negative views of probabilistic sanctions, on the other, might be the product of the well-documented difficulty people have in dealing with probabilities generally.[18] And academics writing about the Blue Bus and related problems are not necessarily immune to this difficulty. But the strong preference for individualized evidence seems to be even more a function of the widespread and systematic underestimation of the probabilistic nature of allegedly individualized evidence, along with an equally widespread and systematic overvaluation of many forms of allegedly individualized evidence. Although there is no fundamental difference between population-based evidence and other forms of evidence, there is a common resistance to using population-based—or actuarial—evidence. But the resistance is mistaken. Someone who claimed to have seen the word "Metropolitan" on the blue bus, for example, would have offered seemingly individualized evidence, but that individualized evidence might still have been based on an observation that occurred on a dark and rainy night from a hundred yards away by someone with poor vision and a financial interest in the outcome. This would count as individualized evidence for the proponents of requiring individualized evidence, but it would be very weak evidence, no matter how individualized it seemed.

Moreover, to repeat a recurrent theme in this book, the allegedly individualized evidence is not as individualized as is often supposed. The eyewitness who reports having seen a blue bus is basing that report on the nonindividualized fact that what the witness has previously perceived as blue has usually turned out actually to be blue. And so too with buses. But a less philosophically obscure example of the same point would come from a witness who reports that someone else was, say, drunk. Reports of drunkenness are usually based on the observer's belief that people who are slurring their words, talking too loudly, and losing their balance are likely drunk. Saying that such-and-such a person was drunk is, in effect, saying that this person exhibited a category of behaviors that probabilistically tend to indicate drunkenness. And the identification of someone as drunk is itself a conclusion based on probabilities. Once we see that characteristics that superficially individualize—"drink," or "bus," or "blue"—are also probabilistic generalizations, the idea of truly individualized evidence is increasingly elusive.

Appreciating the probabilistic dimension of all evidence makes the common aversion to explicitly statistical evidence even more tenuous. Proponents of evidence-based medicine argue that individual treatments should be based on statistical probabilities, but doing so necessarily takes into account the individual patient's group characteristics. Indeed, the entire field of epidemiology is based on statistics, and we rarely see "blue bus" style resistance to basing individual treatments on epidemiological data and conclusions.[19] Nor do we resist the mechanic's diagnosis that the pinging sound coming from the engine is likely the result of using fuel that is too low in octane, even though that diagnosis comes from the mechanic's multiple prior experiences or published data and possibly not even from looking under the hood.

It turns out, therefore, that the kind of statistical evidence that produces skepticism in a trial in court is widely accepted in other contexts. This suggests that the skepticism is rooted not in intuitions about statistics or about evidence, but in intuitions about what the legal system in particular should do, and when and how it should do it. Even if the demand for individualized evidence in the legal system were sound, and I doubt that it is, that demand emerges from views—or intuitions—about the legal system and not about the idea of evidence itself. It is not about the value of using group-level characteristics—statistics—to justify inferences about individual events.[20]

Questions about the liability of the Metropolitan Transit Company are thus similar to questions about whether the reliability of Subarus is evidence of the reliability of *this* Subaru or whether the effectiveness of the Pfizer Covid-19 vaccine on thirty thousand experimental subjects is evidence of its likely effectiveness on one particular patient. And this similarity lays bare that the intuitive resistance to using statistics in legal context is not based on anything about statistics or evidence—it is based on what the legal system should do to people. The intuitions seem to be intuitions about the criminal law that bleed over, not necessarily correctly, into intuitions about law generally, including civil litigation.

Even if the widespread aversion to the use of statistical evidence in law is law-specific, that aversion may still be sound in legal contexts.

Perhaps the law's aversion, and the common support for law's aversion, is based on the idea of excluding statistical evidence as a way of forcing those who would otherwise rely on it to come up with something better.[21] But although creating the incentive to produce the best evidence available is an admirable goal, it is in some tension with the goal of transcending the common failure to ignore or underestimate base rates in reaching conclusions from evidence. Let us return to Subarus. If we cannot rely on the Subaru-ness—the characteristics of the category of which *this* Subaru is a member—of a particular car in assessing its reliability, we are likely to take our assessment of the car's individual characteristics as being more compelling than they actually are, and the characteristics that the car shares with other Subarus or with other cars as being less important as evidence than they actually are, which is precisely the problem that the research about ignoring base rates makes clear.[22] That this car makes a squeaking noise when it goes over bumps is some evidence of its unreliability, but not nearly as strong as this being a Subaru is evidence of its reliability. And if we cannot use its Subaru-ness as evidence, then we will treat the squeaking as being stronger evidence than it actually is. If information about an individual Subaru—or about an individual blue bus, an individual rodeo spectator, an individual prisoner in the prison yard—obscures or crowds out what we can learn from the categories of which those individuals are members, the resulting decisions are more likely to be mistaken. Or so the base-rate literature warns us.

Moreover, "no decision" is rarely an option in court, in policy, or in individual decision making. If statistical evidence is unavailable, there will still be an outcome, and we find ourselves back to Blackstone and the consequences of different types of error. If statistics may not be used to support a judgment against the Metropolitan Transit Company, then Metropolitan's non-liability means non-recovery for the bus driver's victim and the company's negligence. And the question again is whether an error of mistaken liability is worse than an error of mistaken non-liability, the latter entailing, in civil context, non-recovery for the victim of someone else's negligent actions. Similarly, if no prisoner can be convicted in the Prison Yard example, then twenty-four felonious acts go unpunished. And even if, in the criminal context, we properly follow Blackstone in deeming false acquittals as less grave then false convictions, we cannot eliminate false convictions entirely without accepting at least some false acquittals. We are left to wonder whether those who object to the use of statistical evidence fully comprehend that the non-use of statistical evidence will produce mistaken acquittals (which might not be so bad) and mistaken non-compensation of plaintiffs injured physically or financially through no fault of their own (which might be much worse).

One final example should make the tenor of the foregoing even clearer. Let us add some numbers to the Lyme disease example, and imagine that the physician, employing the best techniques of evidence-based medicine, determines from the patient's indications that there is a 96 percent chance that the patient has Lyme disease. And assume that the approved treatment for Lyme disease is a dose of antibiotics. These antibiotics will kill the microbes that produce Lyme disease, but they will also kill some harmless microbes residing in the human body. As a result, there is a 4 percent chance that the antibiotics will kill only harmless microbes. Under these conditions, should the antibiotics be administered?

Hardly anyone would be troubled by administering the antibiotics in these conditions. Yet statistically this is the Prison Yard case, except that micro-organisms take the place of the prisoners. Yes, we should care more about innocent prisoners than we do about innocent microbes, but the point of the example is only to illustrate that resistance to prosecution in the Prison Yard example cannot be based on any mistakes in the statistics, and cannot be based on any defect in the evidence. If such resistance exists, it must be based on the fact that people, understandably, worry more about innocent defendants than innocent microbes. Although that worry may well be justified, identifying and isolating it brings us back to the major point. As a matter of statistical inference, taking the group-level data as evidence of the likelihood in an individual case is inferentially impeccable. What we do with that inference is important, but it is just as important not to allow resistance to the consequences of the inference produce an unwarranted resistance to the inference itself.

Evidence of What?

I want to return to the issue glossed over in the previous section—the extent to which the legal system actually should require evidence of a precisely specified wrong before it is willing to impose liability. For this purpose, recent issues and trials regarding sexual assault provide an important illustration of the issue, and of the problem.

These recent issues surround a common phenomenon of modern life—the frequency with which powerful men are accused by multiple women of having engaged in sexual misconduct, whether rape, some other form of sexual assault, or some other variety of unwanted sexual aggression. Bill Clinton, Bill Cosby, Donald Trump, and Harvey Weinstein are only the most prominent names among those who have been multiply accused in this way, and in each case the accused men have denied each and every allegation. The question that emerges is a question of evidence—what (if anything) did they do, to whom (if anyone) did they do it to, and what (if anything) should society and the legal system do about it?

The allegations against Clinton, Cosby, Trump, Weinstein, and countless other famous and not-so-famous men turn out to be not only of great moral, policy, and political import, but also of statistical and general evidentiary interest. And although posing the issue in terms of what they did and who they did it to seems straightforward, these allegations and how they are considered present an important twist on what is really the first question we ask when we are thinking about evidence: What is it (the evidence) evidence *of?*

It will help if we imagine a hypothetical scenario similar to most of the non-hypothetical scenarios that have become front-page news. Suppose that famous politician Henry has been accused of sexual assault by four women. The accusations have come at different times and at different places, and there is no reason to believe that any of the accusers knew each other or knew of the others' accusations. In other words, and of statistical importance, each of the accusations is independent of the others.[23] But in each case Henry vigorously denies the accusation.

Now suppose that each accusation results in a criminal prosecution. A single accuser testifies credibly, but Henry testifies, at least somewhat credibly, that the events never happened or that any sexual activity was entirely consensual. And there is neither physical evidence nor witnesses other than Henry and the accuser. On these facts, it seems plausible to conclude that the prosecution has established an 80 percent chance that Henry has done what he is charged with having done. But this being a criminal case, the 80 percent chance is insufficient to establish guilt beyond a reasonable doubt. Although, as discussed in Chapter 3, there are debates about whether the beyond a reasonable doubt standard can be quantified, a common view is that beyond a reasonable doubt means at least a 90 percent probability of guilt. Thus, if each of the four accusations goes to trial, and if each of the accusations is proved to an 80 percent probability, Henry will be acquitted in each of four separate trials. And properly so.

But now ask a different question. What if we ask not whether, for each individual case, Henry is guilty, but instead whether Henry has committed at least one sexual assault. Now the probabilities look very different. To be more precise, if there are four accusations, and each of those accusations is .80 likely to be true, then the chances that Henry has committed at least one sexual assault are $1-((1-.80) \times (1-.80) \times (1-.80) \times (1-.80)) = .9924$. Although there is only an 80 percent likelihood that

Henry has committed a particular specified sexual assault, there is a greater than 99 percent chance that Henry has committed at least one sexual assault.

What a legal system should do in such cases is not strictly a question of evidence. Rather, it is a question whether the law, as traditionally understood and designed, is right to refuse to aggregate in the manner just described, or whether, instead, the legal system ought to allow people to be convicted if, as with Henry, it is established beyond a reasonable doubt that they have committed a punishable crime, but not established beyond a reasonable doubt that they have committed a particular specified punishable crime.[24] As here, the evidence often points strongly to the defendant's guilt of something, and indeed something of a particular type, but less strongly to guilt of one particular specified something.[25]

A large part of the legal system's traditional reluctance to punish absent this kind of specification of precisely what the defendant is being punished for seems based on a worry that, taken to the extreme, this approach would permit prosecuting most of us on the theory that we have at some point in our lives committed some punishable crime. Should we permit people to be prosecuted for having committed at least one of some number of quite different crimes? If there is a 40 percent chance that someone has committed an act of shoplifting, a 40 percent chance that the same person has engaged in an act of reckless driving, a 40 percent chance that that person has used an illegal controlled substance, and a 40 percent chance that this person has purchased alcohol for a minor, then there is slightly over a 90 percent chance that they have committed some unspecified criminal offense, but few would approve of criminal conviction of some unspecified crime under such circumstances.[26]

Although the example just given is properly resisted, the resistance may decrease, as with Henry, when the unspecified acts are similar. And the resistance may decrease even further when the context is something other than criminal punishment. If there is a 20 percent chance that someone has committed each of three unspecified acts involving dishonesty, should that person be hired (or retained) as chief of security for a casino? Few managers would hesitate to refuse to hire or to dismiss such a person if already hired, and if that example produces less resistance, the conclusion, again, is that what may properly be thought impermissible when we are considering criminal conviction and likely imprisonment does not look so impermissible in a large number of other very real circumstances presenting the same statistical conclusions reached by the same decision-theoretic methods. With the question of specification as well as with the use of statistics generally, therefore, it is important not to let intuitions and even reasoned conclusions about what the criminal law should do be generalized to conclusions about what should be done or not done regardless of context or consequences.

A Note on Profiling

Most people reading the preceding pages in this chapter would think of the issue of profiling.[27] Decades ago, before racial profiling became publicly salient (although not before it existed), profiling did not have the bad odor that it now exudes. In fact, a 1990s television series called *The Profiler* presented favorably an FBI profiler whose job was to accumulate whatever evidence was available of some crime and then, on the basis of this evidence, construct a profile that narrowed the range of suspects—sometimes to one—so that that small group of prime suspects could be investigated with close scrutiny.

It is unlikely that such a television show would be offered now, twenty-plus years later. And that is because racial profiling—using race as one of the attributes, or even the only attribute, that triggers an investigation—is justifiably widely condemned and widely prohibited within law enforcement, even as unofficially it pervasively persists.

It might seem that there is a disconnect between the condemnation of racial (or ethnic, or national origin, or religious) profiling and the defense of category-based statistical evidence that has emerged from the preceding pages. But the disconnect is illusory. Nothing about the inevitability and desirability of using population-based statistics to reach conclusions about individual acts and individual actors suggests that every statistical inference is statistically valid, nor that every valid statistical inference is normatively desirable.

Part of the condemnation of racial and related profiling is based on the argument, often sound, that some inferences from some classes are simply statistically and empirically invalid. There is, for example, no empirical basis at all for the belief that the class of gay men has, as a class, or on average as a group, less physical courage than the class of heterosexual men, although that generalization was long believed, and persists now. Nor is there any empirical basis, John Henry Wigmore's prejudices (discussed in Chapter 8) notwithstanding, for the belief that women are less honest or accurate than men when they testify in court. It should be obvious, therefore, that nothing I say here about the use of group-level characteristics, whether of people or Lyme-disease-causing micro-organisms, is applicable to descriptions of group-level characteristics that are statistically false.

Even when such descriptions are statistically sound—men over seventy years old have worse hearing and less reliable memory than younger men; women have less upper-body strength than men; African Americans develop high blood pressure more frequently and earlier than others—it does not follow that it is justifiable to use those descriptions as evidence. But here we should distinguish epistemic arguments from normative ones.

Epistemically, even sound empirical generalizations may so suffer from misuse that it is epistemically better to preclude their use. Suppose it is widely believed that French people are better cooks than Russians, and suppose that this generalization has an empirically sound basis as a generalization. But if the operationalization of this belief is that *all* French people are good cooks and *all* Russians are bad, a restaurant that refuses to examine the culinary abilities of individual chefs in favor of never hiring Russians and always hiring the French people may wind up making more mistakes than if it tested individual chefs, assuming that the individual testing was highly reliable, even if not perfect. Sound generalizations can be misused or overused in various ways, but the basic point is that doing so is an epistemic failure. And it is an epistemic failure whose consequences can be lessened by prohibiting group-level generalizations and instead considering only individual characteristics in circumstances where this would produce better aggregate outcomes.

Moreover, a host of moral considerations might in some contexts argue against using even some empirically sound and epistemically useful aggregate characteristics. For example, some reliable statistical indicators are reliable only as a result of previous immoral and often illegal discrimination. Taking the aggregate mathematical ability of women as some (inconclusive) evidence for the mathematical ability of a particular woman might be statistically justified today, but the statistical justification is itself a product of generations (at least) of steering women into certain professions and disciplines (librarian, secretary, nurse) and away from others (scientist, surgeon, mathematician), with the product of that steering being the current differentials. Moreover, it is hardly the case that every statistically sound empirical generalization is appropriately used for every conclusion. The generalization that men as a class have more upper-body strength than women as a class is almost certainly true, but that would hardly justify preferring men over women for the vast range of jobs in which upper-body strength is either irrelevant or of such minor importance that individuals with less strength can be accommodated. Some statistically justifiable generalizations, therefore, are best avoided—not because they are epistemically flawed as evidence, but because they probably reflect or reinforce past injustices.

Thus, even if someone's race, religion, gender, ethnicity, age, sexual orientation, or nationality is in fact evidence for some conclusion, it does not follow that that evidence ought to be used for other conclusions, or even for that conclusion. We don't worry about injustices to blue buses or disease-causing microbes or even rodeo spectators, but there are many reasons to believe that statistical inferences that are usable for such categories may wisely be precluded from others, not because those inferences are statistically invalid, but despite the fact that they are not.

Sampling as Evidence

Article I of the Constitution of the United States provides that there shall be an "actual Enumeration" of the "Persons" in each state for the purpose, originally and still principally, of determining how many representatives in the House of Representatives will be allocated to each state. The actual clause in which the enumeration requirement appears is multiply offensive, containing not only the notorious "three-fifths" clause counting enslaved persons as only three-fifths of a person, but also excluding "Indians not taxed"—which at the time denoted more than 90 percent of the indigenous population of the United States.

Even the less offensive parts of the enumeration clause have been controversial. The US Supreme Court recently declined to decide, for now, the question whether undocumented people were to be counted in the census.[28] But more relevant to questions about evidence are the statutory and constitutional questions, the subject of several Supreme Court decisions, about whether the requirement of an "actual enumeration" allows statistical sampling.[29] If we put aside the statutory and constitutional questions for a moment and consider the issue solely as a question of evidence, we can say that the question we want answered is the question of just how many people are living in a particular state. One form of evidence would be the familiar head counting, in which a census taker goes door to door and actually counts the people living at some residence. And these household-by-household head counts are then aggregated to produce the number of people living in a town, in a state, and in a congressional district. The total number is thus the number of observed residents, which has traditionally been considered good evidence of the number of people actually living in the state. In the modern version, the number of people who answer the census questions online or by mail is considered some evidence, often good evidence, of how many people live in a specified area.

The heads that are counted, however, are not, according to the Constitution, what we really want to know. What we want to know is how many people are living in the state. Traditionally, counting the people available for counting is thought to be reliable evidence of what we want to know. But the result of the counting is not the fact of the matter. The fact of the matter is how many people live somewhere, and the counting is evidence of that fact.

Counting, however, is not perfect evidence, even assuming that there is something we can call perfect evidence. Some people who really do live in the town or state or congressional district refuse to talk to the census taker, and, these days, refuse to respond online and fail to respond by mail. Because such people actually do live in the state, they are part of the ultimate fact. But they do not get counted. The evidence gets it wrong. And in response to this phenomenon, it has been argued that statistical sampling by the Census Bureau would be more reliable than actual counting of actual heads. For now, it appears that, as a matter of statutory interpretation, such sampling is legally impermissible for purposes of allocating congressional seats to the states, but sampling is permissible, used, and also controversial for other purposes.

As is unfortunately the case with most policy issues these days, support for using statistical sampling to count the population has divided along party lines. The political parties don't differ in their views about the abstract question. They differ regarding who will be benefit from one or another answer to a question that, in theory, has no necessary political implications. Republicans tend to oppose sampling in the belief that it will increase the counting of people—disproportionately of lower income and living in urban areas—who are likely to vote Democratic. Democrats oppose exclusive reliance on face-to-face counting for the opposite reason.

The issue, however, is larger than the census. The recent inaccuracies—some would call them spectacular failures—of political polling have not been good for the polling profession generally, but it is worthwhile pointing out that polling, surveying, and all of the other similar techniques are based on the idea of sampling as evidence. If what we are interested in is how many of the country's approximately 150 million voters would prefer Donald Trump to all other potential candidates in the 2024 presidential election, then the best evidence, hardly conclusive, would come from asking all 150 million who they intend to vote for. That would be financially and logistically impossible, so polls sample small percentages of those whose preferences concern us, and then use those results as evidence of the preferences of the larger group. Like all evidence, the conclusion from such polling would be inductive, risky, and, even with the best of sampling techniques, potentially mistaken. But we nevertheless ought not lose sight of the fact that sampling is one of the most prevalent forms of evidence there is.

Sampling, though not by polling, is also a form of evidence widely practiced by manufacturers concerned with quality control. Consider the question of tires. The manufacturers of tires would like to sell tires that will not fail—typically spectacularly, as anyone who has experienced a blowout knows—prior to being driven, say, fifty thousand normal miles. But tire manufacturers cannot test each tire they manufacture, even assuming, counterfactually, that a tire could be tested without impairing its usability. Accordingly, the manufacturers test—and in the process destroy—a comparatively small number of tires and use the results of that testing as evidence of the durability of the full population of tires similar in manufacture to the tested and destroyed tires.

Evidence of the durability of tires is, therefore, just one of the many ways statistical evidence is a central feature of the role of evidence in business, in public policy, and in our daily lives. And statistics derived, accumulated, used, and presented in numerical terms are only the quantitative subset of the larger set of probabilistic, and thus statistical, inferences that are central to the very idea of evidence. Sometimes we are interested in population-level data as evidence with respect to particular members or samples of that population. And at other times, as with census and quality control sampling, we are interested in just the reverse—samples as evidence of population-level or aggregate characteristics. But whether the evidentiary route is from population to sample or from sample to population, the evidentiary inferences are statistical. And so, with or without numbers, is much of the evidence we use, and much of what evidence itself is all about.

Chapter 5

Testimony, and Not Only in Court

LITTLE OF WHAT WE KNOW is based on our own perceptions. This claim may seem surprising, but further reflection reveals its truth. Yes, I know it is snowing outside because I can look out the window and see snow. I know this wine is bad because I taste the mustiness that wine experts call "corking." And I know the orchestra is playing Beethoven's Fifth Symphony because I, personally, recognize its characteristic theme.

But these examples are unrepresentative. I know the date of my birth because my mother told me and because it is written on a document prepared by a public official in Newark, New Jersey. Of course, I did not see, hear, taste, smell, or touch my own birth. I know when I was born not because of direct perception, but because of what others have told me.

This is unremarkable. Much of our knowledge comes from the assertions of others; from *testimony,* in the broad and not court-centric sense of that word. The philosopher R. F. Atkinson is surely right when he observes that "so much of what we believe, not just about the past but about everything, is based on testimony that it is scarcely credible that we could get along without it."[1] Testimony, in this broad sense, consists of the assertions of others, especially the assertions of the others we are asked to credit just because someone has asserted something. So understood, testimony can be written as well as oral, the image of the witness in court giving testimony notwithstanding. I believe it was cold in Montana yesterday because a friend who lives there told me so in a telephone conversation. I believe that the rate of Covid-19 infection in my city is decreasing because I heard it on the evening news. I believe there are bears in the neighborhood, although I have never seen one, because multiple neighbors say that they have seen one. I believe that Indonesia is the fourth largest country in the world in population because I read it on the US Census Bureau's website. I confidently pour a yellow liquid into my mouth because the label on the bottle testifies that the bottle contains lemonade. And on and on. The questions to be addressed here are about the extent to which testimony is evidence for the proposition that the testifier asserts. Or that a testifier asserts to another testifier who asserts it to still another testifier, creating a long chain of testimony whose end link is the person relying on an original assertion passed along through multiple others. The questions about testimony not only are about the status of testimony as evidence, but are also about the extent to which, if at all, that testimonial evidence is different from other types of evidence, about how testimonial evidence compares to personal observation or perception, and about the special evidentiary problems that testimony does or does not create. The focus of this chapter is secondhand knowledge. It is knowledge that comes, not from firsthand observation or experience, but from others' knowledge, typically transmitted by language.[2] The aim of this chapter and Chapters 6–8 is to expose and explore the complexities arising from treating secondhand knowledge as information and as evidence.[3]

The Testimony of George M. Cohan

Most Americans know of George M. Cohan, if they know of him at all, as the composer and entertainer who gave us "Give My Regards to

Broadway," "You're a Grand Old Flag," "Over There," "Yankee Doodle Boy," and many other popular songs of the first half of the twentieth century. But tax lawyers know of Cohan for different reasons. For them Cohan is the central character in what is now known as the "Cohan rule," and it is an important part of tax law and tax practice.[4]

The Cohan rule emerged out of a dispute between Cohan and the Internal Revenue Service regarding his 1921 and 1922 tax returns. Cohan, whose penchant for living large matched his fame, was accustomed to picking up the tab at restaurants and nightclubs for business associates, fellow entertainers, friends, acquaintances, and assorted hangers-on. And when tax time came, Cohan estimated what he had spent on these acts of professional largesse and claimed that amount as a deductible business expense. An auditor for the IRS asked for proof of these expenditures, but Cohan could supply nothing in writing. After all, famous big spenders don't ask for receipts. So Cohan offered as evidence only his own oral representations of what he had spent. The IRS, not surprisingly, refused to allow the deduction. Litigation ensued.

Cohan's dispute with the IRS eventually reached the US Court of Appeals for the Second Circuit, whose jurisdiction encompasses New York, Connecticut, and Vermont. And although Cohan lost on some of his arguments, he prevailed on the question whether his oral representations—his testimony—could count as evidence for his deductible expenses. In a decision written by Judge Learned Hand, perhaps the most distinguished of those American judges who never became Supreme Court justices, the court sided with Cohan.[5] Judge Hand seemed skeptical of Cohan's representations, but he was just as skeptical of the Internal Revenue Service's blanket policy of disallowing any claimed deduction for which there was nothing in writing. What Cohan had *said,* Judge Hand concluded, was evidence of what Cohan had actually done, and the court instructed the IRS to assess Cohan's oral representations more carefully, and without the benefit of a preemptive dismissal of anything that could not be documented on a piece of paper.[6]

The Cohan rule is still with us, although Congress amended the Internal Revenue Code in 1962 to require written substantiation for business travel and various other commonly exaggerated business expenses.[7] And even though it is still not a good idea to claim deductions for which there is no written documentation, Internal Revenue Service agents are nevertheless instructed to recognize that taxpayer oral representations and recollections are evidence and cannot be dismissed out if hand. Written evidence is still better than oral evidence, at least for tax purposes, and the oral evidence needs to be "credible." But oral evidence—oral testimony—remains a permissible, even if risky, basis for a tax deduction.[8] Despite its subsequent narrowing, the tax rule that bears Cohan's name reminds us, and reminds the Internal Revenue Service, that what people say—testimony—can be evidence of the truth of what they are saying.

Treating testimony as evidence requires trusting what the testifier has said.[9] Most obviously, this trust may come from a belief—one itself based on evidence—that the testifier is someone who can be trusted. Perhaps our trust in the truth of what is said—our epistemic trust—comes from our knowledge that what the testifier has said on previous occasions has turned out to be true. Perhaps it comes from knowing that the testifier is the kind of person who does not say things without good reason for believing them true. And perhaps the testifier's position or profession or other source of expertise creates a reason for trust. There may be other reasons as well, but the point is that what someone says, as the Internal Revenue Service still acknowledges, even if grudgingly, is evidence for the truth of what they are saying, at least when they are asserting the kind of thing that there can be evidence for.[10]

The previous paragraph passed quickly over the possibility that the testifier is lying, a topic that will occupy all of Chapter 7, and the possibility that the testifier is honestly mistaken, which we address in Chapter 8. But even more generally, the extent to which testimony can be evidence for a proposition asserted by someone presupposes testifiers who are sincere and competent—that they know what they are talking about. As we will see, these constraints of honesty (or sincerity) and competence (or accuracy, or reliability) are substantial, creating many of the problems with treating testimony as evidence. But as an introduction to the idea of testimony as evidence, we can recognize that testimony is everywhere, that it can be evidence, and that it is perhaps the most predominant form of evidence that exists. Even what little remains of George M. Cohan's dispute with the Internal Revenue Service is a reminder that what people say, even without anything in writing, and even without anything more tangible by way of corroboration, can be evidence for what they are saying.

Hearsay—What's Wrong and What's Right About It

In the midst of the trial of the impeachment of former President Donald Trump in February 2021, the House impeachment managers proposed to call Representative Jaime Herrera Beutler of the state of Washington as a witness. And although Representative Herrera Beutler's proposed oral testimony was eventually replaced with a written statement, both the proposed oral testimony and the actual written testimony raise an important issue. Representative Herrera Beutler's testimony was not about something she had seen or otherwise experienced firsthand. She testified that House Republican leader Kevin McCarthy had told her and others about an angry and expletive-laden phone call between McCarthy and Trump in which Trump had made it clear that he was not going to call off the rioters who at the time were storming the US Capitol.[11]

The House impeachment managers originally sought to use Herrera Beutler's oral testimony as evidence for what McCarthy had told to her, and to use what Herrera Beutler said that McCarthy had said as evidence of Trump's unwillingness to take actions to quell the riot. But if this was to be evidence of Trump's behavior, it required that the members of the Senate believe what Herrera Beutler had said that McCarthy had said, and if the senators believed Herrera Beutler's testimony about what McCarthy had said, they had to believe, further, McCarthy's account of what Trump had said. In other words, this was hearsay. Twice.

Consider also a June 14, 2020, story in the *New York Times* reporting on a recently released book about first lady Melania Trump.[12] The book, by *Washington Post* reporter Mary Jordan, was described in the *Times* article as follows:

> And she [Melania Trump] has also constructed an image of herself that is not always supported by fact. For instance, Ms. Jordan raises questions about Mrs. Trump's claims of being fluent in a number of languages.
>
> "Photographers and others who have worked with her over the years—including native speakers of Italian, French, and German—told me that they never heard her use more than a few words of those language," Ms. Jordan writes.

Now suppose we are interested in the question whether Melania Trump speaks French. And then think about how we might consider the evidence in the *Times* article. If the proposition is that Melania Trump does not speak French, that proposition is supported by the article, which offers itself as evidence for the conclusion that Melania Trump does not speak French. But the reporter who wrote the *Times* article, Maggie Haberman, does not have firsthand knowledge of whether Ms. Trump speaks French. The article merely reports on what photographers and others told Mary Jordan, whose book is described in the *Times* article. And Ms. Jordan also does not have firsthand knowledge of whether Melania Trump speaks French. Ms. Jordan relies on what others have told her. The photographers may know from their own interactions with Ms. Trump that she does not speak French, but the readers of the article must rely on an article by a *Times* reporter, who relies on a book by Mary Jordan, who relies on what the photographers and others have told her. So we have a chain that goes from the photographers to the book author to the *Times* reporter to the reader who might be interested in whether Melania Trump speaks French. This is triple hearsay. And it is risky business.

The law considers hearsay risky for reasons aptly illustrated by the chain that started with the photographers and ended up with the reader of the *Times* article. At every step in the chain—photographer to book author to newspaper reporter to reader—there is a possibility of mistake. And the reader, the one who wants to know whether Melania Trump speaks French, has no way of determining whether there has been a mistake at any of the links, except to rely on the possibly mistaken next link. The reader cannot test what the photographers say except to trust the book author's trusting of the photographers, and the reader has no way of testing the book author except to trust the *Times* reporter's trusting of the book author. And the reader cannot even test the *Times* reporter.

This is why the law has traditionally distrusted hearsay. When a witness in court testifies about what someone else said, and when the jury is asked to accept the truth of what that someone who is not in court said, the normal safeguards of the oath, cross-examination, and observation of the demeanor of the witness are absent. Why, in the extended example above, should we trust the photographers? Why should we trust what the book author said the photographers said? Why should we trust what the reporter said the book author said? Similarly, the law distrusts the statements of those who are not in court, under oath, observed, and subject to cross-examination.

In recent years American law has attached so many exceptions to the rule against hearsay that there is not much of it left.[13] Depending on how one counts, the *Federal Rules of Evidence* contain at least thirty-one exceptions to the prohibition on hearsay evidence, and then the *Rules* add a catchall exception just in case there are forms of reliable hearsay that are not covered by the thirty-one listed exceptions.[14] Going even further, common-law jurisdictions such as Canada and the United Kingdom have pretty much eliminated the exclusion of hearsay, as do many American judges, informally, when there is no jury.[15]

The continuing weakening of the bar on hearsay evidence is explained by the fact that it would be hard to imagine a world without hearsay, or knowledge without hearsay. Perhaps few people care whether Melania Trump speaks French.[16] But many more people care what Representative Herrera Beutler said Representative McCarthy had said former President Trump had said. So much of what we know is based on hearsay, starting with the dates of our birth, that it is impossible to imagine a world in which we did not use hearsay as evidence. Even the quickest scan of a daily newspaper reveals that most of what we learn from so-called news is actually news about what other people have said, and most of why we care about what the people in the news have said is because those people are making factual assertions that we are implicitly being asked to credit. To return to the mob invasion of the Capitol building on January 6, 2021, much of what was reported in the news about that event consisted of various allegedly first-person accounts by those who were there, even though those who provided the accounts typically provided them to journalists, who in turn provided them to the public. Even if we trust the journalists to report accurately on what the participants and observers told them, as we generally do, we are still expected to form our beliefs about what happened on the basis of accounts offered by the people who were there, people whose testimony we cannot observe or cross-examine, and whose accounts we are asked to simply assume are both honest and accurate. We routinely do this, and we would not know much about the world and its goings-on without just this kind of reliance on hearsay. The law's traditional skepticism about hearsay evidence is good reason to think twice about each step in the chain when we evaluate a hearsay statement, but it is important to remember that hearsay evidence is still evidence. And it is usually pretty good evidence at that.

One final cautionary note on hearsay, and on testimony generally: The law says that a statement is hearsay if the out-of-court statement is offered *for the truth of that statement*. That is an important qualification, as the classic example from the legal literature, here modified slightly, makes clear.[17] If my colleague says to me that the dean just told him that she was Joan of Arc, my colleague is not asking me to take the dean's statement as true. Neither of us think that she is Joan of Arc, nor that there is even the remotest possibility that she is. Rather, my colleague is reporting the dean's statement as evidence that she has become mentally unhinged, or as evidence that she was joking. But not as evidence that she is actually Joan of Arc. Only when one person says that some other person said something, and only when we are asked to take what the other person said as evidence for the truth of the proposition asserted, is the problem of hearsay presented.

This understanding of hearsay is relevant to the entire topic of testimony. People say all sort of things, and for all sorts of purposes. When a child comes out from behind a bush on Halloween and shouts "Boo!," she is not testifying, and she is not asking me to believe anything. So too when the train conductor says "All aboard," when the boss says "You're fired," when my friend says "I'm sorry," or, to use another example of so-called performatives from J. L. Austin and speech act theory, some notable personage breaks a bottle of champagne on the bow of a ship and says "I christen this ship *H.M.S. Queen Elizabeth*."[18] Only when someone asserts something that can be true or false do we have testimony, and only then do we confront the myriad questions surrounding the issue of whether we can take that assertion—the testimony—as evidence for what it is that the asserter was asserting.

I Heard It through the Grapevine—
Rumor as Evidence

The problem of hearsay is exacerbated, but also perhaps alleviated, when we are considering whether gossip, rumor, reputation, and other forms collective and unattributed testimony might be considered as evidence. From one perspective, the problems surrounding hearsay seem even worse when the original assertion is not from an individual and identifiable source. When we say that someone has a bad reputation for honesty, or a good reputation for reliability, we are relying on an aggregation of hearsay statements, although we rarely recognize it as such. But hearsay it is, usually thorough multiple iterations of hearsay, and without knowing the source of the original assertion. Whatever the risks of hearsay, they are compounded when we not only have no opportunity to examine the source of the original statement—the declarant, in lawspeak—but when we do not even know who the source or sources are. When we are asked to rely on—to treat as evidence—what some unidentified accumulation of people happen to believe, the justification for believing rumor, gossip, and reputation seems especially thin. And even if we do not go as far as insisting that such sources of knowledge should not count as evidence at all, it seems sensible at the very least to discount heavily the evidence that comes from such unattributed and attenuated sources.

But this is too quick. Perhaps rumor, gossip, and the social mechanisms that produce someone's or something's reputation should be understood not as heightening but as lessening the problems with hearsay. One reason for thinking that rumor, gossip, and reputation might alleviate the hearsay problem, therefore, is that rumor, gossip, and reputation are the collective products of a mechanism that might—and only might—incline toward reliability. Some years ago James Surowiccki, a writer for *The New Yorker,* wrote a popular book entitled *The Wisdom of Crowds.*[19] When groups are diverse and decentralized and when the members are independent of each other, Surowiecki argued, using a number of engaging examples, the groups tend to make better decisions than individuals, better even than highly trained experts making decisions in isolation.

As several critics pointed out, other research casts doubt on Surowiecki's conclusions.[20] Moreover, he may have built so much into his conditions of diversity, decentralization, and independence, especially the last, that the conclusions he reached about wise crowds may have been highly unrepresentative of the behavior of real crowds making real decisions. What the psychologist Irving Janis influentially labeled "groupthink" back in the 1970s is often a large part of how people come to their factual conclusions. And just as collective wisdom may sometimes incline toward truth, perhaps the phenomenon of following the crowd, as people are often prone to do, inclines in just the opposite direction.

The possible wisdom of crowds has in recent years become the subject of more serious academic research, often under the label "collective intelligence"—which is the title of a new academic journal, although its first issue has yet to appear as of this writing. And the Massachusetts Institute of Technology now has the MIT Center for Collective Intelligence. But whether in its popularized or more seriously academic versions, the same issues present themselves.[21] Modern information technology and related advances in artificial intelligence and so-called big data undoubtedly increase the potential for collective intelligence, but the same technology can also be the instrument of collective stupidity. The key question is the extent to which good ideas or true assertions about facts will be more likely to emerge from this or that collective process, or whether instead the same processes that increase the potential for the collective production of good ideas and accurate factual assertions will also increase the potential for the collective production and distribution of bad ideas and erroneous factual assertions..

This debate between the wisdom of crowds crowd, on one side, and the groupthink group, on the other, raises the question whether collective wisdom can be evidence, and whether it is ordinarily better than the noncollective wisdom that is the source of much of our testimonial evidence. If and when the collective wisdom has substantial evidentiary value, it is because of the ability of people, at times, to learn from each other, and, at times, to correct the mistakes that others make. But although some "crowds" are actually diverse, and although many crowds are decentralized, Surowiecki's independence condition limits the value of his conclusions. Most forms of collective judgment are produced by the nonindependent groups that we might, less flatteringly but more accurately, call "mobs." And somewhat less pejorative than "mob" is simply the idea of conventional wisdom, which at times devolves into mere rumor. But whatever label we use, there is a serious question about whether the kinds of things that "everyone knows" can count as evidence for whatever it is that everyone knows, or thinks they know.

It is important to distinguish evidence *that* "everyone knows" something from the fact of everyone knowing something being evidence *for* the something that everyone knows. Consider Donald Trump's frequent assertion, made most notoriously to the crowd of people assembled in Washington, DC, on January 6, 2021—significant numbers of whom became the mob that invaded the Capitol building shortly thereafter. Addressing the crowd on the issue of the integrity of the election, the president said that "everyone knows" that he won the election by a landslide and that "everyone knows" that this obvious outcome was not made official because the election was "stolen."[22] This statement contained (at least) two falsehoods, which must be distinguished. One was the question whether President Trump in fact won the election by a landslide. He did not, so his claim that he had was false. But the other is whether this is something that "everyone knows." That was false too. Sometimes, however, it is true that everyone thinks they know something that is in fact false. Even acknowledging the empirical claim of "everyone" as hyperbole, it is still true that everyone in 1491 knew, or at least thought they knew, that the earth was flat. And to a first approximation, everyone knows now that Marie Antoinette said "Let them eat cake," that Napoleon was short, and that eating shortly before swimming produces muscle cramps. As claims about what it is that everyone knows, or thinks they know, these claims are, roughly, true. As claims about the truth of what everyone knows, or thinks they know, the claims are false.

Once we disaggregate claims that everyone knows something from claims about the truth of what everyone knows, we can focus more carefully on the latter—on the claim that everyone knowing something—or, more plausibly, the consensus knowing something—is evidence for the truth of what it is that everyone knows. The "wisdom of crowds" claim, or the collective-intelligence claim, oversimplified, is that this is so. But the various social, psychological, and political forces leading people to want to align themselves with others—independent of the basis for the alignment—gives pause. In high school some of us wanted to do what the cool kids were doing just because we wanted to be part of that crowd, even if what the crowd was doing was often pretty stupid. And to the extent that such a dynamic exists in other social domains, the ability to rely on the collective wisdom of that domain as evidence for the truth of what the domain believes diminishes commensurately.

The "wisdom of crowds" claim bears an interesting affinity with the "marketplace of ideas" slogan that has been a central part of free speech discourse, policy, and law at least since John Milton asked, rhetorically, "Who ever knew Truth put to the worse in a free and open encounter?"[23] Milton's basic idea, echoed in John Stuart Mill's *On Liberty,* in Oliver Wendell Holmes's claim that the "best test of truth is the power of the thought to get itself accepted in the competition of the market," and in civil libertarian rhetoric for at least the last hundred years, is that the process of collective discussion will incline toward truth—that collectivity produces collective intelligence more than it produces collective folly.[24] Clothed in modern terminology, the claim, as the late Anthony Lewis engagingly put it, is that the collective discourse fostered by a free speech regime is a "search engine for truth."[25]

As a question about evidence, the "marketplace of ideas" slogan raises two different evidentiary claims. One is whether the truth of some proposition is evidence of the likelihood that people will accept it. Obviously, people believe many true propositions. And they believe many false ones as well. And we know, and Madison Avenue knows, that the truth of some proposition is hardly the only determinant of the likelihood that some population will accept it, or even that some significant percentage of some population that will accept it. After all, roughly 30 percent of the population accepts the truth of the (false) predictive and (false) behavioral claims of astrology.[26] Even assuming that truth matters to acceptance, as we hope it does, the identity, authority, and charisma of the person who is asserting something also matter. The same holds for the frequency with which something is said, the technological way in which it is said, the extent to which what is said fits with the prior beliefs of the audience, the way in which what is said satisfies some emotional or psychological needs of the hearer, and much more. Indeed, the long-standing and seemingly increasing acceptance of so-called conspiracy theories provides strong support for the conclusion that people's acceptance of some proposition depends on far more than that proposition's truth.[27] If the question is whether the truth of a proposition is evidence of its likely acceptance—perhaps of less importance in this book—then there is much reason to believe, the faith of Milton and his successors notwithstanding, that although truth matters as evidence, it may matter less than we hope and less than we often suppose. The truth of a proposition, which we know as a result of evidence, is itself not very good evidence, or at least not as good evidence as has long been assumed, of whether it will be accepted by those to whom it is communicated.[28]

More important to us here, however, is the reverse—not the evidentiary value of truth in determining acceptance, but the evidentiary value of acceptance in determining truth. This is the "everyone knows" or "wisdom of crowds" or "collective intelligence" claim—that the fact of acceptance is at least some evidence of the correctness of what it is that is accepted.[29]

On this question, the "wisdom of crowds" claim is one side of the story. But the other side of the story is as skeptical of collective wisdom as evidence as the marketplace of ideas is celebratory. This other side of the story, traceable to the worry about the spread of false rumors during the Second World War, and of a piece with the game of "telephone" that many of us played as children, views collective discussion as the hotbed of misinformation, disinformation, and the basket of human psychological needs that are often in conflict with truth. As falsehoods that are spread widely and quickly by the internet and social media make this hotbed ever hotter, the value of widespread belief as a reliable indicator of likely truth becomes ever smaller.

All the same, evidence that might not be very good evidence is often, although not necessarily, evidence with some value, depending on what we want to with it, or what decisions we want to make as a result of it. The law has long believed, for example, that a person's reputation for honesty (or lack thereof) might be relevant to assessing their credibility and thus the reliability of their formal testimony.[30] The law may be wrong in this, but that long-standing belief suggests that reputation— what everyone knows—may in some contexts have some evidentiary value. And however skeptical we might be about some uses of reputation, including the law's, most of us are comfortable in using reputation evidence when we select our contractors, our restaurants, and perhaps even our babysitters and investment advisors. To the extent that we are relying on collectively produced reputation in this way, we are relying on testimony, even though the original sources of that testimony remain hidden from us. When we rely on reputation, which we often more pejoratively call rumor and gossip, we are relying on also-anonymous assessors of the reliability of what other have told them. This is all the more reason to be especially skeptical of what we can and should understand as indirect testimony. But it might not be reason to discard it entirely.

Chapter 6

Testing Testimony

IN ATTEMPTING TO GUARD against lies and lying, the legal system has long relied, in part, on the oath that witnesses are required to take before testifying. This familiar oath, traditionally sworn on a Bible, purports to oblige the oath-taker to tell the truth, the whole truth, and nothing but the truth. Obviously, the oath is an attempt to prevent lying, and in Chapter 7 we will look at lies, lying, and liars in more detail. An initial question, however, is whether oath-taking provides the kind of assurance that the legal system intends it to provide. And if it does, which as we will see is hardly obvious, does the same apply across the entire range of testimonial statements? We need to look, therefore, both at whether swearing-enhanced or oath-enhanced statements have greater value as legal evidence than those without such purported credibility enhancements, and also whether the same conclusions (or doubts) apply to oaths and swearings outside of the courtroom?

If this were a book of theology, there would be much to say about the value of the oath. Some of that would be about someone's special obligation to God to tell the truth after having sworn unto God to do so. And some would be about what God does to people who lie when they have sworn not to. But this is not a book of theology. Nevertheless, there remains the sociological and nontheological question of the (empirical) extent to which people do or did believe in the religious character and power of the oath. Sociologically and not theologically, we know that many people do believe that they will suffer in the after-life, if not sooner, should they tell a lie after swearing to tell the truth. Of course, I have no way of knowing whether this widespread belief is correct and no way of knowing whether post-death punishment is what actually happens to oath-taking liars. Nor do most readers of this book. Still, some people believe it now, and, importantly, many more people believed it in the past, when the formal oath was first developed. Capi-talizing on this belief in divine retribution, the legal system developed the oath as a way of increasing the likelihood of honesty and perhaps even accuracy in trial testimony.[1]

Although the percentage of people who believe that lying under oath will sentence them to eternal agony in the fires of hell has decreased, the oath persists. And it persists not only for reasons of tradition. It per-sists in part because in many contexts a lie under oath creates a risk of serious legal consequences. It is true that prosecutions for perjury are rare, largely because criminal prosecutions for perjury require the pros-ecutor to prove beyond a reasonable doubt that the witness *knew* their testimony was false.[2] But although perjury prosecutions are difficult and infrequent, they are not unheard of. Moreover, they are often highly publicized, as with former president Donald Trump's friend Roger Stone, whom the president pardoned after he was sentenced to forty months' imprisonment for lying under oath to Congress.[3] And equally well publicized are related crimes such as lying to federal offi-cials, which is what got Martha Stewart sent to prison, and noncrim-inal sanctions for lying under oath, which is what got former President Bill Clinton impeached (but not convicted) and suspended from the practice of law for five years.[4] And if even these sanctions are un-common, we know from the research on heuristics and biases, and as the purveyors of airline crash insurance know as well, that people tend to exaggerate the frequency of unlikely catastrophic events.[5] Consequently, the threat of a perjury prosecution or other official sanction may have a deterrent effect that is greater than the statistical chances of prosecution and conviction would indicate. To the extent that this is so, witnesses in court, reminded that they are under oath, might plausibly tend to tell the truth more than their own moral compass or even self-interest would otherwise suggest.

The phrase "might plausibly" reflects the fact that there is only limited research on the precisely specified question whether oath-taking has a causal effect on the likelihood that witnesses will testify honestly.[6] Plainly there are people who will tell the truth even absent an oath. Or at least we hope so. And equally plainly there are people who will lie even when under oath. That's too bad, but there may not be much that can be done about it. But that leaves a third category, probably the one of greatest importance when we are thinking about the oath, and likely smaller than either of the previous two categories. And this the category of people who will tell the truth when sworn to do so, but would otherwise lie when it suited or benefited them.[7] There is some indication from low-stakes experiments that explicit reminders of obligations to tell the truth, or explicit promises to tell the truth even if not under oath in a technical sense—such as the Ten Commandments' prohibition of lying—have at least some ability to reduce the incidence of lying.[8] But because there is not much other research on the question, and because research on the effects of reminders about the Ten Commandments appear not to distinguish the religious aspects of the Ten Commandments from nonreligious aspects of honesty reminders, we lack a substantial body of empirical evidence on the extent to which, if at all, oaths themselves are truth-promoting, whether in court or out.

Even apart from perjury prosecutions, and even apart from the risk of eternal damnation, the oath, it is said, serves as a reminder of the seriousness—or solemnity, as it is often put—of the proceedings, and thus of the importance of veracity in those proceedings. But although this purported virtue of the oath is often touted, as with the court that announced that "those who have been impressed with the moral, religious or legal significance of formally undertaking to tell the truth are more likely to do so," there is hardly any research indicating whether formal oath-taking, as opposed to less formal reminders, does or does not serve this purpose.[9]

Whether the oath successfully increases the likelihood of honesty in the formal legal process is an important question, but the testimony we are considering more broadly is hardly limited to judicial proceedings. Nor are oaths. Variations on the oath are ubiquitous in everyday life. When someone says, "I swear to God, that's what I saw," they seem to be suggesting that however casual they might normally be about the truth, *this* statement is different. And so too with the large range of equivalents that also seem to have similar quasi-religious origins. "I swear on my mother's grave." "Swear to God, hope to die." "Cross my heart." Or, even more simply, "I swear."

Similar assertions rely less on religious traditions than on conceptions of honor. "Do you give me your word?" Or, unprompted, "I give you my word on this." "You can take my word for it." "As an officer and a gentleman, I give my word." And so on.[10] Similarly, blanket honor codes, such as those in force at the military academies and some of our older colleges and universities, purport to impose an honor-enforced (and sanction-enforced) obligation not to "lie, cheat, or steal, or tolerate those who do."[11]

Honor codes aside, assertion-specific oaths are in some sense curious. When testifiers add these kinds of self-endorsements to their statements, are we then expected to be more skeptical of statements made without them? Is making a statement shorn of "I swear to God" or its equivalents the same as crossing your fingers behind your back, and thus not to be relied on? Or have "I swear to God" and "You have my word" become not much more than throat-clearing, adding little, if anything, to the confidence that the hearer would otherwise have in the veracity of the statement? This hypothesis seems likely, consequently supporting the conclusion that although it would be good to have some way of testing testimony before relying on it, the fact of the testifier giving or not giving an oath, formal or casual, is hardly likely to be a very effective test. Testimony is often good evidence, but it is doubtful that oaths, especially those made outside of formal legal settings, make it very much, if at all, better.

Perry Mason and the Art of Television Cross-Examination

Perry Mason, the fictional defense attorney first created in a series of Erle Stanley Gardner mystery novels and then the eponymous central figure in three different television series starting in the 1950s, was a master of cross-examination. In the typical episode, Mason's client would have been wrongly accused of some horrific crime, usually murder. At the preliminary hearing, or at the trial, Mason would aggressively cross-examine one of the prosecution's witnesses, and under this intense cross-examination the witness would confess that it was he, and not the defendant, who had committed the crime. And occasionally Mason's cross-examination was so effective in pointing to the truth and away from the guilt of the defendant that some member of the spectator's gallery, one who was not even a witness, would stand up in the middle of the trial and, wracked by guilt, blurt out that he (or, occasionally but rarely, she) had actually committed the crime.

All this was fiction. And not just because the stories were fictional. It was fiction because the image of Perry Mason verbally bludgeoning a witness into a confession painted a dramatically unrealistic picture of the nature and effectiveness of cross-examination in testing the truth of testimonial evidence. In reality, witnesses who lie while testifying continue to lie under cross-examination, and witnesses who are simply mistaken reiterate those mistakes when cross-examined. As anyone who has conducted a cross-examination knows, Gardner and the television script writers had the distinct advantage of being able to write the answers as well as the questions.[12] But rarely are real witnesses so cooperative, and actual cross-examination is more commonly a mix of witness stubbornness, compounded uncertainty, and lawyer statements that are as often forms of testimony as they are genuine questions.

The alleged virtues of cross-examination as revealing the truth and exposing falsity received a ringing endorsement a century ago from John Henry Wigmore, at the time the leading scholar of the law of evidence in the United States and perhaps in the entire common-law world. "Cross-examination," Wigmore announced, is "beyond any doubt the greatest legal engine ever invented for the discovery of truth."[13] It is not clear, however, that Wigmore's statement would stand up to the very cross-examination he lauded, and so we should look more carefully at cross-examination as a truth-producing procedure.

In examining the role of cross-examination as an aid to evaluating the truth of testimonial statements, we need to focus, as Wigmore did, on genuine cross-examination. And in doing so, we should exclude the performances, sometimes misleadingly described as cross-examination, that we see with some regularity in congressional hearings. Whatever other purposes such spectacles may serve, haranguing a witness with some combination of questioner-supplied facts and adjective-laden accusations is hardly, an "engine . . . for the discovery of truth."[14] As anyone who has ever moderated a public event knows all too well, there is a difference, often ignored by questioners, between asking a question and making a stump speech, and the typical public legislative or administrative agency hearing contains a great deal of the latter and not much of the former. Indeed, much the same can be said about far too many press conferences, events in which multi-part questions by self-important reporters are followed by vacuous nonanswers from the official at the podium.[15]

When cross-examination operates at its best, it does not, to repeat, lead testifiers to recant their testimony, Perry Mason notwithstanding.[16] And when it operates at its worst, as the sorry history of abusive cross-examination of rape victims shows, it can impede the search for truth, either by casting unjustified doubts on the testimony of witnesses who are telling the truth, or by discouraging such witnesses from even being willing to testify in the first place.[17] Effective and non-abusive cross-examination, though, can elicit information that the testifier might have an interest in not disclosing. It can sometimes, especially by exposing inconsistencies, elicit information by which the receivers of testimony—jurors, prototypically, but many others in many other contexts—can evaluate the honesty and reliability, the credibility, of the testifier.[18] It can reveal sources of bias, conflicts of interest, or simply some reason for believing that the testifier prefers one answer or outcome to another—a matter of some interest if one accepts what the research tells us about motivated reasoning, the topic of Chapter 13. It can also help the evaluator of testimony determine the basis for the testifier's perception. And it can, by the use of follow-up questions, often supply valuable clarification of what may initially have appeared imprecise. If a factual assertion—testimony—is to be useful as evidence, and if and when there is reason to be skeptical about the reliability of such assertions, cross-examination in the broadest sense may supply a useful form of assessment. Such cross-examination need not resemble Perry Mason's, or even real cross-examinations. It may instead be simply the process of taking an assertion as an opportunity to engage the asserter in further clarification, elaboration, or qualification. And thus—as the Internal Revenue Service was grudgingly compelled to acknowledge in its dispute with George M. Cohan—when cross-examination provides the opportunity to scrutinize testimony more carefully, testimony often can supply a useful form of evidence.

Calibrating Testimony

Many people rely on Tripadvisor, Yelp, and related internet resources to choose restaurants, hotels, contractors, and much else. And although the idea of relying on reviews is hardly new, what these services offer that traditional published reviews do not is not only the aggregation of multiple reviews, but also easy access to the reviewing history of each reviewer. Aficionados knew, of course, how to interpret a movie review by the legendary *New Yorker* film critic Pauline Kael or a theater review by the equally legendary Brooks Atkinson of the *New York Times,* just as they know how to evaluate a *Times* restaurant review by Pete Wells now or Ruth Reichl in the recent past. But Tripadvisor and its ilk make the practice far easier. And they do so by allowing the reader of the on-line reviews, with little more than a click or a keystroke, to inspect all of the past reviews of each reviewer.

When the reader of a review consults the reviewing history of the reviewer, the reader is given the ability to *calibrate* a particular review, just as we calibrate (or should) when we add pounds to the reading on a scale that we know reads low and subtract pounds from a reading on a scale that prior experience tells us reads high. So too with the hunters who aim lower than where the gunsight tells them to aim, knowing from past experience that the gunsight leads them to miss high. Before there was very much grading on a curve, and certainly before there were the mandatory curves now current at many colleges and universities, word-of-mouth—itself a form of evidence—told us who were the tough graders and who could provide an easy A. Letters of recommendation are treated similarly when we deliberate over appointments, admissions, hiring, and so on. If we receive multiple letters over time from the same recommenders, recommending different people, we learn that certain recommenders say over-the-top nice things about everyone, and we discount accordingly.[19] And other recommenders are just the opposite, barely having much good to say even about those they recommend. And for those recommenders we inflate. All of this is calibration, and it is not just a question of inflating or deflating. When a restaurant reviewer on Tripadvisor is revealed to have a history of complaining about small portions or too much spice, I know how to evaluate the evaluator, and act accordingly. Similarly for the evaluations coming from evaluators who expect every restaurant to cater to their unreasonable demands. If the demands are described, which they usually are, I can determine which ones are unreasonable, even if an evaluator rarely sees it that way, and then proceed to discount or ignore the ratings of this particular reviewer.

The idea of calibration is applicable to the entire realm of evidence, but it is especially relevant to the use of testimony as evidence.[20] As we will explore in Chapter 7, suppliers of testimony often have an interest in lying, and it would be useful to have some way of minimizing lying and identifying the liars. In Chapter 8 we will look at honest mistake, which is plainly less morally and legally culpable than lying but no less an impediment to treating testimony as reliable evidence. Yet even in the absence of lies or mistakes, testimony is subject to so many shadings, fudgings, hedgings, twistings, embellishments, inflations, deflations, and various other forms of distortion that calibration can be a valuable way for the hearer to evaluate the epistemic worth of what the speaker is saying or what the writer is writing.

One form of calibration that has an especially ugly history is calibration based on the nonindividualized attributes of the testifier. There are many such nonindividualized or group attributes, but the ones most justifiably notorious are those that are based on race, religion, ethnicity, national origin, and gender. Even apart from the exclusions that were based in one way or another on slave status, non-enslaved African Americans were often officially precluded from serving as witnesses in court, as were Indians and sometimes those of Chinese descent.[21] Even when such official exclusions were not in force, informal exclusions of members of the same racial groups were common.[22] Moreover, and especially relevant here, even in the absence of formal or informal exclusions we had (and still have) the prevalence of what Miranda Fricker has aptly referred to as "credibility deficits.[23] People tend to be believed or not believed based on various attributes they possess, even when such attributes have no value in predicting accuracy or honesty.[24] And race has long been foremost among these spuriously predictive attributes.[25]

When it comes to gender, the history is different but no better. Unlike the situation in antiquity, unlike in England in the earliest years of the common law, and unlike in some systems of religious law, women have not generally been precluded from serving as witnesses in modern secular legal systems. Women have, however, long been assumed to be less credible than male witnesses, although there is no evidence to support the assumption.[26] But relying on psychological surveys that would now be considered as methodologically laughable as they are morally offensive, John Henry Wigmore, in his *Principles of Judicial Proof,* first published in 1913 and republished with no change on this point in 1931, claimed that women are more likely than men "to confuse what they have really observed with what they have imagined or wished to occur," and more likely to "fall below [men] in candor and honesty."[27]

Of even greater and more lasting consequence is the fact that women reporting rape and other forms of sexual assault have been thought, again with no supporting evidence, to be more prone to exaggerating or fabricating accusations of sexual assault than other crime victims are to exaggerate or fabricate the crimes they report. As recently as 1975, the California standard (and thus official and mandatory) jury instructions included the so-called cautionary instruction, by which jurors in rape cases were to be told by the judge that "a charge such as that made against the defendant . . . is easily made, and, once made, difficult to defend against, even if the person accused is innocent. Therefore, the law requires that you examine the testimony of the female person named in the information with caution."[28] And this instruction, with its roots in the seventeenth-century writing of the English judge Sir Matthew Hale, was based in large part on the widely believed fiction, just noted, that women were more likely to imagine nonexistent rapes than other people were to imagine other nonexistent crimes against them.[29]

Modern law has attempted to alleviate most of the formal and some of the informal ways in which statistically irrelevant group attributes have been used to discount the courtroom testimony of women and members of racial and other marginalized groups. But that is not to say that such barriers to the accurate assessment of testimony do not persist in legal and non-legal contexts. An entire philosophical program under the name of "epistemic injustice" is focused on addressing many of the problems just described, and many others similar to them.[30] It is important, however, to distinguish the epistemic dimensions of epistemic injustice from those dimensions of testimony and credibility that are unjust but possibly not epistemically so. If there are attributes of classes of people that do predict honesty or dishonesty, or reliability or unreliability, using those attributes to attach an epistemic enhancement or to impose an epistemic discount would not be epistemically problematic even though, depending on the nature of the class, it might still be unjust for other reasons.[31]

Although I know of no racial, ethnic, religious, or gender classes that would fit the foregoing description, other types of classes might be different. The fact that there are laws against age discrimination in employment, for example, and properly so, does not mean that age-based memory impairment is illusory. Even for older adults with no signs of Alzheimer's disease or other forms of dementia, normal aging is highly predictive of at least some memory loss.[32] As a result, being more skeptical of testimonial recollections by people above a certain age— treating those testimonial recollections as weaker evidence, all other things being equal—is not epistemically irrational, even though it might be unjust (and thus avoided or prohibited despite its epistemic rationality) in marginalizing people already marginalized in other ways. And although we cannot choose our ages and thus have only limited ability to control age-related memory weakening, much the same may apply with respect to those attributes that are chosen rather than being beyond the control of the individual. There is no research on whether people who lie for a living—professional poker players, for example, and some telemarketers and telephone solicitors—are less honest than others in other aspects of their lives, but it is not inconceivable that a casual approach to honesty might spill over from one area of a person's life to other areas. The same applies to enhancements rather than discounts. People who are trained in careful visual observation—some police officers, some security guards, members of the military trained in identifying enemy aircraft—might be assumed to be less likely than the rest of us to makes mistakes in perception, and so their testimony about what they saw might be taken as more credible evidence, again all other things being equal, than would the same testimony from someone without that training.

At this point we have shifted to a somewhat broader sense of calibration, and a sense that is different from the testifier-specific calibration that Tripadvisor and Yelp enable with their reviewer histories. The larger point is that when people are evaluating a testimonial statement for its worth as evidence—its probative value, in legalese—they often calibrate that statement based on attributes of some category of which the testifier is a member. Sometimes that calibration will be empirically justified, and sometimes it will not be. Sometimes that calibration will involve a non-epistemic injustice, and sometimes it will not. But even when the calibration is not based on putting the testifier into some larger category, we can still calibrate based on that testifier's own prior testimony. That is what Tripadvisor and Yelp allow us to do. That is what we do when we inflate the testimony about ability from a tough grader (in the precise sense of grading an examination or a term paper or in the less precise context of offering a recommendation) and discount it from an easy one. That is what American law does when it permits "secondary" testimony of various kinds about the likely honesty of the primary testifier.[33] And that is also, if the story of George Washington and the cherry tree were true, which it almost certainly is not, what those who told the story asked the public to do in using a past example of self-sacrificing honesty as evidence of the truth of what Washington was now saying, and of what he might say in the future.

Oath-taking, cross-examination, and various forms of calibration all can help us assess the value of testimony as evidence, although they are primarily focused on oral testimony. But all these devices and strategies are general, in the sense of spanning the entire range of dimensions on which we might evaluate the worth of an item of testimony. More specifically, however, our concerns about the value of testimony are typically of two varieties. One is the possibility that the testifier is lying. And the other is that the testifier is honestly mistaken. These are the specific worries about testimony as evidence that are addressed in Chapters 7 and 8.

Chapter 7

Of Lies and Liars

ONE OF THE MANY PECULIARITIES of the law of evidence is what is called the "excited utterance" exception to the rule against hearsay. The details of the rule need not concern us here, but the basic premise of the rule is that what people say under circumstances of sudden and great excitement—high stress—is especially reliable, and therefore should not be excluded by the rule against hearsay.[1]

On the face of it, the excited utterance exception seems psychologically naive.[2] We have long known that what people say when excited may be vulnerable to the lapses of memory and failures of perception that excitement and stress can cause. If anything, it seems as if excited utterances ought to be treated not as especially reliable, but just the opposite—as especially unreliable.

But that is only half the story. And only the modern half. Back when the excited utterance exception developed, courts were less aware of the various ways in which what people perceived, remembered, and described might be inaccurate. Perception was understood as the primary way in which people gained knowledge, and the possibilities of inaccurate perception, mistaken recollection, and confused recounting were rarely acknowledged. But although the courts and people in general were less attuned to the possibility of honest but erroneous perception, and often oblivious to the risks of honestly mistaken recall and innocently misspoken reports, they were keenly aware of the possibility of intentional fabrication. Lying. Just as the oath developed to try to keep people from lying, the excited utterance exception developed at a time when people were less worried than they should have been about mistakes. But they were very worried, and not less than they should have been, about lies and liars. And so the excited utterance exception was based on the largely accurate view that lying requires advance thought and planning. What people unthinkingly blurt out on the spur of the moment, especially under conditions of high anxiety, is at least what they honestly believe at the time, or so it was thought. The excited utterance exception thus stands as a reminder that the legal system, relying as it does so much on courtroom testimony about events that neither the judge nor the jury have themselves observed, is especially concerned about lying.

Lying is a worry not only in court. Concern about lying has existed as long as there has been lying. The Ten Commandments would hardly have commanded people not to "bear false witness" had false witness not, even then, been perceived as a serious problem. And although the Ten Commandments tried mightily to get people to stop lying, the practice persists. Husbands lie to their wives. Children lie to their parents. Parents lie to their children. Merchants lie to their customers. Criminals lie to the police. The police lie to suspects. Politicians lie to their constituents. Students submitting late papers lie to their professors. Lying, it seems, is everywhere.

Volumes have been written about lying.[3] Sometimes the focus is on why lying is wrong. At other times the concern is with the exceptions— the conditions under which lying might not be wrong, as in the traditional example of lying to the prospective murderer about the whereabouts of his intended victim. And then there are so-called white lies, in which we lie to avoid hurting someone's feelings, and social lies, which are designed to soften the sharp edges of refusals and rebuffs. There are also lies that are the harmless or even necessary part of some practice, such as bluffing in poker, or deceiving an opponent on the football field or the enemy in time of war. And the lies that we call "fish stories" are so common and so commonly discounted that they might not even qualify as lies at all.

Our interest here is neither with the moral rightness or wrongness of lying nor with the moral justifications for the alleged exceptions to the traditional strictures against lying. Rather, the immediate issue is how lying affects the reliability of testimony as evidence. If what people say can be evidence of the content of what they have said—and that is what the idea of testimony is all about—then the value of that testimony is dependent on the truth of what is said. Lies undercut that value, and thus undercut the worth of testimony as evidence. It would be good, as a matter of evidence and not only as a matter of morality, to be able to tell when people are lying, and thus be able to dismiss or discount the testimony of the liar in reaching our factual conclusions.

Not surprisingly, the law has long wrestled with this problem. Given that most of the evidence in a trial consists of testimony, we can easily understand why the law remains especially concerned with that testimony being reliable. And one way testimony might not be reliable is if the witness is lying. Initially, we note that witnesses might lie—and not just be mistaken—if they have an interest in one outcome rather than another. Defendants charged with crimes were long prohibited from testifying in their own defense because of the perception—hardly unfounded—that most people would rather lie than be hanged or imprisoned. And so it was thought that lying by the defendant, even under oath, was so predictable, and therefore a defendant's testimony so predictably unreliable, that it was better not to permit that testimony at all.[4] And the same unease about the effect of self-interest on veracity was applied to civil lawsuits as well, where again the parties were traditionally prohibited from testifying, on the assumption that the pull of self-interest would typically override any perceived obligations to the truth.[5] These prohibitions on defendant and party testimony were eliminated in English law in the early nineteenth century and in most other common-law countries at about the same time, but the worry still persists that criminal defendants will lie to save their skins or their liberty, that defendants in civil lawsuits will lie to save their money, and that plaintiffs in those same civil lawsuits will lie for reasons of retribution or financial gain. The list of reasons for lying is long, and even now it is both permissible and common to cross-examine or otherwise "impeach" a witness in order to elicit the possibility that the witness has an interest in the outcome and is therefore more likely to be lying.

In attempting to guard against lies and lying, the legal system has long relied, at least in part, on the oath that witnesses are required to take before testifying, an oath to tell the truth, the whole truth, and nothing but the truth. As we examined in Chapter 6, the oath, whether formally in court or less formally in many other contexts, has long been a part of numerous testimonial practices. But oaths have only limited value, both in court and out. With the decline in serious belief in an afterlife and in a God insistent on punishing fabricators, with formal sanctions for perjury so rare, and with statements such as "I swear to God" becoming little more than verbal tics, the question remains about to how to guard against lying in a world in which verbal testimony is such an important part of the evidence we use throughout our lives. Although the maxim that the truth hurts is about people's reluctance to face up to difficult facts about themselves, the truth hurts in the broader sense that people often have strong incentives to avoid telling the truth when that truth will be to their personal, professional, social, financial, or other disadvantage. And because the incentives to lie are often great, the incentives to find ways to identify liars and lying have also been great. The better we can identify liars, the more we can rely on testimony.

What Is a Lie?

It was not a good four years for the word "lie." Back when Immanuel Kant was condemning lying in the eighteenth century, and back when Sissela Bok and others were analyzing lying in the twentieth, most people had a pretty good idea of what a lie was. A lie was a false statement used intentionally by the liar to induce the hearer into having a false belief. As recently as 2014, Seana Shiffrin offered a nuanced definition of lying that still contains the basic elements of intended falsity with the aim of deceiving the listener.[6]

Thanks in large part to the Trump administration's casual concern with the truth, much of the public understanding of "lie" has been transformed.[7] The transformation was not the goal of the Trump administration, which was understandably reluctant to use the word "lie" to describe its own behavior, but of the mainstream press as it struggled with how to describe patent falsehoods emanating from what used to be thought of as reliable official sources. Indeed, from the very beginning of the Trump era, members of the press, as well as commentators on the press, engaged in public debates about whether clear falsity alone should be described as a lie. *Slate* generally permitted such an expansive use of the word "lie," and the *New York Times* (eventually) permitted it on its opinion pages. By contrast, National Public Radio and the *Wall Street Journal* decreed that the word "lie" should be reserved for those falsehoods that were plainly intentional, and not merely negligent, even if grossly so, and not merely the product of self-deception, no matter how troubling that self-deception might be.[8]

Although never expressed in exactly these terms, those who encouraged or at least tolerated the expansion of the word "lie" to include a plain falsehood even without evidence of intent appeared to rely on the evidentiary inferences of a blatant falsehood—the very blatancy of the falsehood being taken as evidence that anyone who said something so obviously false must have known of the falsity and therefore knowingly said something false with intent to deceive. If I claim to be the Easter Bunny, to have been awarded the Medal of Honor, or to have run a mile in under four minutes, the obvious falsity of those assertions would seem to count as sufficient evidence of my knowledge of their falsity to justify the label of "lie" even under a traditional definition requiring intent.[9] Similarly, we might infer from the patent implausibility of the claim that "diet slippers" could produce weight loss that those who sold them knew of the falsity of their claims.[10] Indeed, more or less the very question of whether obvious falsity could be evidence of intentional falsity arose in the wake of then-president Trump's now-notorious telephone call to Georgia secretary of state Brad Raffensperger on January 2, 2021, in which Trump encouraged the latter to "find" sufficient votes to change the outcome of the election, at least in Georgia.[11] Public discussion ensued over whether the president had thereby committed election fraud under federal law by "knowingly" attempting to influence the outcome of an election.[12] One view was that because the president believed, however unrealistically, that he had actually won, he could not have knowingly and intentionally (or "willfully," as the statute puts it) attempted to change the outcome. But those who maintained the opposing view argued that because no one, not even Donald Trump, could genuinely believe that he had won, he was attempting to produce a result contrary to what he knew was reality, and had thus violated the law.

Stepping back from this particular event, we can see that those who insist that calling an obvious falsehood a lie even without explicit evidence that the person *knew* their statement was false are plausibly understood not as seeking to change the traditional meaning of the word by removing the requirement of intentionality. Instead they are relying on the inference that saying something patently false, and widely understood to be patently false, would itself be *evidence* of knowing—and not merely negligent, or even reckless—falsity. All the same, it is plain that contemporary journalistic usage is heading in the direction of a willingness to label as a lie anything that is a clear falsehood, even without further evidence that the person accused of having lied knew that what they said was false at the time they said it.

Regardless of the outcome of this ongoing linguistic debate about just what a lie is, the requirement of intent to deceive—intentional falsity—in order for some statement to count as a lie is not only consistent with long-standing usage, but also compatible with most attempts to identify lies. When someone asserts something for which there is no evidence other than their assertion—"the dog ate my homework"—it is useful to know whether they actually believed what they said. Perhaps we should disregard the statement as evidence even if made sincerely, or perhaps not, but if even the person who made the statement doesn't believe it, then neither should we. In other words, although modern usage is becoming increasing compatible with the view that knowing that one's statement is false is not a necessary condition for calling that statement a lie, it is clear that knowing that one's statement is false is a sufficient condition. And if we are worried about people who lie in court, who lie to public officials, who lie on college applications, who lie to health care providers about their eligibility for Covid-19 vaccination, and much more, we should be concerned with trying to root out those whose falsities are intentional. This will not eliminate all falsity, but it will at least eliminate some. As a result, we have witnessed the long-standing efforts, to which we will turn presently, to search for ways of identifying lies under the traditional understanding of what counts as a lie.

Paltering

Traditional definitions of lying have included not only intentionality but also literal falsity. It turns out, however, that getting someone to believe something that is not true often does not require such literal falsity. Suppose a colleague who knows that I am an amateur furniture maker comes into my office and admires my store-bought desk. And then suppose I respond by saying "Thank you." My colleague infers from this that I have made the desk. By saying nothing, I have encouraged this inference, even though it is false. And if I accurately and publicly observe that another colleague is sober today, I have misleadingly suggested that there are other days on which he is not. Or, to return to the student submitting the late paper, if the student who has yet to start on the paper tells me about the close relative who has died, and if the relative has in fact died, the student, in making an accurate statement, nonetheless wants me to believe, inaccurately, that the death was causally responsible for the lateness, even if it was not.

There is a nice but obscure word for this practice of attempting to deceive without saying anything that is literally false—*paltering*.[13] And once we understand the possibility of paltering and recognize its widespread occurrence, we can appreciate the way in which the traditional definition of lying is potentially too narrow when we are concerned with the conditions of social interaction and social trust. For those purposes we have every reason to worry as much about paltering as we do about flat-out lying.

If we are concerned somewhat more narrowly about evidence, however, and even more narrowly about testimony, it is appropriate to focus more precisely on statements that make explicitly factually false assertions. Narrowing the focus in this way may leave paltering and other forms of non-factually-false deception untouched, but the narrow focus allows us to concentrate on the mechanisms that have been used traditionally, and that might be used now or in the future, to determine whether factual statements are accurate or whether instead they are false. When some statement is to be taken as evidence for what it asserts, and especially when there is little or no other evidence leading to that conclusion, we have strong motivations for trying to determine whether that statement—that testimony—is true or false. In legal proceedings, in public policy, and in everyday life we frequently need to determine whether what some statement—the testimony of the testifier—states as a fact actually is a fact. And here, it turns out, there is a long, illuminating history.

Lie Detection—Then and Now, Good and Bad

Among the most noteworthy characteristics of the comic book (and then motion picture) character Wonder Woman is her ability to detect or forestall lying by others. It is not clear whether her Magic Lasso, forged from the Magic Girdle of Aphrodite, was originally intended by her creator to be an implement to secure veracity or instead only to induce submission, but as the character developed over the years, it was Wonder Woman's ability as a lie detector that endured.

Wonder Woman may or may not be interesting in her own right.[14] But what is particularly noteworthy is that her creator, William Moulton Marston, a senior faculty member in the Harvard University Department of Psychology at the time, was also the inventor, in the 1920s, of one of the early polygraphs—lie-detection machines. And that itself is of particular interest because the judicial decision that rejected the courtroom use of Marston's polygraph—*United States v. Frye*—has had a lasting impact in two different ways.[15] One was in establishing what was for a long time, and what still is in some states, the test for determining whether scientific expert testimony would be admissible in legal proceedings.[16] And the other was in launching a century of official skepticism about lie-detecting technology and expertise, a skepticism that, at least for courts, persists even as the technology has improved dramatically.

Marston's polygraph was not the first. That honor apparently belongs either to Cesare Lombroso, a prominent criminologist who in late nineteenth-century Italy invented a device that purported to use measurements of blood pressure to identify lies, or to James MacKenzie, a Scottish cardiologist who created a similar device at about the same time premised on the same basic theory.[17] The theory is that telling a lie is more stressful (or requires more mental exertion in other ways) than telling the truth, and that the heightened stress is reflected in higher blood pressure. Subsequent advances, including Marston's, and including an even more sophisticated polygraph devised by John A. Larson in 1921, improved on Lombroso and MacKenzie by including respiration rate as an additional indicator of knowing deception. And post-Larson polygraphs, especially the one invented by Leonard Keeler in the 1930s that is the principal precursor of the modern polygraph, have added galvanic skin response and heart rate.[18] Even with the improvements, however, the basic principle throughout has remained the same—that there are physiological markers of deception, and that the physiological markers of stress level are chief among the physiological markers of deception. Stress, in other words, is evidence of deception, and this too-crude observation is at least the starting point for most of the far more sophisticated physiological approaches to lie detection.

The physiological markers of deception, including more contemporary approaches to be discussed presently, are to be distinguished from behavioral markers. Most people, including most jurors listening to witness testimony in court, believe that certain behaviors are reliable indicators of lying. One of those behaviors is looking directly at the questioner, the common belief being that liars will avoid eye contact.[19] Similarly, liars are generally believed to speak less confidently than truth-tellers, to fidget and display other overt signs of nervousness, and to look down rather than up even apart from the question of eye contact. And there are others as well. But most of these beliefs are false.[20] Or, to put it more precisely, the behavioral cues that most people, including most police officers, believe are indicators of intentional deception are nothing of the sort.[21] Belief in the soundness of these unsound behavioral indicators of lying leads ordinary people to be quite poor at distinguishing liars from truth-tellers. Indeed, most of the studies on interpersonal lie detection reveal that even people who are consciously aware of the indications they are watching for, and even people seemingly trained to identify liars, are scarcely better than random.[22] Courts have traditionally rejected lie-detection technology for use at trials, and most courts still do (although some states, such as New Mexico, tend to allow it).[23] And their support for this policy tends to be the view that "the jury is the lie-detector in the courtroom."[24] But this view is inconsistent with the fact that jurors, like people in general, are simply not very good at lie detection.

Here, as elsewhere, one of the most important questions to ask about any evidentiary conclusion, especially conclusions purporting to cast doubt on some piece of evidence or some method of obtaining evidence, is "Compared to what?" The question to be asked about any form of lie detection, therefore, is not whether the method is perfect, and not whether it is highly accurate, but whether the method is better than lie detection through the use of all of the folk wisdom, urban legends, uninformed amateur psychology, and countless other varieties of conventional but mistaken approaches that people have traditionally used to evaluate the credibility of testimony, both in court and out. Although the reliability tests on polygraphs vary widely in their results, even the most cautious or skeptical conclusions put the reliability of the modern polygraph as being at least 70 percent, both for the identification of true statements and the identification of false ones (the two not necessarily being the same), with the more common conclusions being that polygraphs tend to be 80 to 85 percent accurate in identifying both true and false statements.[25] The 2002 National Research Council report's conclusion that the traditional lie detector, administered competently, could identify deception at a rate that is "well above chance" but "well below perfection" and not having "extremely high accuracy" captures what most of the research concluded then, and still concludes now. But even that level of accuracy dwarfs the accuracy of the nontechnological alternatives used by ordinary people, including the ordinary people who sit on juries.

Various modern techniques for lie-detection are different from the traditional polygraph, but they do not reject the basic principle that deception tends to produce measurable physiological indicators. It is not clear how much better, if at all, any of these techniques are than the traditional polygraph, but it seems clear that they are no worse.[26] One of these techniques, periorbital thermography, with accuracy rates around 75 percent, measures the temperature around the eyes, and is based on the premise that the rate of blood flow around the eyes is especially sensitive to stress and thus correlates with deception.[27] Near-infrared-spectroscopy, with similar or slightly greater accuracy, assesses the optical properties of brain tissue, properties that again have been shown to vary with stress level.[28] And electroencephalography, sometimes referred to as "brain fingerprinting," measures the electrochemical emissions of the brain, in particular brain wave P300, in response to various stimuli, with the theory being that the level of emission is a measure of consciousness of guilt, and with consciousness of guilt being a measure of deception.[29]

All of these techniques are still in use and are still being developed, as is the traditional polygraph in its best form. Much of the contemporary attention to lie detection, however, has focused on the use of functional magnetic resonance imaging—fMRI, "brain scans"—to detect deception.[30] Even here the basic idea is the same. Common notions notwithstanding, brains do not light up when engaged in certain tasks, and fMRI scans do not take pictures of brains. Instead, an fMRI scan measures and displays a physiological response to various activities. For lie detection purposes, fMRI is used to measure the extent to which certain regions of the brain recruit higher levels of oxygenated hemoglobin when the possessor of that brain is being deceptive than they do when that person is telling the truth.

Research seeking to advance these technologies continues apace, with the largest single track of the current research being done by neuroscientists using fMRI approaches. And although much of that research is being done in the service of pure science and knowledge for its own sake, at least some of the interest is fueled by the wide range of practical uses for such technology, and not only in the courtroom or other parts of the criminal justice system. A no longer extant company called No Lie MRI, Inc., for example, recognized that prosecutors and defense attorneys might not be the only ones interested in identifying liars—the rest of us might be interested as well, especially when we distrust our spouses, our business collaborators, or the people who are trying to sell us houses and cars.

But we are getting ahead of things. The issue before us starts with the proposition that testimony can be evidence, but that its value as evidence increases as our confidence increases that the testifier is not trying to deceive us, whether by literal lying, by paltering, or in some other way. We thus seek a way of assessing the value of an act of testimony as evidence by determining the likelihood that the testifier is lying. When Marston's polygraph (crude by modern-day standards) was rejected as courtroom evidence, the rationale for its rejection was that the methods had not been generally accepted by any relevant scientific or professional community. As noted above, this test of general acceptance has been replaced in all federal and most state courts by a focus on reliability and accuracy rather than acceptance, a question to which we will return in Chapter 9. But despite the change in the nature of the test, the traditional judicial skepticism continues. There are exceptions. As noted above, New Mexico now generally allows polygraph evidence subject to constraints of relevance and avoidance of prejudice, and a number of federal courts have been open to accepting it in particular cases. But these are exceptions, and courts persist in ruling that evidence based on lie-detection technology is inadmissible, even as the degree of reliability increases.

In the popular press, and also in much of the scientific literature, especially the neuroscience literature, there has been widespread skepticism about the use of any of these techniques, even the best of them, for courtroom use.[31] That skepticism seems based on two related factors, each of which deserves closer scrutiny. One is the worry that the current level of reliability is nowhere near high enough to justify using it to convict people of crimes and deprive people of their liberty. And of course this is right. Even the most optimistic conclusions about the best of the modern lie-detection techniques rarely have a level of reliability above 90 percent. It is clear, therefore, that the use of lie detection by itself, even assuming that the use could somehow circumvent the constraints of the Fifth Amendment's bar on compulsory self-incrimination, would be insufficient to justify a criminal conviction. But if lie detection is not good enough alone to prove guilt beyond a reasonable doubt—which it is not—is it good enough to show, on behalf of a defendant, that a reasonable doubt exists?[32] Suppose that some eyewitness testimony, whose hardly certain reliability we will explore in Chapter 8, places the defendant at the scene of the armed robbery, but the defendant claims that the eyewitness was mistaken and that he, the defendant, was two hundred miles away and in a different state at the time of the crime. In that context, it is hardly obvious, to put it mildly, that we should deprive that defendant of the opportunity to support his alibi defense with the result of a polygraph or fMRI examination showing that he was 85 percent likely to have been telling the truth. Or perhaps even that the witness against him might have been lying. In other words, what is plainly insufficient to support a conviction under the beyond a reasonable doubt standard might nevertheless be sufficient to defeat a conviction precisely because of that standard.

A second source of skepticism is the worry that jurors and maybe even judges will take lie-detection evidence as being more reliable than it actually is. Jurors, it is said, will see an fMRI scan, which they erroneously believe to be a picture of a brain, and take this as absolute proof of lying or truth-telling, which of course it is not. Interestingly, however, research on exactly this question by neuroscientists Martha Farah and Cayce Hook shows this worry to be unwarranted. In the face of claims that brain scan images have a "seductive allure" for laypeople, Farah and Hook experimentally demonstrate that there is nothing about a brain scan that makes it inordinately influential.[33] All sorts of evidence might, of course, be overvalued, but Farah and Hook show that overvaluation of fMRI evidence is no more likely than overvaluation is for any other type of evidence.

At this point it is important to bear in mind that, even in courtroom contexts, judges and jurors prohibited from knowing lie-detection results are not going to exit the jury box and go home. And they are not going to refuse to decide. Neither of these is a permitted option, even though something like that—simply not offering or publishing a conclusion—is an option for the scientist whose experiments neither confirm nor disconfirm a hypothesis. Unlike scientists, however, judges and juries must reach a decision at a particular time. And if in making that decision they are unable to use the results of lie-detection science or technology, they are going to evaluate credibility in the same way that lay people always have—by relying on the widely, but not wisely, accepted indicators of deception that dominate lay decision making, popular culture, and television dramas, but whose empirical basis is far more fragile than the empirical basis of a wide array of lie-detection techniques. Here, as is so often the case, "Compared to what?" is the right but too-rarely asked question.

Leaving the Courtroom

That lie-detection technology turns out to be better than the courts think it is, and better than some of popular journalism thinks it is, explains why it is so widespread outside of the legal system. Government uses it to screen job applicants, especially for law enforcement, intelligence, and national security positions, especially but not only by evaluating the accuracy of the representations on employment applications and in interviews. Government security and intelligence agencies use it not only to evaluate existing and potential employees, but also to assess the accuracy of the information they receive. Insurance companies use it to determine the veracity of claims and the claims records of their insureds. And although a federal law called the Employee Polygraph Protection Act of 1988 prohibits polygraph screening of employees and applicants by private employers, it contains exceptions for the pharmaceutical and security industries.[34] Less commonly, public figures sometimes use polygraph results to attempt to rebut claims that they have engaged in some variety of misconduct, as Virginia lieutenant governor and then-gubernatorial candidate Justin Fairfax did in seeking to challenge the two accusations of sexual assault made against him.[35] And sometimes those who make such accusations use polygraph results to buttress their accusations when they are called into question, as Christine Blasey Ford did when her claims that then-nominee and now Supreme Court Justice Brett Kavanaugh had sexually assaulted her when the two were teenagers were called into question.[36]

Indeed, given the accuracy level of most forms of lie detection, it is perhaps surprising that there is not more use of it by those whose public claims have been directly challenged. Some of this reluctance might be a spillover from widespread knowledge that lie detection is not generally usable in court. And some might be a function of public skepticism flowing from public knowledge of the possibility that one can "beat" the lie detector if properly trained, and especially if you get to pick your own technology and technician. And some might result from the fear felt by people engaged in public disputes about the factual truth of their statements that exposed deception might be fatal to their public claims. Better, perhaps, to rely on confident assertions of truth than on imperfect technological endorsements of that truth. That said, however, it is hardly irrational to wonder whether someone who is unwilling to use the best of modern lie-detection technology to bolster their public claims might have reason to be afraid of what that technology might reveal.

When the lie-detection potential of fMRI began to become known, the potential for such use out of the courtroom was not lost on some entrepreneurs. No Lie MRI no longer exists, and another, Cephos, barely does, both companies having relied heavily and mistakenly on the likelihood that their methods would eventually be accepted for courtroom use, especially in noncriminal cases involving matters such as business disputes and child custody. But others have taken their place, one being the Utah-based company Converus, which uses a device it calls EyeDetect to measure pupil size and other aspects of the eye, and which the company claims to be able to detect deception with 86 percent accuracy.[37] The Arizona company Discern Science International, with its origins at Arizona State University, employs a device it has named Avatar to analyze a collection of facial microexpressions, and claims that its device also approaches 90 percent accuracy in identifying those whose answers to a digital customs agent are not truthful.[38] Others have joined the fray, and even more undoubtedly will, recognizing that the interest in ferreting out lies and liars is as old as lying, and that the demand for both is unlikely to decrease.

Two Larger Lessons

Buried in the previous sections are two larger lessons that are not only about lies and lying, and not only about testimony. And it is worthwhile, if only for purposes of emphasis, to repeat both of them. One is the recurrent question "Compared to what?" Evidence is the path we travel in determining whether some statement about a fact is true or testing some factual hypothesis. We do not start with evidence. Instead we start with something we want to know, with a question about the likely truth of some factual assertion or the soundness of some hypothesis of interest to us. To make this point, the great philosopher of science Karl Popper once began a lecture by instructing his audience simply to "observe." Puzzled by the instruction, the members of the audience eventually understood that Popper wanted them to grasp that unguided observation, even if not technically impossible, is generally pointless.

And that is why we start with some hypothesis or topic or statement of fact that interests us and not with unsorted and unfocused evidence.

If we have a hypothesis we want to evaluate or a question to which we seek—and often require—an answer, we start with a need for evidence. And what is important about evidence being need-based is that the need allows and sometimes forces us to recognize not only that evidence comes in degrees, but also that sometimes imperfect evidence is the best we can do. Weak evidence is better than evidence-free guessing, and slight evidence is better than superstition. Of course, better evidence is better than worse evidence, and it is often useful to require the best evidence we can get. Nevertheless, worse evidence, at least in this sense, often is better than nothing.

The second lesson, which follows from the first, is that whether some form of evidence is good enough depends on what follows from there being sufficient (or insufficient) evidence. That was one of the important lessons from our discussion of the burden of proof in Chapter 3. It is also the lesson that emerges from the difference between lie-detection technology being good enough to put people in prison, which it plainly is not, and lie-detection technology being good enough to keep people out of prison, which it very well might be. Indeed, even more with respect to policymaking than with the truth or falsity of a particular factual hypothesis, evaluating evidence in light of its potential use and in light of the consequences of its sufficiency is vital. Evidence that is not strong enough to justify a restriction of individual liberty might be strong enough to justify a government warning, and evidence that is not strong enough to ban an otherwise legal product might be strong enough to justify an individual consumer in refusing to purchase it. Not only as we evaluate lies and lying, and not only as we evaluate testimony in general, a pervasive question about evidence, whether in individual bits or in the aggregate, is not whether it is good, but whether it is good enough.

Chapter 8

Can We Believe Our Eyes and Ears?

MORE THAN 130 TELEVISION stations in the United States label their local news broadcast as "Eyewitness News." Or so says *Wikipedia,* which tends to be good evidence for this sort of thing, even if not for everything. And because the label designates a style of local news reporting featuring camera crews rushing to the scene of newsworthy events and reporters breathlessly interviewing participants in ongoing happenings, the image these stations wish to project is that of the reliable firsthand witness.

But just how reliable are eyewitnesses? More precisely, often we want to know how reliable are the representations, as evidence, of those who have claimed to have seen something firsthand. Or, less commonly, to have heard something firsthand. Or, even less commonly, to have tasted or smelled or touched something firsthand. The question, the answer to which might not be the same for hearing, smelling, tasting, and touching as it is for seeing, is not just about lying, which we have explored in Chapters 6 and 7. Rather, it is about the even more common phenomenon of honest mistake by those whose firsthand accounts we are asked to believe just because of their firsthandedness—just because they were *there.*[1]

The reliability of eyewitnesses—or, more accurately, the unreliability of eyewitnesses—has become prominent in recent years.[2] Eyewitness accounts have always been a pervasive source of information and knowledge, but much of the recent prominence is due to the subsequent exoneration of people who have been convicted of crimes they did not commit. It turns out that the largest number of these exonerations have involved trials in which an erroneous conviction was based on what was subsequently discovered to have been a mistaken eyewitness identification of the unfortunate, actually and factually innocent defendant—the defendant who simply didn't do it.[3] Such mistaken eyewitness identifications, however, come in three varieties, which we need to disaggregate. The first is the one most people imagine when they think of eyewitness mistakes—a failure of perception. For example, believing you saw a bird when what you really saw was a bat. Or believing you witnessed a shoplifter when the person leaving the store with the goods had actually paid for them. Or believing you saw Chris when you really saw someone else of Chris's approximate height and weight dressed the way Chris dresses. Second is a failure of memory—perceiving something accurately at the time of perception but remembering that perception inaccurately some days, weeks, months, or years later.[4] For example, knowing at the time of witnessing an automobile accident that the blue car that ran the stop sign was a Toyota but (mis)remembering much later that it was a red Honda. Or knowing when you were growing up the telephone number of your childhood home but mistakenly thinking now that it was a different one. And third is a failure of reporting—inaccurately reporting what you accurately saw and now accurately remember. An example would be describing what you accurately saw and accurately remembered as sleet in a way that your listeners believed that you were describing snow.

All these failures, and more, have produced a healthy skepticism in recent years about the value as evidence of eyewitness accounts. And much of this skepticism has had admirably important effects on the legal system. The procedures for identifying a perpetrator in a lineup, for example, have been changed substantially in recent years to lessen the possibility of a mistaken identification caused by manipulative law enforcement tactics designed to steer the identification in the direction of the individual that the police had already decided had committed the crime.[5] In addition, skepticism about criminal convictions based solely on the testimony of one eyewitness has produced the further investigation that frequently reveals that a conviction and subsequent incarceration were based on a demonstrable factual error. Mistaken eyewitness identifications, sometimes revealed by credible recantations by the single witness, have, it turns out, produced the single largest number of post-conviction exonerations. Indeed, the risks of mistaken identification, even by those who claim to have observed the defendant actually committing the crime, are sufficiently substantial that some states, starting with New Jersey, now explicitly instruct jurors about the possibility of error in an eyewitness identification, a possibility that the typical lay juror is inclined to ignore or minimize.[6]

Even outside of the legal system, honest mistakes by those who claim to have observed something "with their own eyes" are widespread.[7] And so too with people who insist they have remembered something, even though mistakes of memory are as predictable as mistakes of perception.[8] There is thus good reason to doubt that eyewitness accounts of past events are evidence that we should treat as invariably reliable just because it is provided by people who purport to have seen or even experienced firsthand what they are now reporting to us.

But recall the lesson of horses and zebras from Chapter 2. It is true that neither memory nor first-person perception are as accurate as they have traditionally been understood to be. And it is important that we know this, especially because of the consequences in the criminal justice system and occasionally elsewhere of the overvaluation of first-person or eyewitness accounts. Still, most—indeed, a lot more than most—eyewitness accounts are accurate, and as such can be evidence of what the eyewitnesses claimed to have seen. And most memories are accurate as well, providing, again, evidence of what those describing what they have seen, heard, or experienced have in fact seen, heard, or experienced. We all have a list of things that we have remembered inaccurately, but even a long list of inaccurate recollections pales in the face of what for almost everyone is a far longer list of accurate recollections. I may have forgotten what I had for breakfast yesterday or where I left my keys today, but I remember, correctly, a very large number of other things about yesterday and today. That both perception and memory are often flawed is not inconsistent with perception and memory being even more often accurate and thus of evidentiary value. Even though eyewitness accounts have traditionally been overvalued as evidence, it is possible that recent revelations about this overvaluation, and its consequences, have led to substantial undervaluation.

One cause of what may well be the contemporary *under*valuation of eyewitness accounts is, as just noted, the common tendency to overcompensate for recently discovered flaws of one sort or another. Disappointed believers often become radical disbelievers, and some of the contemporary skepticism about eyewitness accounts may be a function of just this kind of overreaction when people who used to believe that eyewitness accounts were always or almost always reliable become aware of how such accounts may be mistaken. The publicity about exonerations in the criminal justice system has shone valuable light on the consequences for individuals of the traditional excess reliance of eyewitness accounts generally and eyewitness identifications in particular. But it is important to remember that although a mistaken identification in a criminal prosecution can result in the incarceration or even execution of someone who is innocent, not all mistakes in first-person accounts have the same dire consequences. Recalling Blackstone and the way in which the errors of mistaken conviction are properly treated as much more serious than the errors of mistaken acquittal, it is entirely appropriate to treat the mistakes of an inaccurate eyewitness account in the criminal justice system as especially grave, and accordingly to be willing to suppress or discount some number of accurate eyewitness accounts in order to avoid a smaller number but more serious inaccurate ones. We do not know how many guilty people would have been acquitted had juries been (properly) instructed to be skeptical about eyewitness identifications, but it would be surprising if that number were zero.[9] An attitude or disposition of skepticism about eyewitness accounts, being of necessity general rather than event-specific, will be skeptical of accurate eyewitness accounts as well as inaccurate ones, with the consequence being that some number of accurate eyewitness accounts will be mistakenly discarded as inaccurate. Moreover, and as we saw in Chapter 3, coming to believe that an eyewitness account was not beyond a reasonable doubt accurate is consistent with it being probably accurate—even though, if that is the only or primary evidence, it is appropriately insufficient for a criminal conviction. And that is why at least some—we do not know how many, but it would be remarkable if it were none—of those who, on the basis of recent revelations and research about the failings of eyewitness identification, have been properly found not to have been guilty beyond a reasonable doubt may well have been probably, but only probably, guilty of the crime of which they were charged.

Once we leave the criminal justice system, however, Blackstonian skewing is by no means the only or the necessarily correct approach to any question about how we should treat eyewitness accounts as evidence. Treating the use of mistaken eyewitness accounts as more serious than the non-use of accurate accounts is what the law ought to do when it is prosecuting people for alleged crimes and threatening them with incarceration, or worse, but that conclusion comes at a cost of overall accuracy. When we exit the criminal courtroom, the same sacrifice in overall accuracy may no longer be appropriate. Consider the question whether I should return to the restaurant where a year ago I enjoyed the best chocolate soufflé I have ever had. My recollection of that exquisite soufflé leads me to want to return. But perhaps the soufflé was not as good as I now remember it. Or perhaps it was a different restaurant. Or perhaps it was a cheese soufflé and not chocolate. Or maybe it was chocolate mousse and not a chocolate soufflé. All these things are possible, and the awareness of false memories and maybe even false perceptions alerts me to such possibilities. But there are worse things in the world than ordering a disappointing chocolate soufflé or going to a restaurant in the expectation of having one and discovering that it is not on the menu and never has been. Being imprisoned for a crime you did not commit, for example. And although the chocolate soufflé example may be extreme, it illustrates that mistakes of perception and of recollection might be more serious in some contexts than in others. As a result, it is wise to remember that although mistakes of this kind are always possible, they are rarely probable. And the larger lesson, which pervades all the chapters here on testimony, is that although it is correct to be somewhat skeptical about testimony as evidence of what the testimony asserts, or at least to be aware of the possibility of false testimony, it is not necessarily correct to treat an item of testimony as having a lower probability of truth than it actually has.

Much of what was in the foregoing pages became highly relevant during the Senate trial of the impeachment of Donald Trump in February of 2021. Perhaps ironically, and perhaps hypocritically, much of the recent concern about the accuracy of eyewitnesses and first-person accounts appeared to go out the window as the impeachment proceedings in the House of Representatives and then the trial in the Senate unfolded. Some members of Congress saw little need for witnesses or other evidence, and that was because they were *there*. They could make their judgments, these members of Congress alleged, on the basis of their own experiences and their own observations, but with seemingly little recognition of the possibility that the very traumatic nature of those experiences would have rendered their observations more suspect rather than more reliable. And so too for many of the rest of us, who saw the events on television as they were happening and then multiple times thereafter. If eyewitnesses are to be distrusted, are all of us to be distrusted in terms of what we saw on television on January 6, 2021?

The answer to that question is not straightforward. For one thing, an impeachment trial is not a criminal trial, and no one is going to be imprisoned or executed solely because of the Senate's verdict. Accordingly, it might be appropriate to rely more on our commonsense confidence in observation even though it can (fairly rarely) go astray. In a criminal trial, with imprisonment or even execution looming, it is fully justified to guard against the small but not nonexistent possibility of mistaken first-person observation, as the New Jersey courts have led others in doing. But in a proceeding other than a criminal trial, perhaps relying on the likely correctness of an eyewitness observation makes more sense than guarding against its unlikely incorrectness. Nevertheless, it is a point of some amusement or irony that many of the most skeptical voices about the dangers of relying too much on eyewitnesses appeared strangely silent with respect to the most eyewitness-dependent event in recent memory.

As a . . .

There is a tedious consistency in the opening lines of the letters to the editor that most newspapers print on or near their editorial pages. Although the letters deal with all varieties of subjects and express all varieties of points of view, a remarkably high percentage of them begin in the same way: "As a . . ."

"As a retired firefighter, . . ." "As an earthquake survivor, . . ." "As a psychiatrist who has treated many cases of claustrophobia, . . ." "As a victim of a hit-and-run accident, . . ." "As a college student, . . ." "As a recent immigrant, . . ." "As the descendant of grandparents who died in the 1918 influenza epidemic, . . ." And so on and on and on.

What is interesting about the "as a . . ." claim is that the reader is asked to treat what the letter writer says as more reliable—as better evidence—because of the letter writer's first-person experience. Sometimes the "as a . . ." claimant is, plausibly and often usefully, engaging in an act of self-credentialing, as with, "As a former winner of a Nobel Prize in medicine, I believe that the most effective way of controlling the Covid-19 pandemic is . . ." Or "As the author of seven books about climate change, I have become convinced that the principal cause of the melting of the polar ice cap is . . ." And sometimes the self-credentialing will not be about expertise, but about an opportunity to perceive that is likely better than the reader's. "As someone standing outside the Capitol building on January 6, 2021, . . ." "As someone who was working in a bank on Wall Street on September 11, 2001, . . ." "As someone who once ate a home-cooked dinner at Julia Child's house, . . ."

Such self-credentialing is common, understandable, and often useful for the reader. But if we set aside the self-credentialing that describes the writer's source of genuine expertise or a genuine advantage in perception, we see a different variety of the "as a . . ." claim as especially common. Here the letter writer is not claiming the authority of professional or expert knowledge, and maybe not even the ability to observe that others lacked, but instead the authority of the survivor, the participant, the victim, or some other form of first-person experience. And then the question, plainly related to the issues about eyewitness identification that we dealt with in the previous sections, is the extent to which someone's participation in some event gives them some sort of special authority or special insight into that event solely by virtue of their participation, such that we should treat their account as evidence having significant weight.

Now things become more complicated. Sometimes the authority of the person who was there is based on an opportunity for perception that the receiver of the testimony probably did have—for example, the person who was at the Capitol on January 6, 2021, and who may have been able to see something that the rest of us could not. And sometimes being a participant provides the motivation to learn more. A person who is afflicted with a disease might be motivated to read more about it, and to follow the research more closely, than others whose interest in the disease is less personal. Members of Mothers Against Drunk Driving (MADD) whose children were killed by drunk drivers have profound reason to learn more about drunk driving, its causes, and its possible cures than do those of us not so personally affected.

All of these qualifications duly noted, it remains the case that it is common to give some kind of special testimonial, and thus evidential, weight to participants solely because they were participants. Yet it is not clear that simply being a participant is necessarily a source of greater knowledge or greater insight. For one thing, being there can be distorting as well as enlightening. A driver injured in a minor traffic accident is not only likely to have a particular view about who or what caused the accident but may also see the accident or the injuries as more serious than they would appear to a less involved observer. And the same applies to being a victim more generally. People with afflictions sometimes caused by environmental agents—toxic waste dumps, lead pipes, polluted water supplies, and such—often have opinions about what has caused their affliction, and often they attribute the affliction to some newsworthy toxic agent. Frequently those opinions are correct, but they are not correct by virtue of the affliction being theirs and not someone else's. People may know the cause of their broken arms, but the fact that hair loss is sometimes caused by secondhand smoke does not give the person whose hair is falling out any special insight into whether secondhand smoke was the cause, despite how frequently victims offer such opinions on the evening news.

Quite often someone claiming the authority of first-person experience talks of having a particular *perspective*. The former member of

Congress does indeed have a perspective on Congress different from those of us without that experience. But does that perspective confer value as evidence on what the person with that perspective has to say? The perspective of the insider is indeed a perspective not shared by outsiders, but outsiders have perspectives too, and the outsider perspective is not shared by the insider. Does the insider perspective, by virtue of its insider-ness, confer more reliability or more reliability as evidence for some conclusion? That depends on what the conclusion is, or what the insider claims to know that non-insiders do not.

One of the most profound observations about the insider perspective was offered by Izaak Walton in his 1653 *The Compleat Angler*. Here Walton warns the reader that no advice from a fisherman on how to fish would be worth considering if the fish could talk. And although I think I can tell you about university teaching from my perspective, there is little reason to believe that this perspective is more valuable than that of the students, or, even better, the clients my law students will eventually serve.

This idea is familiar to many of us from the Indian parable about the blind men and the elephant, most familiar these days from the 1873 poem of that name by John Godfrey Saxe. As the parable goes, a group of blind men are taken to "see" an elephant, but, being blind, they cannot actually see the elephant. So each touches a different part of the elephant, and generalizes—analogizes—what an elephant is like from the particular part that he happens to touch. One touches the trunk and imagines an elephant as being like a rope. Another touches the leg and believes an elephant is like a tree. Still another touches the elephant's side and thinks an elephant is like a wall. And so on. And if there is a lesson from the parable, it is that partial perception is just that—partial.

The parable of the blind men and the elephant holds a valuable lesson for thinking about the authority of first-person or direct experience. Participants, perpetrators, victims, bystanders, and others—all others, in fact—have a standpoint, or a perspective, or a lens through which they view an act, an event, a state of affairs, or anything else. And although relying on the accounts of eyewitnesses may be more valuable as evidence than some of the contemporary skepticism might warrant (or so I have been arguing here), relying on the accounts of participants may be less valuable than some of the contemporary celebrations of so-called lived experience might warrant. Insofar as some perspectives have traditionally been ignored, that is a huge problem, and one in desperate need of remedy. Plainly some of the call to recognize those experiences and the feelings they generate is the morally generated and morally justified plea to stop ignoring the perspectives of those whose perspectives have long been ignored.[10] But those perspectives are still perspectives, and their value as evidence needs to be understood as such. The accounts of those who say, "It happened to me," just like the accounts of those who say, "I was there," have value as evidence, but that value, which is to be distinguished from the moral values of inclusion, may, as with eyewitness testimony, suffer from the flaw of being overvalued as evidence—just as first-person accounts often suffer from being morally undervalued.

The Camera Doesn't Lie—Or Does It?

Back when all cameras used film (or, even earlier, when they used glass plates), photographs were understood to be especially reliable evidence of what they were photographs of. Not many people know what Mount Everest or an emperor penguin looks like, but they think they do because they have seen pictures. And the same for Franklin Roosevelt, Charlie Chaplin, and Jacqueline Kennedy, all distinctive-looking people who were photographed countless times but were never the subject of memorable paintings or drawings.

For those of us who claim to know what those people, places, and animals look like, our evidence for that knowledge comes entirely from photographs. And like the evidence that comes from eyewitnesses, photographic evidence has long been understood to be particularly reliable evidence, even if not perfect evidence, of the characteristics of the people, places, and events that the photographs are photographs of. The photograph has long been understood as being like the report of an eyewitness, only better.

Susan Sontag, among others, knew better. And so do most serious photographers. In *On Photography,* Sontag demonstrated just how much a photograph was the product not only of what the photograph was a photograph of, but also of numerous choices made by the photographer.[11] Most obvious is the choice of what to leave in and what to take out, not because of any fancy darkroom or Photoshop or retouching techniques but simply by virtue of where one aims and where one does not, or how close or far away the camera is from what it is that the camera sees. Consider, for example, a still-discussed episode from the 1959 Boston mayoral election, in which the underdog, city councillor John Collins, defeated the heavy favorite, John Powers, who was then president of the Massachusetts state senate. Powers had long been reputed or rumored to be associated with gamblers and other organized crime figures, and Collins capitalized on this by using in his campaign brochures and making available to the newspapers a photograph of Powers with a particularly notorious bookie. The Collins campaign, however, had cropped out of the same picture a third individual, the revered Cardinal Richard Cushing. Being associated with a known gambler had bad implications, and being associated with Cardinal Cushing had good ones, so the cropping, which may have helped Collins in this election but which dogged him for years afterwards, made what was originally an innocuous photograph look far more sinister than it actually was. And those who saw the cropped photograph were none the wiser.[12]

As with eyewitness accounts, the view that it's a lie to say that "the camera doesn't lie" can be taken too far. Noticing the frequent errors made by eyewitnesses can blind us to the fact that most eyewitness accounts are mostly right. Similarly, recognizing that a photograph reflects the choices and perspective of the photographer—as well as the results of optical, chemical, and, these days, digital processes—blinds us to the fact that a photograph is usually pretty good evidence of some aspect of what the photograph is a photograph of. The same holds for what the television camera shows—the storming of the Capitol on January 6, 2021, being the most salient recent example. A philosopher of art, Kendall Walton, reminds us that a photograph is more than just a depiction or a description. It is importantly "transparent" to what is being photographed in the way that seeing something through a microscope or telescope is different from the descriptions in prose and poetry and depictions in drawings and oil paintings.[13] Of course photographs can be distorted and even fabricated. The government of Nepal, for example, has just taken steps to revoke the climbing permissions of two mountaineers whose photograph of themselves on the top of Mount Everest was exposed as a complete fraud.[14] And even nonfabricated photographs reflect the standpoint, the perspective, the theories, and the values of the photographer as well as the mechanical, optical, and, now, digital properties of a human-created device. But there is a reason newspapers give us photographs and not drawings, why television news often seems more informative than radio news, and why Matthew Brady's Civil War photographs tell us something that the roughly contemporaneous oil paintings of Édouard Manet or the drawings of Francisco Goya a generation earlier do not.[15] As evidence, photographs are far from perfect and far from "pure." But their value as evidence is different from and often better than other means of conveying much the same information.

A photograph is thus best understood as testimony, of a mechanical variety. As with all testimony, it might be distorted. It might be incomplete. Depending on the skills and motivations of the photographer, it might be a complete fabrication. Simon Brann Thorpe's war photographs use only toy soldiers and fabricated landscapes. For Thorpe, photographing what is itself artificial emphasizes the creative role of the photographer and downplays the role of that which a photograph is a photograph of.[16] Just as we have come to understand that not everything that someone reports is true, we have also come to understand, assisted by commentators like Sontag and photographers like Thorpe, that not all photographic testimony is accurate. But here we are back to the question "Compared to what?"

The legal system's approach to photographs reflects the law's traditional and at times peculiar preference for oral testimony. So, traditionally, a photograph will be admitted as evidence only if someone—not necessarily the photographer—testifies that the photograph accurately represents what the photograph is supposed to be a photograph of.[17] And although photographs authenticated and used in this way are typically referred to as "pictorial testimony," the photograph is not so much testimony as it is the adjunct to someone else's testimony—in the manner of a chart or a graph. A photograph used in this way is thus analogous to the witness who holds out her hands in support of her testimony saying that the person she saw was "this tall."

More recently, and spurred by the proliferation of hidden and not-so-hidden cameras that used to be situated only in banks and are now located almost everywhere, photographs taken by such devices can be used as evidence—as a "silent witness"—as long as there is testimony by the installer, operator, or someone else who can testify that what the camera photographed was what the camera saw and what was actually "there" when the camera recorded the image.[18]

Plainly most of the considerations that apply to photographic testimony apply to nonphotographic sound recording as well, and to videotape in all of its permutations. Indeed, the law again has had to wrestle with the problem of videotapes that portray one side's version of the events with such seeming realism that jurors are likely to believe that they are seeing what actually happened, as opposed to one side's version of what actually happened.[19] But through all of these technological developments, from Louis Jacques Daguerre's earliest cameras to the most contemporary forms of digital imaging, from Thomas Edison's first phonograph to state-of-the-art electronic recording, the issues are the same, even if they vary in degree.[20] All of these techniques can convey what they record and are thus analogous to human beings who convey via testimony what they have seen, heard, or otherwise experienced. But like human beings, photographs and recordings also can lie, palter, fudge, hedge, slant, and embellish. The question, though, is not whether they can. The question is whether they do. And just as a slanted story often supplies more information than no story at all, a photograph can and typically does provides more and better information than a verbal description or a drawing, both of which typically involve a substantially higher ratio of human creativity and intervention than technological reproduction.

Perhaps the best analogy here is to the locks on our cars. Even in my small city of 50,000, I am pretty sure that there are a few hundred people who in a space of just a few minutes can unlock my locked car and drive it away without benefit of a key. But I lock my car anyway, because I recognize that what *can* happen usually does not, and because I recognize that making things more difficult decreases the likelihood of theft, even if it does not eliminate it entirely. Similarly, although it is possible that the photographs of the assault on the Capitol on January 6, 2021, were complete fabrications, and even though it is probable—actually, certain—that they reflect the perspective, in the broadest sense of that word, of the photographer, they are not only far better than nothing—they also give an impression that is undoubtedly highly accurate, even if not perfectly accurate. And so too with the video recording of police officer Derek Chauvin's killing of George Floyd, and, even earlier, the video of football player Ray Rice assaulting his wife in an elevator. In cases such as these, it is possible that the perpetrator's denials would have been believed, but the photographic evidence added such a degree of reliability that flat-out denials became implausible. And thus both incidents are valuable reminders that although photographs and videos can be distorted, misinterpreted, and occasionally even fabricated, they often serve as far better evidence than first- or second-hand testimony, which can also be distorted, misinterpreted, and fabricated, and often to an even greater degree.

The lessons about photography, therefore, track the lessons about eyewitness or other forms of first-person testimony. Skepticism is justified, but complete skepticism is not. Of course we should recognize that the inevitable human choices are as inherent in photography and sound recording as they are in human descriptions. But if the right amount of skepticism produces the conclusion that photographic evidence is far from perfect, we should remember that evidence that is far from perfect—just like almost all other evidence—is far from worthless.

Chapter 9

Of Experts and Expertise

ON OCTOBER 14, 2020, then-judge and now-justice Amy Coney Barrett was asked at her confirmation hearings by then-senator and now-vice president Kamala Harris whether she believed that climate change was happening. In the grand tradition of Supreme Court nominees for at least the past thirty years, Justice Barrett hedged, fudged, and dodged, responding that she would not express a view on such a "politically controversial" matter as climate change.[1] And although Barrett's characterization of climate change as *politically* controversial was totally accurate, she was nevertheless widely criticized for implying that climate change was scientifically controversial, even if that was not what she actually said.[2]

Although some of the people who criticized Barrett for what they thought she had said, or what they thought she had implied—or for not saying what they wished she had said—really do know quite a bit about the science of climate change, most of Barrett's critics did not. Nor do most of the rest of us when we believe, correctly, that climate change is both real and of potentially catastrophic proportions. Instead we take the word of scientists. And not just this or that scientist, but the *consensus* of scientists who work on such matters. They are the experts, and for

145

most of us the evidence of climate change comes neither from our own perceptions nor from our own research, but instead from what we believe the scientists have concluded. What the scientists—the experts—tell us is our evidence for what we believe. The scientists rely on evidence, but *our* evidence consists of what the scientists have said.

The reliance on expertise is a variation on the themes that pervade the use of testimony as evidence generally, which was the focus of Chapters 5, 6, 7, and 8. When people rely on the scientific consensus in believing that climate change is real, substantially human-caused, and leading to a catastrophe of epic proportions, they are relying on the testimony of scientists. The scientists, we believe, or at least most people believe, are the experts. And their conclusions are based on evidence, or so we hope and assume. But for the rest of us, *our* evidence is what the scientists have said. We rely on the testimony of the scientists. And relying on the testimony of experts, or on the collective testimony of an expert community, is different from relying on someone who claims to have firsthand knowledge. Indeed, it is different enough that it deserves to be in its own category, as it is in law, as it is in this book, and as it is elsewhere.

It is no coincidence that Justice Barrett was asked about climate change. The issue is not only politically charged, but also presents a particularly good example of an issue in which relying on expert opinion is, roughly, essential. True, there are experts in auto mechanics, furniture making, and physical fitness, but these are all domains in which many people have a bit of lay knowledge, and in which they therefore often believe (sometimes mistakenly) that their lay knowledge is sufficient, and in which they consequently believe (again, sometimes or even often mistakenly) that they have enough knowledge to be able to distinguish the genuine experts from the poseurs.[3]

Climate change—like rocket science and brain surgery, to take the two examples of highly technical and complex knowledge whose inaccessibility to the untrained is a staple of popular culture—is different.

Putting aside those people who are ignorantly convinced that climate change is happening because it was warm last week, or the people who are equally ignorantly sure that climate change is not real because it was cold yesterday, most of the rest of us are forced to rely on expert opinion. But then we must figure out who the experts are, and here we run into problems. How are we, as nonexperts, to determine who the experts are in areas about which we know nothing?[4] Isn't it necessary to be an expert oneself to know who the experts are? And to know whether what they say can be relied on?[5]

There are several rejoinders to this worry about nonexpert evaluation of expertise, which appears to be necessary when nonexperts treat expert conclusions as evidence. First, nonexperts often have the ability to identify and evaluate the rationality of what experts conclude, even if the nonexperts do not understand the underlying methods and conclusions. When so-called experts offer conclusions and the reasons for those conclusions that are internally contradictory or rely on implausible initial premises, nonexpert assessment can reject the expert conclusions even if the assessors are not themselves aware of the expert methods that are allegedly being used. You do not have to be an astronomer to know that the moon is not made out of green cheese, and if somewhat purporting to be an astronomer says that it is, then non-astronomers have good reason to reject what is advertised as an expert conclusion. Getting back to earth, literally, when an expert experimental psychologist claims to have proved the existence of a paranormal ability to see the future, those with ordinary (nonexpert) knowledge have reason to doubt the soundness of the expert conclusions even if they are not themselves experts.[6] At least sometimes, one need not be an expert to know when the experts have gone off the rails, and, conversely, when they have not.

The more important rejoinder to the worry that nonexperts cannot evaluate expertise about which they themselves have no expertise is that nonexperts can still identify and rely on the external trappings of expertise even if the nonexperts cannot identify and evaluate the expertise itself. These external trappings might include things like Nobel Prizes, tenured professorships at Cal Tech and MIT, grants from the National Science Foundation, and fellowships in widely recognized honorary professional associations such as the American Association for the Advancement of Science, the National Academy of Sciences, and the Royal Society. When we rely in the credentials of experts to establish their expertise, we are relying on what we as nonexperts know about the credentialing practices of various institutions. To be sure, lay knowledge of such credentials and credentialing practices might itself be less informed than the knowledge that insiders have about those credentialing practices. Still, such credentialing knowledge is likely to be more accessible to external observers than are the expert practices for which the credentials are evidence.

Using such externally observable indicators of expertise is hardly perfect. Consider phrenology. The so-called science of phrenology was more or less invented by the Austrian physician Franz Joseph Gall at the close of the eighteenth century, flourished in the early and middle nineteenth century, and did not die out until the beginning of the twentieth. The basic idea behind phrenology was that it was possible to determine a person's psychological attributes and behavioral proclivities by examining the exterior terrain of their skull. People with hills or valleys in certain places would likely be aggressive or passive, smart or stupid, selfish or altruistic, and so on. And back when phrenology flourished, it had most of the external trappings of any other academic or scientific discipline. It had professional associations, professional degrees, professional peer-reviewed journals such as the *American Phrenological Journal,* conferences at which papers were presented, widely used textbooks, manuals of best practices, endorsements by prominent intellectuals such as Harvard president Josiah Quincy, and much else.[7] But phrenology was still, to use the term recently reincarnated by President Biden, malarkey. None of the cranial markers of psychological makeup or behavioral tendencies actually mark or predict anything at all, as we now know.[8] And so all of the external indicators of useful expertise, indicators that frequently *are* reliable, failed miserably in the case of phrenology.

Much the same can be said about astrology today. The British-based Astrological Association publishes the *Astrological Journal* and the *Astrology and Medicine Newsletter.* Other astrology journals, most of which resemble serious academic journals in their formatting, referencing, footnoting, and much else, include *Above and Below: Journal of Astrological Studies,* the *Geocosmic Journal,* and *ISAR International Astrology,* the last published by the International Society for Astrological Research. Various astrology organizations hold conferences, offer courses, and provide credentials. But unlike phrenology, astrology still attracts and retains a vast number of believers.[9] And this level of belief persists in the face of numerous serious academic studies of astrology's basic premises about the relationship between astrological sign and personality, behavior, and predictions of the future—studies that have confirmed that astrology's basic premises are false: knowing the position of the planets and stars at the moment of someone's birth tells us nothing at all about that person's psychological makeup or behavioral attributes.[10] Other than as nonscientific amusement, astrology has been repeatedly shown to fit into the malarkey category, notwithstanding its external trappings of academic legitimacy.

Phrenology and astrology stand as warnings against taking the external indicators of an area of expertise as sacred. These external indicators might be some evidence of genuine knowledge, but they are only evidence, and here the evidence points to something that is not true. And when evidence going in one direction is dwarfed by better evidence for the opposite conclusion, it is a mistake to move from the weaker evidence to a conclusion that only the evidence on one side might support. The fundamental caution provided by phrenology and astrology is that externally visible credentials and related indicia of evidential soundness might be misleading, and that some field's self-created mechanisms of self-validation might still lead us astray.

If we are wise to be cautious about those external indicators of genuine and valuable expertise that are accessible to nonexperts, then we are back to the original problem. We started with the problem of nonexpert assessment of the value as evidence of expert conclusions and opinion, but if that inquiry only leads us to nonexpert evaluation of credentials and related markers, we have not made much progress. Why should we take the validating practices of the National Academies of Science more seriously than those of the Astrological Association or the International Society for Astrological Research? We should, of course, but why? Why should we take a degree in theoretical physics from MIT as a better indicator of true expertise than a degree from the kind of for-profit educational institution that used to advertise on matchbooks back when people used matchbooks? More precisely, why should we take the allegedly validating indicators seriously if we don't actually know very much about astrology or about the scientific disciplines represented in the National Academies of Science? The examples of phrenology and astrology caution us against relying too heavily, or at least solely, on *internal* criteria of the soundness of expert opinion, in the sense of members of an expert community self-validating the expertise of that community.

At this point the recent history of American law on the subject of expert opinion has something to teach us. As described in Chapter 7, William Moulton Marston's crude lie detector was the central character in what for many years was the American judicial system's reliance on solely internal criteria of expertise. For reasons that are slightly beside the point here, experts are allowed to say things in court that nonexpert witnesses cannot. Experts can offer opinions about hypothetical examples, but nonexperts must testify only about things as to which they have personal knowledge. Experts can offer opinions based on the accumulated knowledge in their discipline in ways that nonexperts cannot. And experts can offer opinions and conclusions regarding matters where nonexperts would be restricted to hard facts.[11]

Whether this bifurcation between expert and lay testimony is a good idea is not our concern here.[12] But the bifurcation does make it necessary for judges to determine who is an expert and who is not, and to assess which forms of knowledge involve expertise and which do not. When a court was faced with the question in 1923 whether Marston's lie detector would qualify for the greater leeway granted to expert testimony, the court said that it would not, basing its conclusion on the fact that neither Marston's device nor the science on which it was based had been "generally accepted" within the relevant scientific community.[13] In other words, the test for expertise was internal, and if (and only if) some expert community validated some method or approach could it then count as legitimate expertise.

Eventually most courts, and the US Supreme Court, were confronted with what I have characterized as the phrenology problem. Or perhaps we should call it the malarkey problem. Certain communities of specialists have their own internal criteria, but there is no guarantee that satisfying those internal criteria would actually produce useful evidence or useful knowledge. A good example of this came in 1996 when a New York University physicist named Alan Sokal sent a fabricated and content-free collection of meaningless jargon and fashionable references purporting to establish the nonobjectivity of the existence of gravity to an academic journal in cultural studies, and the journal then proceeded to accept it for publication.[14] But the article was even worse than malarkey. It wasn't just wrong; it was nonsense. The basic point of Sokal's hoax was to expose the emptiness of a particular journal, and, by implication, an entire field. The larger lesson is that even if fields can be trusted to say who or what satisfies the field's own internal standards and who or what does not, that does not tell us whether the field or its standards say anything that is externally true or valuable. Phrenologists can tell you who is an expert phrenologist, but that doesn't tell the rest of us whether to listen to expert phrenologists about disease, personality, behavior, or anything else.

Recognizing this kind of problem, the Supreme Court, which has authority over evidentiary rules in federal but not state courts, ruled in 1993 that the internal criteria of some field might be somewhat relevant in determining expertise, but that external criteria of reliability must be applied as well.[15] Even if some phrenologist had won some mythical Phrenologist of the Year award five years running, that phrenologist could qualify as an expert for purposes of testifying as an expert in the federal courts only if it could be demonstrated that phrenology actually had the ability to produce reliable evidence.

And this brings us back to climate change and global warming. To return to the issue as framed in Chapter 1, there are two evidentiary issues at work here. One is about the evidence that scientists consider in concluding that there is climate change, that it is caused by humans, and that human action might mitigate its consequences. And the other is about the evidence that politicians, non-science-trained policymakers, and citizens use in determining that there is global warming. And although the former is far beyond the scope of this book, the latter is of crucial importance. If the evidence that politicians, policymakers, and citizens have for the existence of global warming consists largely of the testimony (including the conclusions) of scientists, then how should those in the groups composed on nonscientists—the politicians, policymakers, and citizens—evaluate and weigh that testimony?

One answer to this question is the one supplied by the Supreme Court—expert testimony must meet external standards of reliability. But what the Supreme Court said about the use of expert evidence in the legal system contains a lesson that is not restricted to expert evidence in courts of law. Outside of the courtroom, and in inquiry generally, there are certain standards of soundness that transcend particular fields. That is what the Supreme Court appeared to have in mind in talking about "reliability." Insofar as a field, whether nuclear physics or phrenology, makes causal or predictive claims, those claims can be tested by externally accessible means. Those external means include the basic principles of evidence and inquiry, as well as fundamental principles of statistical inference. There might be other such overarching principles of rational inquiry as well, but the fundamental idea is that there are methods and criteria, not exclusive to any particular field or discipline, that allow us to evaluate the soundness of entire fields without getting trapped in the internal phrenology problem. Perhaps the true skeptic might obsess about what makes the basic principles of inquiry, evidentiary inference, statistics, and mathematics sound, but as long as we can leave those worries to philosophers, the rest of us can rest on the assurance that there are ways to evaluate the soundness of entire fields, and thus of the experts within it, that do not require us to rely solely on the very experts whose reliability is precisely the matter at issue.

Thus, when we rely on climate scientists to tell us about the causes and potential consequences of climate change and global warming, we are not relying only on climate scientists to tell us that climate science is reliable. We would no more leave it at that than we would rely on Saudis or Texans to assure us about the importance of fossil fuels. But climate science is itself based on the learning from other fields, and the value of those other fields has been tested against the basic principles of scientific inquiry and scientific validity. Insofar as climate science rests on physics, geology, and chemistry, along with the foundational principles of science in general, we have enough evidence of the soundness of those fields to have at least some confidence in the fields, such as climate science, that they have spawned.

In addition, we can often, even if not necessarily, have confidence in a field if it has survived under circumstances in which there are incentives to attack its methods and its conclusions. One reason phrenology was eventually exposed as worthless was that physicians challenged it and phrenology did not survive those challenges. So too with skepticism

about climate science. Oil companies, airlines, and automobile manufacturers have for many years had an obvious interest in the predictions about global warming being false.[16] Those predictions have not
yet been shown to be false—despite the fact that there has been no lack
of trying—and this in itself gives us good reason to take what the scientists, the experts, have said as good evidence for their conclusions.

To recapitulate, the question for us here is not *why* scientists have
concluded that climate change is real, that it is caused by certain activities of human beings, and that the rate of change, especially of
warming, can be slowed in certain ways. *That* topic has been the subject of a huge and burgeoning scientific literature.[17] Even those aspects
of that literature that dissent from some aspects of the consensus, or
the mainstream, acknowledge the central claims, even as they quarrel
about issues at the edges. For us, therefore, the question is not what
produced those central claims, but, instead, why we as nonscientists
ought to treat those central claims as evidence for the nature and causes
of climate change. The lesson of this section is that the answer is
"Because the scientists have said so"—and this lesson, with its complications, pervades the entire subject of expertise as evidence.

On Watching, Perhaps Too Closely, What We Eat

The bottle of apple juice I purchased this morning contained a large
label announcing that the juice contained "No GMOS." The apple juice
also did not contain a vast number of other things, such as arsenic,
strychnine, and bat guano, but the juice company did not see any reason
to announce that fact. It announced the absence of GMOS—genetically
modified organisms—because the company perceived, correctly, that
many people object to food products containing such substances, or
that are in some way the product of GMO technology.

What makes this issue relevant, especially when examined in conjunction with the issue of climate change, is that GMO technology, like

climate change, is also the subject of a scientific consensus. But unlike with climate change, about which we are told we should have significant worry, here it turns out that the scientific consensus, at least in the United States, tells us not to worry. So what is going on here? If the consensus of science and scientists on the dangers of climate change is sufficient to justify major public policies and substantial public agreement, why is a similar consensus about the non-dangers of GMOs seemingly less influential in molding public policy, corporate behavior, and public opinion?

I want to spend a bit of time examining the GMO controversy, but one bit of preliminary brush-clearing is important. Some people object to GMO technology because it interferes in some way with the natural development of natural products. Given that for at least a few thousand years nature has given us disease, earthquakes, tornados, hurricanes, and floods, among other natural disasters and catastrophes, it is hardly clear that deferring to what nature without human intervention provides is necessarily a wise strategy. Perhaps Katherine Hepburn, playing Rose Sayer in *The African Queen,* was right in observing that "nature is what we were put in this world to rise above." But whatever moral or religious truth there is in the "let nature alone" view, it is one I enthusiastically put aside here.[18]

In the context of this book, the more interesting claim by GMO opponents is that GMOs should be avoided, condemned, or banned because they present a non-negligible possibility of physical harm to humans, animals, and the environment. The issue is partly about the precautionary principle discussed in Chapter 3, a principle that cautions inaction—conservatism—in the face of almost any uncertainty.[19] But deferring questions about the precautionary principle for the next few paragraphs, the point is that many people believe, for nontheological reasons, that the risks created by GMOS are, even if far from certain, quite substantial.

What makes this particular topic of special relevance here is that the consensus of American scientists is to the contrary. Although the consensus of scientists is that climate change is real, human-caused, and potentially catastrophic, the consensus of scientists—sometimes even the same ones—is that the dangers of GMOS are somewhere between nonexistent and exaggerated. And what makes this relevant issue especially interesting is that the political valence of the controversy tends to be the reverse in the two cases. To oversimplify, most of the skepticism about climate change, its causes, and its dangers comes from the political right. But much of the skepticism about GMOs comes from those who would consider themselves left of center politically, and who are in fact left of center on a wide range of other issues. Given that both cases involve trusting the expert testimony of scientists, can this difference be explained?

One hypothesis is that herd mentality is at work. Following the crowd. Sometimes for good epistemic reasons, people follow crowds because they believe that the crowds usually get it right. Recall from Chapter 5 the discussion of collective intelligence and the alleged wisdom of crowds. But often people follow crowds because they desire to be associated with a certain group of people. We wanted to hang out with the cool kids in high school because they were the cool kids. Period. But here there is also the important evidentiary issue highlighted in the previous section. What do experts know, how do we as nonexperts know who the experts are, and how, why, and when should we take what the experts say as evidence for what the experts are saying? As we will see in Chapters 10 and 11, this is not just about the physical sciences, but for the moment let us stick to physical (or natural) science, perhaps the most obvious area of expertise there is, and the area in which the expertise is often least accessible to the nonexpert. Perhaps, whether rightly or wrongly, I can reach my own conclusions about art, literature, and wine, but I simply have no view whatsoever about the scientific processes or reasoning that leads to the conclusion that GMOs are safe, or, for that matter, harmful. And the issue is confounded even more by the fact that GMO skepticism is considerably greater in Europe, even among scientists, than it is in the United States.[20] Because we would not expect the physical phenomena involved in GMOs to vary with geography, the fact that American and European views on this issue are so different, even among scientists, suggests that the issues producing the disagreement are at least partly political and sociological rather than scientific.[21]

An important issue here—which is perhaps related to questions about the precautionary principle, and perhaps related to the difference between American and European views on the precautionary principle—is the question of what we should make of an absence of evidence. Assume that the consensus of American scientists is correct that there is little evidence ("no evidence" would be too strong) that GMOs are harmful to human health or to the environment. Strictly as a matter of language and logic, the absence of evidence of harm does not entail evidence of the absence of harm. This is a general principle, not restricted to GMOs. But even once we recognize that the absence of evidence is not the same as evidence of absence, and that the absence of evidence does not logically or rationally entail evidence for absence, a further question remains. Can the absence of evidence nevertheless, inductively and not deductively, be some evidence of absence? And here things are not so clear. GMO skeptics, or GMO opponents, might revert to the precautionary principle, believing that in the absence of evidence, especially about things we put into our mouths, we should not assume safety. Better safe than sorry. But the precautionary principle is a principle not of science but of policy. If the science tells us that GMOS are, on the best current knowledge, harmless, then a policy that would restrict them anyway on the basis of the precautionary principle is a policy that cannot be said to be following the science.[22]

Still, the absence of evidence can be evidence of absence when it follows actual efforts to prove presence. If no one had addressed the issue of GMO safety at all, we might conclude *only* that there was no evidence of GMO harmfulness. But given that we have now seen at least several decades of unsuccessful attempts to establish that GMOs are harmful, and given that there are financial and political incentives in support of (and, of course, also in opposition to) those efforts, then the existence of non-prevailing opposition is itself some evidence for the conclusion that GMOS are not harmful. If I have never tried to do a hundred pushups, then perhaps I have no evidence that I cannot do a hundred pushups. But if I have regularly tried to do so, and if I have regularly failed, then I have evidence that this is something that I cannot do. The same holds, now, for GMOS, whose harmfulness appears yet to be established despite vigorous efforts to do so.

The issue of GMOs, therefore, is of a piece with the issue of climate change, the opposite political and social valence of the two issues notwithstanding. If we adopt the principle that what the consensus of scientists say is good evidence for what they are saying, then we have good evidence for the dangers of climate change and similarly good evidence that GMOs are not dangerous. Conversely, those who remain skeptical about the harmlessness of GMOS in the face of relatively authoritative conclusions of scientists and scientific groups about that harmlessness should have to explain why they accept the relatively authoritative conclusions of many of the same scientists and many of the same groups on the issue of climate change. The idea of authority is content-independent in the sense that relying on authority means taking the source of a conclusion as at least a reason for accepting it. In the language of countless exasperated parents whose attempts at reasoning with their children have failed, "because I said so" captures well what is at the heart of the idea of authority and thus of deference to that authority. That so many of those who reject the same sources of authority as evidence with respect to GMOs that they accept with respect to climate change suggests that they are relying not on authority at all, and thus not on the idea of expertise at all, but instead on something best explained by sociologists and political scientists.

Vaccination, Then and Now

As I write this, one of the biggest topics in American public policy is vaccination. Most of the controversies surrounding the topic relate to the supply and administration of Covid-19 vaccines, including controversies over who should be given priority in being vaccinated and how the world's limited supplies of vaccines should be apportioned— controversies that will persist as long as supplies are limited and the ability to administer vaccines remains limited. But one issue is how to deal with the fact that many people are unwilling to be vaccinated. Some of that resistance comes from some portions of the African American community, for whom the (long-standing and not Covid-19-specific) resistance is based on ugly episodes in the past where African Americans were used as experimental subjects, typically without choice, as in some of the prison experiments, and often without disclosure of the risks even when participation was allegedly voluntary.[23]

The resistance of some minority communities in the United States to vaccination is a crucial policy issue, but of immediate relevance to this part of this book is the resistance of many others, including many white evangelicals, not only to Covid-19 vaccination, but also to vaccination generally, a resistance that long precedes Covid-19. Vaccination skepticism, after all, has been around for a long time.[24] The most relevant form of pre-Covid-19 vaccine skepticism is the belief that vaccination is a risk factor for autism. And here the politics are murkier. It appears that climate-change skepticism tilts to the right, and that GMO skepticism tilts to the left, but vaccination skepticism seems to know no ideology. Believers in a causal relationship between vaccination and autism, or between vaccination and other untoward ailments and conditions, exist throughout the political spectrum. Yet although vaccination resistance spans the full range of vaccines, much of the pre-Covid-19 resistance was focused on the MMR (measles, mumps, rubella) vaccine and the claim that it was a substantial risk factor for autism.

Vaccination skeptics may come in all political and ideological varieties, but regarding vaccination the scientific evidence is even clearer. Perhaps fueled by the size and persistence of the belief that there is a connection between vaccinations and autism, and also by the fact that non-vaccination has potentially disastrous community-wide consequences, there has been serious scientific testing of the hypothesized connection, and once again the conclusion has been that no such connection exists.[25] And here, to reprise an issue mentioned earlier, it is not that there is no evidence to support the connection. It is that there is evidence—strong evidence—to support the conclusion that there is no connection. Perhaps there is more evidence for the connection between vaccination and autism than there is for the existence of the mysterious "Q," who some people believe is ridding the federal government of evil forces, or than there is for flying saucers coming to earth. Still, there is now overwhelming evidence that there is no connection between vaccinations and autism—evidence that has come from cutting-edge scientific studies filtered through peer review and the other mechanisms of scientific validity.

Again, most of us have no way of directly knowing whether there is a connection between vaccinations and autism. Drugs do cause side effects, and on the face of it the claim that autism could be one of the side effects of a particular substance being introduced into the body in a particular way is not as preposterous as the claim that the Democratic Party has been infiltrated by a cadre of Satanist pedophiles. Still, we do have evidence of the absence of any connection between vaccination and autism, and that evidence, for most of us, comes from the testimony of scientists, either individually or collectively. That is not only good evidence, but it is also of a piece with much of the evidence on which we base our daily lives. If we can trust the testimony of scientists that climate change is real and that GMOs are not harmful, then for the same reason we can trust the scientists that vaccination is not a cause of autism, despite the insistence of a large number of nonscientists.

On the Idea of a Consensus

It would be a mistake to say that there are no dissenters to the claims that climate change poses significant dangers or the claims that GMOs and vaccination present no dangers. There are even dissenters within the relevant scientific communities. Nonetheless, we who are outside the relevant expert communities are asked, even in the face of the disagreement of some experts, to rely on the evidentiary weight of there being a *consensus* of experts, the occasional dissenter notwithstanding.

What exactly is a consensus? If there were strict boundaries to the relevant domains of expertise, we could treat those domains as if they were legislatures, and simply take a vote, with the majority, or two-thirds, or three-quarters, being the threshold for being able to say that the consensus of scientists is that global warming is real, just as the consensus of the Electoral College was that Joe Biden is the president, and just as the Virginia General Assembly decided, by consensus, to abolish the death penalty.

Expert communities, however, are not like this. One reason is that the judgment of expert communities does not make something so. It is only evidence of something. And this is unlike the determinations of the Electoral College or the Virginia General Assembly, whose very actions produce an outcome, just as two people saying "I will" before a duly empowered official produce a marriage. In contrast, the conclusions of experts are evidence, and those conclusions are rarely the formal judgments of an organized body whose rules determine when the body will issue an evidentiary pronouncement and when it will not. Rather, we often confront the slippery idea of a consensus. And the idea of consensus is slippery not only because the idea does not contain numerical thresholds, but also because the idea of a consensus incorporates some equally slippery sense that some of the constituent voices are to count for more than others. One person-one-vote may be a (sometimes observed) principle of democracy and of constitutional law, but it is not necessarily the principle of what is to count as a consensus. If 50 professors of medicine at the country's leading medical schools, in conjunction with 30 physicians who are officers of the country's major medical societies, all agree that vaccination is not a cause of autism, then even if there are a total of 80 physicians in the United States who say just the opposite, then we can (and should) still say that the medical consensus is that no causal relationship exists.

Implicit in the forgoing conclusion is the idea that a consensus, even if partially numerical, is even more substantially sociological. We cannot know what counts as a consensus within some profession or expert community unless we know something about the sociology of that community: Who counts and who does not. Which forms of publication are to be taken most seriously and which are not, or less so. Which methods are accepted and which are rejected. And like any sociological inquiry, the sociological account of what is to constitute a consensus records the pathologies of the community as well as its strengths. When we say that the consensus of some community is such and such, we implicitly accept that community's own inclusions and exclusions, its own hierarchies, and its own forms of discrimination, some of which are good and some of which are not. Accordingly, saying that the consensus of science supports the conclusion that climate change is real, and that the consensus of medicine supports the conclusion that there is no connection between vaccinations and autism, brings us back to the problem that dominates this chapter: Nonexpert reliance on expert conclusions is as irrevocably problematic as it is irrevocably necessary.

The Limits of Science and the Limits of Expertise

The philosopher Nathan Ballantyne has given us a very nice phrase— *epistemic trespassing*.[26] The idea is that although there are people who know things that others do not, and although it is both necessary and desirable that we rely on such superior knowledge as evidence, members of various knowledge communities have a tendency—one we should guard against—to claim a knowledge and an expertise that go beyond the grounds for their knowledge and expertise.

The phenomenon is familiar. Public letters published as newspaper advertisements frequently tout the number of Nobel Prize winners who agree with the letter's conclusion, even if those conclusions do not relate to what the Nobel Prize winner won the Nobel Prize for. In Ballantyne's language, these Nobel Prize winners are trespassers, and we should beware of them. But although epistemic trespassing appears problematic, and appears to involve unwarranted claims of unjustified expertise, we might still take some qualifications and credentials as proxies for more remote forms of expertise, and thus treat the testimony of epistemic trespassers as worthy of evidential weight. Nobel Prize winners in the natural sciences are probably more intelligent than the average person, and for this reason alone we might treat what they say about areas outside their expertise as evidence. We also might suppose that natural-science Nobel Prize winners are more knowledgeable about science in general than the average person, and so what a Nobel Prize winner in chemistry thinks about some proposition in physics might be entitled to greater evidentiary weight than what some equally accomplished poet or sculptor thinks about the same proposition. Less obviously, we might assume that scientists are more concerned with the accuracy of empirical observation than most people, and so we might treat the observational testimony of a Nobel Prize winner in the natural sciences as being especially likely to be accurate and thus worthy of evidential respect.

The more serious problem of evidential trespassing, one that is not addressed by Ballantyne, comes from the frequency with which experts, most commonly scientists, engage in the particular form of evidential trespassing that we might characterize as *policy hegemony*—the assumption that an expert in the empirical or even theoretical aspect of some domain has some sort of privileged position with respect to what some public policy ought to be with respect to that domain's empirical, factual, or descriptive findings.

Let us start with a controversial and widely known example. In July 1945, Leo Szilard, the physicist most responsible for the design and development of the atomic bomb, drafted a petition to President Harry Truman. The petition was signed by many of the other scientists involved in the bomb project, and it urged Truman not to use the bomb that they had helped to develop against Japan except under certain narrow conditions.[27] Largely because of the resistance to the petition by senior members of the military and Secretary of War Henry Stimson's staff, the petition was never delivered to Truman or Stimson. But there is no indication that Truman would have heeded the requests in the petition even had he seen it, and the bombings of Hiroshima and then Nagasaki were inconsistent with what Szilard and his co-petitioners desired.[28]

The basis for the argument in the petition was the scientists' awareness of the enormous destructive capacity of the bomb. But although there is no reason to believe that President Truman had any more idea of what makes an atomic bomb work than I do, it seems clear from the historical record that at the moment when he authorized the dropping of the bombs on Hiroshima and Nagasaki, Truman knew the extent of the bombs' destructive capacities. This being so, the question turns to what the scientists knew that Truman did not. Obviously, there were empirical and predictive issues, still debated, about how many lives would have been lost had there been a land invasion instead of an atomic bomb attack. There were also empirical and predictive issues about what would have been necessary to induce the Japanese to surrender prior to Hiroshima, and then after Hiroshima but prior to Nagasaki. Moreover, there were and remain immense moral issues, still debated, about how a president in time of war should value the relative importance of American and enemy lives, and so too with military and civilian lives. Issues also arise about the extent to which dropping the bomb would have encouraged further nuclear proliferation, and about what the consequences of that proliferation would have been. But with the exception of the way in which the last question may require knowledge of what it would have taken for other countries to build a bomb, none of these questions fell within the domain of expertise of those who had enabled the building of the bomb. Szilard's aims were morally admirable, but there was no reason Truman should have listened to Szilard and his co-signers more than to anyone else with equally morally admirable goals.

Plainly there are cases in which an expert in some area has, because of that expertise, reason to learn about things in the vicinity of that expertise that others might not know. But that was not the case with the bomb. In making the decision about the costs and benefits, to put it crassly, of dropping the bomb, Truman had as much evidence as the scientists. We can question, therefore, whether in petitioning Truman the scientists were relying on any relevant expertise they had that Truman did not. No doubt their involvement gave them a feeling of personal responsibility, and in that sense writing the petition was totally understandable, both personally and morally. But none of that goes to the question whether Truman, had he seen the petition, should have taken what the scientists said about actually using the bomb as coming from the vantage point of comparative expertise, and it is not at all clear that it did.

Much the same can be said these days about climate change. Climate scientists can tell us, and should tell us, about what the world will or might look like in 2050 or 2100 if we do not cut back on fossil fuels, for example. But on the question whether a given amount of welfare (or utility, or pleasure, or even financial) sacrifice now is worth guarding against what might happen in thirty or seventy years, again it is hardly clear that climate scientists have any comparative expertise. The issues are undoubtedly vital, but once the scientists have used their expertise to tell us what is happening now and what can happen in the future, the question of what to *do* is no longer a question about which scientists have the kind of expertise that should lead others to treat their policy prescriptions as evidence of what ought to be done.

The issue of this kind of policy trespassing or policy hegemony is particularly salient in the area of Covid-19. Despite the urgings of many scientists—including the most prominent and respected scientist on the issue, Dr. Anthony Fauci—to "follow" the science, whether and how to follow the science is not wholly or ultimately a scientific question. Scientists can and should tell us what will happen if we do or do not take certain measures, but whether to take those measures, especially if they have costs in the largest sense, is not a scientific question. Just as the ability of traffic analysts to tell us how many lives would be saved if the speed limits on interstate highways would be reduced to fifty miles per hour does not tell us whether to take that step, epidemiology not tell us how to balance some amount of increased epidemiological risk with some other amount of loss of personal liberty or loss of economic activity.

None of this should be taken as suggesting that it is ever right to go against the science. Nor as suggesting that policy goals should lead us to ignore or distort or contradict the science. If that is all that following the science means, then there is no reason to doubt that that is exactly what we should do. But if following the science means following the scientists in *their* assessment of the correct balance between health and economics, or health and liberty, then there is reason to hesitate. These are monumental policy decisions, of course, but they are not policy decisions with respect to which those who supply the appropriate first words about the empirical questions are the ones who ought to have the last word about what we should do.

Chapter 10

The Science of Crime

WHEN MOST PEOPLE THINK OF EVIDENCE, they think of crime and crime detection. Assisted by several generations of television and more than several generations of crime novels, most people believe that evidence is what detectives look for when a crime has been committed, and what prosecutors present to the jury in order to ensure that the perpetrators get their just desserts.

This understanding of evidence is not wrong. Although the premise of this book is that evidence is much more than just the traces left at a crime scene, the kind of evidence that is featured in countless mystery novels and on television shows such as *CSI* and *Law and Order* nonetheless represents an important part of the world of evidence, a part that commonly goes by the name "forensics." Fingerprint evidence has long been the best-known form of forensic evidence, but there are also voiceprints, shoeprints, tire marks, bite marks, tool marks, ballistic examinations, handwriting analysis, hair and fiber matching, and many more, including less well-known ones such as the analysis of blood spatter patterns. And now there is DNA.

Most of these forensic techniques have long enjoyed largely favorable portrayals on television and in popular fiction. In recent years, however, there has been heightened scrutiny of most of the forms of forensic evidence that have for generations been accepted with little or no controversy, not only on television but also in real trials in real courtrooms. In 1993, in *Daubert v. Merrell Dow Pharmaceuticals,* the US Supreme Court insisted that scientific and expert evidence be of a type that has been established as reliable.[1] And among the consequences of this increased attention to scientific reliability has been spate of exonerations of individuals whose criminal convictions were shown to have been the result of shoddy forensic techniques.[2] Indeed, even fingerprint evidence, long considered the gold standard of forensic techniques, has been called into question.[3] Perhaps most importantly and most influentially, an extensive 2009 report by the National Research Council challenged almost all of the methods long used by forensics experts in and out of law enforcement, claiming not only that the reliability of those methods was open to question, but also that the methods used to determine that reliability had traditionally failed even the most basic requirements of experimental validity.[4]

Modern critics of long-accepted forensic techniques have identified multiple problems. One is the tendency of forensic experts, when testifying in court, to exaggerate the conclusiveness of their results, frequently with the use—or overuse—of words like "match" and "certain."[5] And sometimes even with the testimonial assertion that the probability of error was "zero."[6] Such conclusions and characterizations are problematic, in part, because they can misleadingly suggest that it is inconceivable that anyone other than the defendant on trial could be the source of the forensically incriminating evidence. If a ballistics examiner, for example, locates with a microscope a similarity (or multiple similarities) between the marks—the striations, or the "lands" and "grooves"—on a bullet as well as the imperfections in the interior of a gun barrel that can create such marks (and similarly with the marks on a shell casing and the imperfections on a firing pin), trained and experienced examiners can to a high probability estimate that this bullet was fired from this gun.[7] But there is a difference between a high probability and a certainty, and courts and lawyers have been concerned that describing this high probability as "certain" or as a "match" will mislead jurors into thinking that the imperfections on the interior of a barrel are necessarily unique, which is not true, and that the comparison between these imperfections and the marks on the bullet is a straightforward matter involving little or no judgment on the part of the examiner, which is also not true. For these and other reasons, for example, Judge Jed Rakoff of the US District Court for the Southern District of New York limited the expert ballistics witness for the prosecution in a criminal case to saying in his testimony only that some bullet was "more likely than not" to have come from a particular gun, a probabilistic assessment that certainly did not overstate the evidentiary value of the evidence and the expert's conclusion, even though it may well have understated it.[8]

Related to the problem of exaggerated reliability are questions about the validity of the testing procedures that lead to conclusions about the reliability of some forensic technique. Traditionally, forensic scientists have argued for the reliability of their methods by reference to the high percentage of convictions that have resulted from their examinations and subsequent testimony. But this approach to validation suffers from multiple and obvious flaws. One is that the testimony may have influenced the jury conviction, thus eliminating the untainted "ground truth" that is necessary for rigorous validation. If we are interested in the extent to which ballistics examination, for example, can identify a gun possessed by the defendant as the murder weapon, then we need to know whether the examination actually identified that gun as the source of bullet in the victim's body. But if we know only that this gun produced this bullet because the jury said so, and if the jury's saying so was at least in part a product of the examiner's saying so, then the existence of the jury verdict as evidence of the method's reliability is worthless. Moreover, juries are not required to explain the grounds for their verdict, and it is impermissible for a judge to require a jury to sub-divide its verdict into particular answers to particular questions.[9] Consequently, the fact of a conviction is consistent with the jury having disbelieved or otherwise disregarded the ballistics examiner but having nevertheless convicted the defendant because of other evidence. Indeed, much the same can apply to a prosecutor's initial decision to prosecute. If a prosecutor went forward with the prosecution only if all of the evidence was extremely strong, including the non-forensic evidence, then the fact of conviction tells us almost nothing about whether the forensic evidence itself was a causal factor in the decision to prosecute.

Although such flaws have plagued almost all of the forms of forensic identification evidence, recent developments have forced some of the various forensic subcommunities to conduct the kind of legitimate testing that would begin to resemble genuinely scientific method and thus provide sound, even if not conclusive, evidence of the reli-ability of their methods. Were we actually to know—by test firing, for example—which of a large sample of bullets comes from a particular gun and which does not, and if we were then to give the ballistics ex-aminer a sample of bullets and a sample of guns and ask that examiner which bullets came from which guns, we would then be able to deter-mine the extent—the error rates—to which an examiner identified a bullet as coming from a gun when in fact it did not, and the extent to which an examiner identified a bullet as not coming from a particular gun when in actuality it did. Recently at least some of the forensic sub-communities have done all of this in response to the 2009 National Research Council report.[10] And when this is done, we then do have gen-uine scientific support for the value of the method as evidence. In fo-rensics, as elsewhere, the question of the worth of some fact or test or method *as* evidence is itself something that can be established—or not—*by* evidence.

I have used ballistics identification as an example, but the same is-sues persist for almost all forensic identification techniques. Was the hair found at the scene of the crime the hair of the defendant? Did the cotton fiber in the getaway car come from the coat of the person accused of the bank robbery? Was an empty gas can in the vicinity of the fire evidence that the fire was intentionally caused by a human being—arson? Were the defendant's fingerprints on the gas can evidence that the defendant was the arsonist? Is the similarity between the handwriting on a ransom note and the defendant's handwriting on a birthday card to his mother evidence that the defendant is the kidnapper? If the marks on the skull of a victim was beaten to death are similar to the marks on a pipe wrench owned by the defendant, is this evidence against the defendant, and, if so, of what strength? And so on. In all of these examples there are, of course, innocent explanations for the evidence, but the existence of such innocent explanations goes to the weight of the evidence and not to its admissibility.[11] As long as this kind of evidence makes it more likely than it would have been without the evidence that the defendant was guilty of the crime charged, the existence of innocent explanations does not preclude treating the identifying forensic evidence as having evidentiary value.

Handwriting examination provides another good example of the use, misuse, and validation of forensic evidence. But in looking at handwriting identification evidence, we need to make it clear initially that we are not talking about the purported ability of some purported experts to assess personality traits allegedly revealed by the subject's handwriting. There are people, billing themselves as experts, who claim, often profitably, to be able to determine from someone's handwriting whether that person is shy or extroverted, cautious or daring, empathetic or selfish, frugal or generous, and much more. Those claims of expertise—graphology—might possibly have slightly more validity than phrenology, but not much more, and probably have none at all, as multiple serious studies of this type of graphology have established.[12]

Putting the pseudoscience of graphology aside, therefore, what is now before us is the handwriting equivalent of ballistics identification—the

identification of a person by use of handwriting comparisons. Just as a
bullet can show, even if not conclusively, which gun most likely produced it, handwriting similarly can point, again not conclusively, to
the identity of the writer.[13] And if the guilty person wrote a ransom
note or used a forged signature to cash a check made out to someone
else, for example, handwriting identification claims to be able to determine whether the defendant was actually the person who wrote or signed
the incriminating documents.

Here again the issues parallel those raised by ballistics identification.
Professional handwriting identification experts have long touted the accuracy of their methods, but the existence of few rigorous tests of
those methods led many commentators to express a degree of skepticism even greater than that expressed about ballistics.[14] After the Supreme Court's 1993 *Daubert* decision, and especially after the 2009 National Research Council report, however, the community of professional
handwriting examiners, their organizations, and those who would use
their testimony added considerable rigor both to the methods and
to the testing of those methods. The reliability of handwriting identification still lags considerably behind that of ballistics identification,
though, and far behind that of fingerprint identification.[15] Yet handwriting identification by professionals well exceeds nonprofessional
identification, and most recent studies put the error rate for professional
handwriting identification examination at somewhere between 15 and
20 percent, meaning that the accuracy of an identification of a piece of
unverified handwriting as coming (or not coming) from a particular
individual whose handwriting is known is somewhere in the vicinity
of 80 to 85 percent.[16] This would hardly be enough, by itself, to prove a
defendant guilty beyond a reasonable doubt, but it is plainly enough
to satisfy the minimal standards for its admissibility as evidence. Between the minimal standards for the initial admissibility of any evidence and the maximal standards of proof beyond a reasonable doubt,
however, we have, after *Daubert*—the requirement to satisfy the stan-

dards for expert or scientific evidence, standards that are higher than for normal admissibility but not as high as the standards necessary for conviction on that evidence alone.

Once again, and as with ballistics, the courts have been divided on whether expert testimony about similarity in handwriting is sufficient to satisfy the heightened standard for expert evidence.[17] And we can speculate that this standard is heightened even further, albeit without acknowledgment, when the question is whether the evidence can be used by the prosecution in a criminal case. A useful example of the difference between what is necessary to satisfy the heightened, and perhaps further heightened, standard for expert scientific evidence and what is necessary for that evidence to be relevant in the first place comes from the 1995 federal court decision in *United States v. Starzecpyzel*.[18] The defendants were accused of stealing more than a hundred works of art from the obviously wealthy aunt of one of the defendants, then forging the aunt's signature on documents consigning the works to Christie's and Sotheby's for sale at auction, and thereafter directing the auction houses to remit the proceeds to Swiss bank accounts controlled by the defendants. Needless to say, this scheme constituted multiple crimes under federal law. In order to prove the scheme at trial, and thus to prove that the signatures on the consigning documents were forged, the prosecution sought to use several forensic document examiners to testify that they had examined other documents signed by the aunt as well as the consigning documents and had come to the conclusion that the signatures on the latter were forgeries. When the admissibility of this expert testimony was challenged, Judge Lawrence McKenna of the US District Court for the Southern District of New York concluded that the expert's methods not only were not science but could even also be characterized as "junk science." The experts and their approach, he said, possessed neither a rigorously delineated methodology nor very much in the way of testing-based assurances of the accuracy of whatever methodology they used. Yet having come to that conclusion, and thus to the conclusion that the ability to identify a signature as a forgery was not scientific, Judge McKenna nevertheless proceeded to allow the document examiners to testify. There are many types of evidence that are not science, and whose validity cannot be established by scientific methods, he acknowledged, but that might still have admissible probative value, not as science but as legitimate and helpful practical testimony by an expert in some practical field.[19] The evidence was thus admitted, the consequence being that the defendants were convicted and each sentenced to several years in federal prison.

In allowing the evidence to be used despite its nonscientific character, Judge McKenna drew a useful analogy between this form of expertise and the expertise of a harbor pilot. The expertise of a harbor pilot, the judge reasoned, came from long and successful experience, experience that could constitute expertise even if those possessing it did not have a structured and tested methodology. For Judge McKenna, the basic point of the analogy was to support the conclusion that various forms of experience might still qualify as expertise, even if that experience could not be scientifically tested or even grounded in testable hypotheses. We could not, after all, do a test in which multiple harbor pilots were asked to use multiple methods of piloting the ships under their control in order to see which ships arrived safely at the dock and which ones sank as a result of hitting unseen reefs. We might further analogize Judge McKenna's harbor pilots to drivers whose insurance companies set their premiums or give them safe driver discounts by virtue of the drivers possessing an accident-free record for some number of years. Most safe drivers cannot explain why they are safe drivers, other than uttering a few platitudes about paying attention and not driving too fast. And safe drivers do not subject their approaches to rigorous testing by changing one aspect of their driving to see if that produces accidents. And, importantly, the insurance company does not care. All the insurance company cares about is that someone's long accident-free record shows that them to be a safe driver. Similarly, and as Judge McKenna concluded, long and successful experience can qualify someone as an expert, thus giving their judgments value and weight as evidence, even if their practices and methodology are far removed from anything resembling science.

The formal legal basis for Judge McKenna's decision is now obsolete, the Supreme Court having subsequently ruled in a different case that even nonscientific evidence must meet some sort of standard of reliability before it can be admitted as the testimony of an expert.[20] But even if the reliability of various experience-based forms of expertise, such as harbor piloting, cannot be established with scientific rigor, there are alternative, even if less rigorous, indicators of reliability that are still permissible, and the kind of nonscientific and individual-judgment-based expertise that Judge McKenna allowed would still be allowed today. More importantly, and of relevance to evidence generally and not merely to forensic evidence in criminal trials, there are many forms of evidence that are not science, and that cannot be scientifically tested. Recall from Chapter 2 the physician whose diagnoses are based on long experience rather than laboratory experiments or clinical trials. The nonscientific nature of such evidence, and the non-rigorous testing of the reliability of such evidence, undoubtedly weakens its evidential value. But weaker evidential value is not the same as no evidential value, and the lessons of nonscientific forensic evidence are important throughout the realm of evidence and inferences based on evidence.

The examples of ballistic and handwriting identification merely scratch the surface of a vast literature and an even vaster history about forensics and criminal investigation. The combination of the Supreme Court's now-decades-old insistence on indicators of reliability for the admission of all forms of expert evidence, and the roughly contemporaneous rise of concern about the erroneous conviction of innocent defendants, has called into question much of the conventional wisdom about forensic evidence, the forensic science that has long been taken to be valid and reliable by lawyers, judges, the police, the public, novelists.

and television writers. But the lessons to be learned are lessons about evidence generally, and not just about the kind of evidence that is left at the "scene of the crime." And to that we now turn.

Recurring Lessons

The recent history of forensic techniques provides ample grounds for caution about the reliability of those techniques, but that history also, albeit less obviously, provides grounds for being cautious about the caution. Literally by definition, the field of forensics is about crime, and identifying the perpetrators of crimes is typically in aid of using the legal system to punish them, often by imprisonment. It is thus easy to see why the evaluation of forensic evidence exists largely in the context of the potential use of such evidence to put people in prison, sometimes to execute them, and almost always to do at least something unpleasant to those convicted of a criminal offense.

Because the use, misuse, and evaluation of forensic techniques has so overwhelmingly been situated within the criminal justice system and its long-standing and desirable requirements of proof beyond a reasonable doubt, it is tempting to move quickly from the inability of some forensic technique to prove guilt beyond a reasonable doubt to conclusions about the overall weaknesses of that forensic technique. That temptation, however, should be resisted. And it should be resisted for two reasons that have recurred throughout this book. The first is that whether evidence is good or bad, sufficient or insufficient, depends on what we are going to do if the evidence is sufficient. How much evidence we need is a function of the question "For what?" Even in the criminal justice system, forensic techniques that would be insufficient to support a conviction, perhaps even in conjunction with other evidence, might well be sufficient to prompt an investigation and might also be adequate to lead investigators to look in one direction or at one suspect rather than another.

Moreover, as discussed in Chapter 7 in the context of lie detection, evidence that would plainly be insufficient by itself to prove a defendant's guilt beyond a reasonable doubt, and that might even be inadmissible in conjunction with other evidence in light of the legal system's concern for the rights of defendants, might nevertheless be more than sufficient to allow a *defendant* to establish that there was a reasonable doubt as to his guilt. If a defendant were to offer testimony by a ballistics expert that the bullet extracted from a victim "matched" a gun owned by someone other than the defendant and who had a motive for killing the victim, we can wonder whether the judges who balked at terms like "match" would have done so in this context. Consequently, we can also wonder whether some of the work that is being done by the "beyond a reasonable doubt" burden of proof is also casting a shadow on questions about the validity of some forms of evidence more generally, perhaps distorting the evaluation of evidence in the service of ensuring (or double-ensuring) that only the most plainly guilty of defendants are actually convicted.[21]

The history of ballistics identification again provides a useful and sobering lesson of this last point. Scorn toward such evidence is nowadays more common than it used to be, and it is now and then referred to as "junk science."[22] But the original uses of ballistics evidence were not for the purposes of putting people in prison but instead for keeping them out. Although there had been some earlier and laughably crude attempts at ballistics identification, the first such identification that even approached systematic rigor was the one that saved Charlie Stielow from the electric chair. Stielow, a mentally challenged handyman in upstate New York, had been tried, convicted, and sentenced to death in 1916 for the murder of his employers. But the combination of his lawyers' efforts and a sympathetic governor secured for Stielow an affidavit and subsequent testimony by a self-trained ballistics expert who established that Stielow's gun could not have been the murder weapon, the prosecution's case notwithstanding. Stielow was exonerated and released.[23]

Stielow's case is a dramatic example of how evidence that might be properly deemed insufficient to support a criminal conviction might still be sufficient to support an acquittal or exoneration by raising a reasonable doubt about some defendant's guilt. And we can say the same for other forms of forensic evidence that appear deficient when used by the prosecution in a criminal case. Handwriting identification examiners, for example, whose reliability was established only by their record of convictions and thus whose reliability was insufficient to satisfy modern standards of reliability, might still have such extensive experience that we would—and should—be reluctant to dismiss their testimony as to the potential deficiencies of a prosecutor's evidence to the contrary. And in a civil case, where denial of genuine liability is as wrong as mistaken imposition of liability, again what is not good enough for the prosecution in a criminal case might be considered to be good enough for an injured plaintiff in a civil case. Admittedly, the tenor of the previous several sentences is in tension with the law's traditional and still-persistent view that the admissibility of evidence does not vary with the type of case or the party or side that is offering the evidence. But the case of Charlie Stielow and other factually innocent defendants who have been wrongly convicted may suggest that the law's traditional indifference to the source and purposes of evidence should perhaps be open for reevaluation.[24]

Linked to the question "For what?" is the question "Compared to what?" Not only do we need to know the purposes for which a piece of evidence is being put, or the hypotheses it is being used to test, before we know whether the evidence is relevant, whether we should consider it, and how much weight we should give it, but we also need to know what alternative evidence will be used if the evidence under consideration cannot be used. And that inquiry includes the possibility of "none." If some piece of evidence is not usable, but we are forced to make a decision, perhaps the decision will be made on no evidence at all. This may not be the typical way in which the question "Compared to what?" arises, but it is still essential, for forensic evidence and elsewhere, that we understand the alternatives before we too quickly say that some type of evidence is not good enough.

Consider again the case of handwriting comparison. In American law, lay comparisons of handwriting—sometimes comparisons offered by witnesses and sometimes comparisons performed directly by the jury—are plainly accepted for the preliminary purpose of authentication and have frequently been accepted as relevant substantive evidence.[25] If a layperson familiar with someone's signature testifies that the signature on a document whose authenticity is disputed is the signature of the person whose signature the witness knows, that testimony will commonly be admitted, even recognizing that the weight to be given to that testimony is ultimately for the jury to decide. Even worse (or better, depending on your point of view), the jury itself is sometimes allowed to assess whether one signature or piece of handwriting is similar to another, and is permitted to do to with no expert assistance at all. If in the *Starzecpyzel* case the expert had not been permitted to testify as to the dissimilarity between the signature of Ms. Goldstone (whose art it was) and the signature on the consignment documents presented to Christie's and Sotheby's, that determination would likely have been left for the jury to make. The question then is not whether expert handwriting identification comparison is good, but, again, whether it is good enough. And the question of whether it is good enough is substantially a function of what the jury (or judge) would have done in the absence of that expert testimony.

And, finally, we should not forget the Blackstonian idea of preferring the errors of false acquittal to the errors of false conviction. If we update Blackstone's insight into the language of decision theory, we can understand him as saying that determining guilt or innocence is an exercise in decision making under uncertainty, and that designing procedures for making that decision involves selecting among necessarily imperfect decision procedures. And although some of the problems with forensic evidence might be corrected without cost, supposing that we can do so for most of those problems seems Pollyannaish. Not only do almost all of the remedies come at some cost in the literal financial sense, but they also often, even if not necessarily, come at the kind of cost that Blackstone first recognized. In most cases. fixing the procedures that have produced many of the recent exonerations in order to guard against false positives will involve increasing the number of false negatives. For example, prohibiting a ballistics expert from describing an identified similarity as a "match" is likely to lead at least some jurors to discount that expert's conclusions more than the science or the statistics would justify. It seems likely, therefore, that across a large enough array of cases, excluding admittedly imperfect forensic evidence will produce the erroneous acquittal of more guilty defendants than would be produced by the beyond a reasonable doubt standard operating alone. That consequence is real, but whether that consequence is a price worth paying is a determination that the evidence alone cannot make. It is common these days to identify the failures of forensic science and consequent false convictions as something like "shocking."[26] And insofar as those failures can (and should) be corrected at little cost and with no change in the number of false acquittals, then shocking they are. But if some of the forensic failures can be corrected only at some cost, and only by shifting the ratio of false convictions to false acquittals, then the very existence of those failures may be less shocking and more inevitable than may initially appear.

A Note on DNA

Although forensic identification by the use of fingerprints, ballistics, handwriting, and much else still dominates the forensic world, all of these techniques are in some way quaint. We are, after all, now in the era of DNA. Because the chances of two people having identical DNA is much smaller than even the chances of two people having the identical fingerprints—to say nothing of two people having identical handwriting or two guns producing bullets with identical markings or two people looking the same to an eyewitness—DNA investigation holds out the promise of offering dramatic improvements on all of the other known methods of forensic identification. Indeed, it is curious that DNA identification is so often described as "DNA fingerprinting," suggesting that fingerprint identification is the ideal, and ideal to which DNA analysis aspires. But that gets it backward. Fingerprint analysis, for all its reliability, is not as reliable as has long been assumed, and DNA analysis, done properly, is vastly better.[27]

That DNA analysis is vastly better than the alternatives for many or most forensic purposes does not mean that it is without problems. One of those problems is that what DNA analysis has the potential to do is not always how it is implemented in practice. Samples are lost, contaminated, and mislabeled. Or miscollected in the first place. Or even if not lost, contaminated, mislabeled, or miscollected, they may be only partial. Moreover, the chemicals used in the analysis may have expired. Or the analysts may be inexperienced, incompetent, or poorly supervised. And so on. For DNA analysis, as with almost any other human activity, it is a mistake to confuse some technique's potential if done perfectly with the actual performance of the technique. It may be rare for the examiner to spill a milkshake on the sample, but that extreme and hypothetical image is a reminder that there is a difference between theory and implementation, and a difference between ideal and actual performance. Most legal decisions on the use of DNA as evidence, therefore, are less about the science than they are about how that science is applied by fallible humans and laboratories in particular instances.[28] In fact, the inquiry is best understood as involving three parts. First there is the science; second there are the techniques for implementing the science; and third is how those techniques have been carried out on particular occasions.[29] And even if the first of the three is now well accepted, the second and third have the potential for making what is extraordinarily reliable in theory often far less so in practice.

The second area of concern emerges from the fact that DNA testing is partial, in the sense that even the best currently available techniques do not and cannot look at all of the alleles in all of the polymorphic sites. In simple language, currently it is only possible to examine some parts of the DNA profile, even with the best of techniques. And although no two people (except for identical twins) have truly the same DNA, two (or more) people might be identical in those parts of the DNA profile that it is now possible to examine. Then the question moves from theoretical certainty to practical probability. But here things get tricky—because we are no longer in the realm of almost immeasurably small possibilities that someone other than the defendant could have produced the DNA found on, say, the murder weapon or the door handle of the stolen car. Rather, we are dealing with probabilities such that it is at least conceivable that the DNA was produced by someone other than the defendant. And so, to use an entirely made-up number, suppose the chances are one in ten million that someone other than the defendant left this particular DNA sample on the murder weapon. That's a big number, but it also means, in theory, that there are thirty-three people in the United States who are as likely as the defendant to have left their DNA on the murder weapon. And if there are thirty-three such people, then the probability that it was the defendant is not much more than 3 percent, at least if we were to consider this and no other evidence.[30]

This is obviously a dramatically oversimplified example. But the basic point of the example takes us back to Reverend Bayes. If the police could have rounded up all thirty-three of these people, and if there were no other evidence at all, then the 3 percent figure would be correct. But the defendant is the defendant because of other evidence, despite the fiction—and it is a fiction—of a genuine presumption of innocence. Given that there is other evidence against the defendant—place of residence, age, motive, opportunity, and so on, then the question is what the DNA comparison, or match, does to the probability that *this* defendant is guilty. If we start with a probability of 1 / 330,000,000—that the defendant was simply a random resident of anywhere in the United States picked up off the street (or selected by a nationwide lottery) to be a defendant—then what the DNA adds is plainly not enough, even though it does increase substantially the probability of the defendant's guilt. But that, of course, is not how the criminal process works. At a trial, various other pieces of evidence, including the theoretically irrelevant fact that it is *this* defendant who is on trial, will lower the 330,000,000 pool to a much, much smaller number. And then the existence of a DNA match between the defendant's DNA and the DNA found at the crime scene, given the extraordinarily small possibility that any other member of *that* pool could have been a match, is what gives DNA evidence its statistical power and thus its power as evidence. Once we recognize that the presumption of innocence is a fiction, and that the prior probability of the defendant's guilt is much higher than 1 / 330,000,000 by the time the DNA evidence is introduced, we can see that what the DNA evidence does is raise a non-negligible prior probability to a much higher posterior probability, often enough to convict.[31]

Or often enough to exonerate. An important feature of the DNA "revolution" is the frequency with which DNA analysis has been used to show that people previously convicted of crimes either could not have committed those crimes or at least might not have with a sufficiently high probability to raise a reasonable doubt.[32] And so, although there is no room here to explore all of the scientific, statistical, legal, and moral issues that the widespread use of DNA analysis has spawned, in one respect the fact of numerous DNA exonerations reinforces one of the themes that pervades this book—whether evidence is good depends on whether it is good enough, and whether it is good enough depends on what it is to be used for. That is why fMRI lie detection, which may not yet be good enough to put people in prison, might be good enough to keep them out. And that is why it is a mistake to think of DNA solely in terms of apocalyptic 1984 scenarios in which massive DNA databases invade our privacy and make it impossible to escape even our minor transgressions. That would indeed be something to worry about, but the same revolutions in DNA and big data that make it more difficult for the guilty to avoid detection also make it more difficult to convict the innocent. And that is to be celebrated and not lamented.

Chapter 11

The Ever-Expanding Domain
of Expertise

FOR ONLY $129 YOU CAN TAKE an online course from IAP Career College, at the end of which you will receive a certificate designating you as a "lifestyle expert."[1] Relatedly, the actress Gwyneth Paltrow also designates herself as a lifestyle expert, though it is not entirely clear what makes her a lifestyle expert. Or for that matter what makes anyone a lifestyle expert. What do lifestyle experts know that the rest of us do not? Each of us, after all, has a lifestyle. And those of us who more or less like our lifestyles might even think we are, at the very least, expert about our own lifestyles.

It is easy to mock lifestyle experts, but their very existence suggests that there are all sorts of experts, most of whom are not, and do not purport to be, scientists of any kind. Although the forensics experts discussed on Chapter 10 vary in the scientific rigor of their methods, most of them at least purport to be doing something close to the science we explored in Chapter 9. Not so, however, with those whose expertise is in music appreciation, art authentication, body language, wine tasting, literary criticism, and various other endeavors of greater or lesser respectability. What remains to be addressed, therefore, is the question of expertise as evidence where the very nature of the expertise is far more elusive than it is in the case of scientists.[2]

Consider, for example, chicken sexing, a topic that most of us have not actually ever considered.[3] But the practice really does exist, and it is genuinely important. Although it is not particularly difficult to distinguish a male from a female chicken once the chicks are more than a few weeks old, that turns out to be too late. Given the nature of the modern chicken-raising and egg industries, determining the sex of a chick almost immediately after hatching is crucial to the success of the industries and the individual companies involved in those industries. And so there has been the emergence of a cadre of expert chicken sexers.[4]

Two things are important about chicken sexing. One is that it works. Experienced expert sexers can apparently get it right about 98 percent of the time, although novices do barely better than 50 percent. In other words, novices are no better than random, but experts are a great deal better. And the second thing is that most of the experts cannot provide a very precise description of just what method they use to achieve this 98 percent success rate. And even if they could provide some description of their methods, it is unlikely that they could give a satisfactory analysis of why those methods work. In the same way, we suspect that even the most successful baseball pitchers do not have much understanding of the physics of curveballs, even though they know that the ball curves and know how to make it curve.

As we have seen, one form of evidence that occupies much of our evidentiary universe comes from the testimony and conclusions of experts. We know there is climate change because scientific experts, in ways that most of us cannot comprehend, have determined that there is and have announced that determination publicly. We know that vaccination works, and with few side effects, again because of the work of scientists, who then report their conclusions to the rest of us. And so too with the safety of GMOs, the flight control system of a lunar probe, the efficacy of radar, and, for most of us, even the physics of the internal combustion engine that moves the automobile taking us from one place to another. And we saw in Chapter 10 that many of the contemporary controversies surrounding forensic evidence, such as the validity of handwriting identification, focus on whether such evidence is scientific in the same way that climate science, rocket science, and brain science are scientific.

Other forms of expertise do not look like science and do not purport to be science. Chicken sexing, for example. And yet they work. The challenge, accordingly, is to consider the evidentiary status of such forms of expert judgment when they claim to provide us with information and thus of evidence. If a chicken sexer says that this chick is a male, is that evidence that the chick is indeed a male? And how good is that evidence? This is the question to be addressed, with the benefit of examples that may be less obscure and more useful to most of us than chicken sexing.

Is It Really a Rembrandt?

One of the best-known examples of qualitative, impressionistic, non-scientific, but nevertheless highly respectable expertise is art authentication. In January 2021 a painting entitled *Young Man Holding a Roundel,* by Sandro Botticelli, sold in a Sotheby's online auction for $92.2 million dollars.[5] That is a lot of money for a painting. Or for anything else, for that matter. And much of that amount was a function of the fact that this was by all accounts a genuine original Botticelli actually painted by Botticelli. Had it been a really good reproduction—one that accurately reproduced the colors and even the brushstrokes and the surface texture of a Botticelli, and that looked authentic to most laypeople and maybe even to some art professionals—its value would have been measured in the hundreds or maybe the thousands but not in the tens of millions. Even if it had been a genuine original oil painting, its value as "attributed to Botticelli, "studio of Botticelli, "circle of Botticelli," "follower of Botticelli," "manner of Botticelli," or "after Botticelli" would have been but a small fraction of the price that was actually paid.[6] Similarly, but with even less value, had it been a hand-painted actual oil painting that was a forgery, no matter how indistinguishable the forgery may have been from a genuine Botticelli.

The $92.2 million figure for this Botticelli may be extreme, but it illustrates the fact that a great deal of money, in addition to pure historical or academic interest, turns on the ability to authenticate a painting as being a genuine, original work of the artist who is claimed to have painted the painting. Or sculpted the sculpture. Or drawn the drawing. And therefore we have experts in art authentication. The question, then, is what makes them experts, and why their expert conclusions should have such great evidentiary weight.

Before turning directly to the question as just posed, a few clarifications are in order. First, and perhaps most importantly, we need to distinguish authentication from evaluation. There are art experts who purport to be able to explain why Claude Monet's *Water Lilies* is a better painting than the same artist's *Woman with a Parasol,* and why Monet is a more important and better artist than his fellow impressionist Armand Guillaumin. But these judgments are different from art authentication, for two reasons. First, these judgments are heavily infused with questions of taste. Monet being a better painter than Guillaumin is, say the experts, not simply a matter of taste in the same way that vanilla fudge ice cream being better than chocolate chip is a matter of taste. But taste and preference are relevant to comparing artists or works of an artist in a way that the authenticity of a work of art, at least in theory, is not. For authentication, there is a fact of the matter. Experts might differ in their conclusions about authenticity, but they agree that what they are attempting to determine is whether, in our earlier example, an actual person named Sandro Botticelli actually applied paint to create a particular painting on a particular canvas. Even when the evidence for what the fact of the matter is might be inconclusive, that evidence is marshaled for or against a conclusion about a fact that is not itself uncertain. Botticelli either painted this painting or he did not.

A good contrast to fact-focused art authentication is wine tasting. Although (some) wine experts can identify a wine's grape variety, region of origin, and, sometimes, vintage year in a blind tasting, and although the existence of an actual fact of the matter about a wine's origin and production makes wine identification similar to art authentication, most of what wine experts report, usually with the assistance of uninformative adjectives such as "shy," "naive," and "authoritative," are their own tastes and preferences, albeit tastes and preferences informed by extensive experience.[7] Still, the typical wine evaluation by a wine expert is not the identification of an actual fact like the painter of a painting or the sex of a chicken. And in that sense art authentication by art experts involves the attempts by the experts, on the basis of evidence, to identify some fact about the world.[8]

An expert judgment about the authenticity of a work of art, therefore, can be measured, at least in theory, against the actual authenticity of the work. Actual authenticity is the object of art authentication, and it is to be distinguished from the way in which the monetary value of a work of art may be a function of the authenticating judgment—the evidence—of the experts. The dollar value of a Monet compared to a Guillaumin may be at least somewhat a function of what the experts have said just because it is the experts that are saying it, but authentication is different. Perhaps an authentic Botticelli is valuable as authentic because all of the Botticelli experts agree that it is an authentic Botticelli. But if it turned out that the expert judgment was mistaken, as with the Han van Meegeren-created "Vermeer" discussed in Chapter 2, the value would all but disappear.[9] For authentication, even if not for valuation, the expert judgment is evidence of something else—authenticity—and rarely, and never conclusively, an end in itself.

As a final qualification, we need to set aside issues about the distinction between authorship and authenticity. Especially these days, even the authentic artists may not be the ones who physically create the objects properly attributed to them. Prominent contemporary artists such as Sol Lewitt, Damien Hurst, and Jeff Koons often—perhaps typically—sign their names to objects fabricated solely by the assistants in their studios. But if the assistants create an object under Lewitt's supervision, and Lewitt then signs that object or acknowledges in some other way that it is his, that object is then an authentic Lewitt even if we might have a philosophical debate about what it means for this to be a Lewitt. That is an interesting and important issue, but it is not an issue about evidence, and it is not our issue. Here we are concerned only with distinguishing the authentic Lewitt, or Botticelli, or Rembrandt, from copies, fakes, forgeries, and misattributions. And for this issue the question of evidence is of crucial importance.

These qualifications out of the way, we have arrived at the heart of the matter. We are interested in the truth of the factual proposition that an actual human being named Sandro Botticelli in or around 1480 painted the painting now known as *Young Man Holding a Roundel*. We are not interested in whether this is a better painting than a triptych by Francis Bacon that sold for more than $80 million earlier in 2020, or in whether the Botticelli was "really" worth $92.2 million dollars. All we care about is whether Botticelli painted it.

At this point the role of experts takes center stage.[10] And here there are similarities to and differences from the kinds of expertise we have already considered. It would be nice if, for art authentication, we could do the same kinds of tests that the best of forensic identification experts and their organizations are conducting these days, even if they have long resisted it, and even if it took the Supreme Court ruling in *Daubert v. Merrill Dow Pharmaceuticals, Inc.* to get them to change their ways.[11] Following what the best of the forensic scientists in the best of the forensic sciences are now doing, and following as well what real scientists in their laboratories have long done, we could ask Botticelli to give us, say, fifty paintings, each accompanied by his personal sworn and polygraph-tested testimony that he in fact painted them. And then we could commission a group of accomplished art forgers to paint fifty paintings in the style of Botticelli, and then ask the forgers to swear, again with state-of-the-art polygraph testing, that they and not Botticelli painted them. We would then give the hundred paintings, unidentified as to their authenticity but whose authenticity was known to the tester, to the alleged Botticelli experts and ask them to tell us which are the real Botticellis and which are the forgeries. And when all of this was done, we would have, both for each expert and for the community of experts, a measure of their reliability as identifiers of positives (painted by Botticelli) and negatives (not painted by Botticelli). This would yield the error rate of false positives and the possibly different error rate of false negatives.

Of course, this is a fantasy. Botticelli has been dead for a very long time. Moreover, he did not paint a sufficient number of paintings to provide a large enough sample size. And so forth. But if we think of this as a thought experiment, it tells us something precisely because of its fantastic character. It tells us that the expertise of the Botticelli expert is of a variety different from that of the forensic expert. In part the expertise of the art authenticator resembles the expertise of the physician whose confidence in her diagnoses and treatments comes from long experience. But even there the physician knows that the patients she diagnoses in a certain way and treats in a certain way get better. And she knows that some of her diagnoses have turned out to be mistaken, because the symptoms did not improve, although they did when she shifted to an alternative diagnosis. But this approach does not appear applicable to the Botticelli expert.

So what makes a Botticelli expert an expert? What kinds of evidence do art authentication experts use to reach their conclusions? And once a Botticelli expert has reached a conclusion, what is it that warrants the rest of us in treating that conclusion as evidence of a painting's authenticity—as a genuine Botticelli?

A considerable amount of the art authenticator's expertise the lies in an encyclopedic knowledge of the lives of particular artists at issue. Botticelli lived in certain places at certain times, and a painting of some location in a particular year during which Botticelli lived far away would be some evidence of the painting's lack of authenticity. And so too if the painting represented a subject alien to what the experts know about the artist.

More significant is the question of style. The color we now know as Titian red is so named because Titian characteristically used it in his paintings, and so the presence or absence of that color would be evidence for or against its authenticity as a genuine Titian. The same is true for Vermeer's distinctive blue and the very different but equally distinctive blue created by Yves Klein and produced by a process that Klein had patented. In addition, experts in the style of a particular artist know the form of the brushstrokes, what the brushstrokes say about the brushes used, and a great deal more. This great deal more, however, does not, for most experts, include the artist's signature. That may seem surprising, but not so much on further reflection. Forging a Salvatore Dali painting, to take the example of a frequently forged artist, is quite difficult, even if it is far from impossible. But forging Dali's signature, even as characteristic as it is, would be well within the capacity of even a novice forger.[12] Once we get beyond the signature, there are so many characteristics of the style of a particular painter that the evidence relied on by the experts is substantially the evidence that is based on knowledge of these characteristics. Just as someone running out of a bank wearing a ski mask and carrying a bag is evidence that that person robbed the bank because people so clothed and so behaving are usually people who have robbed a bank, a particular style of brushstroke is evidence that the painting was by, say, Botticelli, because of the authenticator's generalized knowledge that Botticelli usually used brushstrokes of this style and most other painters did not. And although this might hardly be conclusive, it is an example of the type of evidence that, combined with other evidence of characteristic style, will lead the experts to the conclusion that the work is authentic—or not.

Less crude, or at least less subjective, are the modern techniques of genuinely scientific inspection of a painting. X-ray analysis, carbon dating, fiber analysis of the canvas, infrared reflectography, mass spectrometry, chemical analysis of the paint, and much more can tell us when (and sometimes where) a painting was painted, and although the typical Botticelli experts may not know how to use such techniques, they know the people who do and where to find them.[13] Moreover, microscopic examination can reveal, in ways that visual inspection might not, such things as whether the particular style of brushstrokes or paint application did or did not resemble the painter's distinctive style. And there is a great deal more of this variety.

Several things are important about this kind of expertise. One is that it is subjective in the sense of involving imprecise judgment.[14] A brushstroke style is likely to be more or less like Botticelli's rather than clearly his or clearly not. Second, much of this is expertise is about knowledge rather than technique. Although the line between the two is fuzzy, there is a difference between being an expert on Botticelli and being an expert skier. Or even an expert painter. And third, and often most importantly, an attribution of authenticity is likely to be an aggregation of multiple, scattered, and uncertain pieces of evidence rather than being the product of one piece of evidence that is conclusive one way or another. Indeed, experts in art authentication, just like expert chicken sexers, sometimes cannot explain just what it is that leads them to their conclusions. For the expert art authenticator, these multiple factors are often accumulated and described under the mysterious label of "connoisseurship" and the equally mysterious "eye" of the expert.[15]

Once we appreciate both the subjectivity of individual items of evidence of authenticity and the way in which an attribution is the result of a subjective accumulation of multiple subjective determinations, we can also appreciate that the conclusion to be drawn from these multiple items of evidence is itself subjective. Fingerprint examiners have worked out, and have used until recently, detailed protocols for determining when there are sufficient points of similarity—typically between twelve and twenty, depending on the laboratory and the jurisdiction in which it is located—between two fingerprints to be able to declare that one fingerprint matches another.[16] But few analogs exist in the world of art authentication. Moreover, some of the subjective determinations might have more evidentiary value than others, and so it is not merely a matter of counting the similarities and the differences. One Botticelli expert might attribute a painting to Botticelli on the basis of eight authenticating pieces of evidence and only one relatively insignificant outlier, but another might be satisfied neither with the number of items of positive evidence nor with the alleged insignificance of the outlier, thus leading that expert to be unwilling to declare the painting authentic. Moreover, the final verdict of an individual authenticator will also be a function of that authenticator's own burden of proof. One authenticator might be looking for something close to proof beyond a reasonable doubt, while another would be satisfied with the equivalent of clear and convincing evidence.[17]

Given all of this subjectivity, it is not surprising that the experts will frequently disagree. And then the question for the "consumer" of an attribution—the museum, art historian, auction house, purchaser, editor of a *catalogue raisonné,* and so on—is what to make of the disagreement. Presumably the consumer will have an also subjective and largely sociological sense of who the best experts are and whose opinion is entitled to less evidentiary value.[18] But there will also be judgments—again subjective and even assuming that the experts have equal evidentiary weight—about how much agreement is necessary and how much disagreement is fatal.

A good example of the latter comes from a recent dispute about the authenticity of a painting by the mid-twentieth-century modernist painter Florine Stettheimer. As reported by the *New York Times,* the painting was to be offered for sale by Skinner's, a Boston-based high-end auction house.[19] But although several Stettheimer experts had declared the work authentic, another Stettheimer expert concluded that neither the subject nor the style were compatible with Stettheimer, leading this latter expert to declare the painting inauthentic. Skinner's then withdrew the painting from the sale, providing as a reason the "difference of scholarly opinion." Given that, according to the *Times,* multiple Stettheimer experts were satisfied with the disputed painting's authenticity, the implication is that, at least for Skinner's, anything short of unanimity would be insufficient to satisfy them. Skinner's, after all, has its own reputation to think of, and it is not implausible to suppose that they operate under their own version of the precautionary principle discussed in Chapter 3. But that leads us back to our recurring issue of the relationship between the amount of evidence required—the burden of proof—and the consequence of that requirement having, or having not, been met. The very fact of disagreement may have been disqualifying for Skinner, but perhaps it would not have been so for collectors deciding how to label the paintings on their walls, and perhaps even not for a museum. If subsequent evidence proves a museum wrong in its attribution and labeling, it simply takes the painting down, or relabels it according to the now-less-certain attribution.[20] But if a prominent auction house (or gallery) sells a painting subsequently shown to be inauthentic, the reputational (and financial) consequences may be much more severe.

What emerges from all of this is the irreducibly subjective judgment involved in the conclusions of an art authenticator, and in the decisions by the consumers of such authenticators, about whether to accept an authentication, and for what purpose. But as Judge McKenna said with respect to handwriting analysis, subjective does not mean worthless.

Perhaps art authentication, like handwriting identification, is imprecise, subjective, open to interpretation, vulnerable to disagreement, and undeniably unscientific. But evidence that is the product of such imprecise, subjective, interpretive, and unscientific judgments can still have value as evidence, even if that value is less than the evidentiary value of a properly designed controlled laboratory experiment. Moreover, as the example of art authentication is designed to illustrate, there can still be people who are experts in areas other than science and whose expertise is not scientific. Where and when such expert judgments are reliable—whether they should be treated as evidence by others, and, if so, of what weight—is typically the result of acceptance of those judgments over time. Treating acceptance as the measure of reliability, however, has much the same odor of circularity as it does for traditional forensic science. But just as with traditional forensic science, authentication evidence for which the assurance of validity is only that the judgments have survived the test of time and that they have not been falsified in an obvious way may still, in some contexts and for some purposes, be the best we can do. And often the best we can do is good enough.

Evidence and History

The evidence that art authenticators use is evidence about the existence—or not—of some concrete historical event. Did a man named Sandro Botticelli paint *Young Man Holding a Roundel* in or around 1480? Did Johannes Vermeer or Han van Meegeren paint *Christ at Emmaus?*[21] Once we see that controversies about the authenticity of works of art are historical controversies—What did a particular individual painter do or not do at a particular time and place in the past?—we enter into the much larger world of controversies about historical events, about the evidence deployed as weapons in those controversies, and about the conclusions of historians and others *as* evidence.

Did Lee Harvey Oswald have assistance in assassinating President John F. Kennedy?[22] Did Nicola Sacco and Bartolomeo Vanzetti murder a paymaster and a guard in an armed robbery of a shoe company in Braintree, Massachusetts, in 1920?[23] When did the Maori first arrive in what is now New Zealand?[24]

As with our discussion of art authentication, a few preliminary clarifications and qualifications are in order. First, the discussion here will focus on what we might think of as questions of hard singular fact. "Singular" in the sense of one act or event and not an aggregation, and thus different from the also-factual claim that "industrialization accelerated rapidly in late nineteenth-century Britain." And "hard" in the sense that a contemporaneous observer would have been able to say with a high degree of certainty that the event did or did not happen. By contrast, many historical questions and controversies are about factual issues that resist straightforward answers, and are substantially interpretive, such as questions about the causes of World War I or whether lead pipes led to the decline of the Roman Empire. Even interpretive questions presuppose certain facts that are then interpreted, and therefore issues about historical interpretation do involve determinations of the hard facts of the past. But to keep first things first, we first have to know what, concretely, happened—and for such questions the issues of evidence about hard singular facts are both preliminary and essential.

Historians are also concerned with issues that are more are more normatively evaluative. One prominent example is the truth or falsity of the controversial claim in the *New York Times*'s 1619 Project that the preservation of slavery was "one of the primary reasons" for the American Revolution, a claim that attracted objections from a group of distinguished and otherwise sympathetic historians.[25] Again, the controversy was substantially about the interpretation of large themes in American history, even as those offering competing interpretations each premised their interpretations on more concrete facts. So too with historical questions that involve counterfactual speculation, such as the question whether the sinking of the *Titanic* could have been prevented if nearby ships had paid better attention, or whether less self-confident physicians could have saved President James Garfield after he was shot by a deranged assassin.[26]

Interpretive, evaluative, and counterfactual historical questions, which are very much the stock in trade of academic historians, undoubtedly involve evidence, but they also—especially the interpretive and evaluative questions—involve subjective judgments of importance and value. Other questions are more purely factual. Trivially, many people believe that George Washington's false teeth were made out of wood, but there is a factual answer to the question whether they were, however elusive that answer might be to us now.[27] The inconclusiveness of the evidence may make the fact of the matter elusive, or at least it did in the past, but there still is a fact of the matter that, in theory, makes some hypotheses about the makeup of Washington's teeth right and others wrong. Somewhat more consequentially, we do not know whether Anne Boleyn had an adulterous relationship with her own brother, that being one of the charges that led to her beheading in 1536.[28] And more consequential yet is the claim that there were no people living in what is now northern South Africa when the first Dutch settlers of that area—the *Voortrekkers*—headed northward from what is now Cape Town in the seventeenth century, a claim that was long part of the apartheid narrative and justification, and has long been resisted, with strong evidence, by anti-apartheid forces.[29]

All these questions, and countless more, involve the use of evidence. We cannot ask George Washington what his teeth were made of, nor interrogate Anne Boleyn about her sexual practices, nor literally observe the terrain of southern Africa in the seventeenth century to see if there were any people there. When we do not have the relatively primary information that comes from first-person accounts or observations—information that is itself not necessarily certain, as we saw in Chapter 8—we are forced to rely on evidence and inferences from often uncertain and conflicting evidence as we attempt to answer such straightforward factual questions.

Although some philosophers of history have argued that historical factual inquiry is different from other sorts of factual inquiry, it is hardly clear that this claim is correct, as other philosophers of history have insisted with equal vehemence.[30] For one thing, we are accustomed to using evidence to reach conclusions across space, which may not be fundamentally different from doing so across time. I did not live in 1914, but nor have I ever been in Uzbekistan, and thus there seems little cause for supposing that knowledge, or at least my knowledge, of what occurred in 1914 should be thought of as different in kind from knowledge about Uzbekistan. In both cases I must rely on testimony, and perhaps on testimony through multiple iterations. That testimony might of course be mistaken, and multiple iterations may increase the possibility of error, but the evidence that we use to learn about spatially remote events is not fundamentally different from the kinds of evidence we use to learn about temporally remote ones.

Indeed, much the same applies to any form of inquiry other than direct observation. Even if we assume that direct observation and memory are infallible, which of course they are not, as we discussed in Chapter 8, most of our knowledge comes from some form of testimony. And so too does historical knowledge. We know about the medical treatment (mis)administered to a dying President Garfield because of what people who were there said, because of what the people who heard what they said then reported to others, and so on for the past almost 150 years. Historical inquiry, at least and especially about singular facts, is fundamentally a process of evaluating testimony and evaluating hearsay. But that is hardly unique to the events of the distant and not-so-distant past.

These days historians increasingly use a battery of modern and sophisticated methods, including computerized analysis of texts and large data sets and techniques of cutting-edge natural science such as carbon-dating of artifacts and chemical examination of fibers and even bodily emanations.[31] And especially in the use of these and other scientific approaches, the techniques of the historian increasingly resemble even more at least some of the techniques of the art authenticator and the forensics expert. But, again, there is little about the pastness of the past that makes the evidence used by historians different in kind from the evidence that is used whenever we have no immediate access to the facts that interest us. Few of the methods of historical research—including reliance on testimony, the use of multiple hearsay, the examination of documents, and the analysis of physical objects, for example—are different from the way in which evidence is used in court. Trials, after all, also involve reconstructing events that are not happening in real time.[32] And the evidence that courts use to make up for this epistemic distance is in many respects of the same variety that historians use to make up for epistemic distance, even if that distance is typically greater for the historian than it is for the judge and the jury.

At bottom, therefore, the building blocks of historical inquiry, even interpretive and evaluative history, are the singular facts that historians access and identify by using evidence. Some evidence might be strong and some might be weak, and conclusions from the evidence are typically the product of multiple items of evidence. Just like verdicts in court. Just like the factual conclusions of investigative journalists. And just like the everyday factual conclusions that we reach regarding contemporary acts and events.

There is one respect, however, in which historical inquiry is different, at least according to some influential commentators on historical methodology. Unlike everyday assessment of evidence by ordinary people in their daily lives, unlike most of the assessments of evidence in public policy settings, and even unlike the assessment of evidence by judges and juries, some of these influential voices about historical methods, often using the label "source criticism," prescribe relatively specific rules for the weighting and prioritization of items of evidence.[33] Physical objects are to be preferred to testimony, for example. Testimony is given greater weight if it is closer in time to the described event. Eyewitness testimony is to be preferred to other forms of testimony. And in some ways these "rules," softer or harder depending on the author and on how they are used by the historian, resemble the "two witness" rule required by the US Constitution for prosecution of treason and the "two source" rule often employed in much of traditional print journalism.[34]

Although these prescriptions, and other like them, are not different in kind from what people normally do, and not that different from how judges and jurors normally evaluate evidence, what is noteworthy is the attempt to reduce these ordinary principles of evidentiary evaluation to explicit guidelines, or even rules. It is not surprising that these guidelines often come from commentators in countries whose legal systems follow the civil law and not the common-law tradition. For although common-law judges and juries are rarely in modern times given rules about how to evaluate or weight the items of evidence that are admitted for their consideration, the civil law, following its Roman law origins, is different. Civil-law principles of evidence often include just these kinds of rules of weighting and priority, rules that nowadays are alien to the common-law universe.[35] And so just like civil-law judges (rarely are there juries in the civil-law world) are frequently expected to follow official rules for the evaluation of evidence, historians are being urged to do much the same thing, even if, obviously, less officially.

This brief excursion into the methodology of the expert historian has larger lessons. Perhaps what makes the historian an expert is knowledge (knowing what) about a particular area or period or person, as opposed to a distinctive approach (knowing how) not shared by others.

Good historians use evidence the way good judges and good thinkers use evidence, and that is to be applauded. But when we think about why and when we should treat the judgments of historians as evidence for the truth of the conclusions they reach, we may find that the basis for treating those conclusions as evidence is more similar than we might have supposed to the basis for treating any other source of knowledge as evidence.

Chapter 12

The Relevance of the Past
to the Present

ON FEBRUARY 19, 2021, Senator Bernie Sanders of Vermont was asked his views about the then-pending nomination of Neera Tanden to be director of Office of Management and Budget. Because Tanden had been sharply and personally critical of Sanders when she worked for former secretary of state Hillary Clinton some years earlier, questions arose about whether the tone of her criticism of Sanders, as well as of many Republicans, would persist were she to become director of OMB. In response to the questions to him, and to Tanden's pledge to be "radically different," Sanders said, "I worry less about what Ms. Tanden did in the past than what she's going to do in the future."[1]

Two years earlier, on February 25, 2019, Trump administration press secretary Sarah Sanders (no relation to Bernie Sanders) cautioned those in attendance at a White House press conference not to believe the allegations being leveled against the president by his former lawyer and "fixer" Michael Cohen. "It's laughable," Sanders said, "that anyone would take a convicted liar like Cohen at his word."[2]

Stepping back from the political combat that framed both of these events, the comments of Bernie Sanders and then of Sarah Sanders raise important issues about the evidentiary significance of past acts—and not only criminal convictions—in reaching conclusions about someone's subsequent or likely behavior. Should the fact that Tanden had used strong and personal invective in the past be taken as evidence of her proclivity to do so again in the future? Does the fact that Cohen lied in the past make it more likely than we would otherwise suppose that he is lying now? Is Cohen's past lying *evidence* of his current lying? In insisting that Cohen should not be believed now because he had lied in the past, Sarah Sanders was asking her listeners to rely on the venerable adage "Once a liar, always a liar." Or, to the same effect, "Leopards never change their spots."

But are these slogans sound? Or was Bernie Sanders on firm ground in saying, possibly sincerely and possibly not, that past actions may not be very good evidence of future or even current behavior? And is the thought behind "Once a liar, always a liar" applicable not only to lies, liars, and leopards, but also to human behavior in general? Did Virginia governor Ralph Northam's racist performance in blackface while in medical school make it more likely than otherwise that he would engage in racist acts or make racist decisions while in office?[3] Should President Biden's mandatory F for plagiarism in a law school course in 1965, combined with his subsequent unattributed uses of the language of other political figures in some of his own campaign speeches, be taken as evidence against the veracity—or the originality—of anything he says now?[4] Does Martha Stewart's 2004 felony conviction for lying to federal officials provide evidence for distrusting her recipes or the products she recommends?[5]

Consider also tennis at the highest professional level, where players frequently falsely claim an injury in order to secure an additional time out, or sometimes to avoid continuing to compete in a match they are destined to lose.[6] If some player claims a non-obvious injury, should the referee (or the doctor, for that matter) take into account that player's past record of false injury claims in assessing the likelihood that this time it is a genuine injury? The same question arises in professional golf, where it is sometimes contested whether a player has intentionally adjusted the ball or the terrain in order to make a subsequent shot less difficult.[7] If the tournament officials are unsure about the truth of an accusation of this form of cheating, is the accused player's past record of rules infractions relevant for the officials in making their decision now?[8] And if the player is the president of the United States, does a record of cheating on the golf course provide some evidence of likely dishonesty in the performance of official presidential duties?[9]

Often in such cases, a common argument against using someone's previous behavior as evidence for what they might have done now is that what is past is past. Just because someone has done something before does not mean that they will necessarily do it again, and especially under different circumstances, so the argument goes. But would those who make that argument accept a late-night ride from someone who had been convicted on three previous occasions of driving while intoxicated, or, criminal convictions aside, from someone they knew to have been involved in multiple automobile accidents? And why did the *New York Times*, in reporting on a 1991 subway derailment that killed five passengers and injured another two hundred, think it important to inform its readers that the motorman operating the train had some months earlier ignored a red signal while operating his train, and that he had, still earlier, been reprimanded several times by the Transit Authority for violation of the Authority's rules?[10] The *Times*, we suspect, believed that the motorman's past conduct was relevant in determining whether on this occasion he had been acting negligently, or had been once again violating the rules of the Transit Authority. Whatever we may think of the more complex examples of Governor Northam and President Biden and Martha Stewart— examples that likely are colored by political or personal preferences of admiration or animosity—few people are likely to fault the *Times* for thinking that the motorman's past acts are relevant to evaluating his claim of innocence on this occasion. The same goes for the tennis pro who says that this time the pain is real, or the professional golfer who professes innocence when accused of less-than-honorable behavior.

Past acts are commonly considered to be relevant in predicting *future* behavior, which is why convicted child molesters do not get hired as camp counselors or TSA agents, and why confessed plagiarists rarely secure positions as college professors. And although evidence is crucial both in predicting future behavior and in determining the events of the past, the immediate focus here is on the relevance of past acts in attempting to determine under circumstances of uncertainty the facts of something that has already happened. Prediction is indeed important, but so is determining what occurred in the past or what is happening now under conditions of uncertainty. Still, it is worth bearing in mind that for all of these inquiries, whether forward-looking, backward-looking, or present-looking, the question is whether what someone has done in the past is evidence of what they did later, what they are doing now, or what they might do in the future.

The Law's Peculiar Attitude

One reaction to questions about the relevance of past acts to assessing the likelihood of subsequent behavior is to wonder how anyone could possibly doubt that past behavior is evidence, and often good evidence, of subsequent behavior. Past acts are of course relevant, as Sarah Sanders and all of us know. Common experience and everyday decision-making provide countless examples of our willingness to use earlier actions as evidence as to what someone might subsequently have done. If a friend asks me to believe that he has been cheated by a cashier at a local store, I am more likely to believe him if I had been cheated by the same cashier at the same store a month ago. True, Governor Northam's political supporters might argue against making much, if anything, about his past lapses, as would those who are fans of Martha Stewart, or politically sympathetic to President Biden, or would like to believe Michael Cohen. But parents do not hire convicted child molesters as babysitters. Banks do not employ security guards who have been released on parole after having served time for bank robbery. And it is pointless to try telling your insurance company that your three previous accidents should not cause them to raise your rates or cancel your policy because the accidents you have had (or caused) in the past do not show that you are more likely than anyone else to have or cause accidents in the future. Your insurance company knows that your past record is relevant to assessing your subsequent behavior, and most of the rest of us operate in the same way when we decide who to trust, who to believe, and who to hire to fix our cars or repair the plumbing. Faced with a question about *who* did something now, or *what* someone did now, our fingers quickly point to the person who has done something similar in the past, or to what some person has done in the past. Captain Renault in *Casablanca* spoke not only for countless police officers, but also for most of the rest of us, when he memorably referred to rounding up "the usual suspects."

Yet however odd it seems to ignore past acts in trying to figure out whether someone has done something on this particular occasion, that is exactly the typical and long-standing practice of the legal system. Rule 404(b) of the *Federal Rules of Evidence*—a rule that governs trials in federal courts, that serves as the model for the rules of evidence in most states, and that reflects a long-standing approach throughout the common-law world—provides that "evidence of a crime, wrong, or other act is not admissible to prove a person's character in order to show that on a particular occasion the person acted in accordance with the character."[11] Put aside the issue of character for the moment. We will return to that shortly. Stripped of the character question, what this rule says is that past acts, including but not limited to past crimes and past wrongs, cannot be used to show that someone committed that kind of act on the occasion in question. That the defendant has committed three bank robberies in past years cannot be offered in evidence by a prosecutor trying to prove that the defendant has committed the particular bank robbery he is now charged with committing. In a typical lawsuit emerging out of an automobile accident, and in which both drivers claim that the other driver negligently caused the accident, the plaintiff is not permitted to show that the defendant driver has been found liable for negligent driving on multiple previous occasions. And if Michael Cohen were now to be charged with perjury for allegedly once again lying during a court proceeding, the jury will never hear about his past conviction for pretty much the exact same crime.

Is the law being irrational? Why would the legal system insist on excluding evidence of what anyone with any common sense knows to be relevant? If banks will not hire convicted bank robbers as security guards, why can't juries take past bank robbery convictions into account in trying to decide whether someone committed the bank robbery with which he is now charged? If insurance companies can use our past accident records in setting our rates, why can't courts use those same accident records in seeking to judge whether some accident was our fault?

Not surprisingly, the law has several responses to what at first glance seems perverse. One response implicitly recalls a theme common in more than a few movies.[12] Someone, typically a juvenile male, has gotten into trouble as a result of, say, stealing a car or committing an assault during a gang fight. He goes to prison, and, upon release and seeking to "go straight," looks to find a job. But employer after employer asks whether he has a criminal record, and, learning that he has been convicted of a crime, refuses to hire him. And he then objects that this is unfair, and that his past acts should not be held against him. He has, he complains and pleads, already "paid his debt to society."

In excluding past crimes and other wrongs that have produced some sort of penalty (including a judgment in a civil lawsuit based, say, on negligent driving), the law might be understood as agreeing with our unfortunate parolee. If someone's past conviction and imprisonment for a crime can now be used against them when they are charged with a different crime, are they not being punished once again for the past crime? If having to pay money as a result of a verdict in a civil suit following a finding of negligent driving can then be used in a subsequent civil suit again charging negligence, is the driver at risk of being penalized once more for his past negligence? It is unfair, so the argument goes, to use someone's past wrongs against them in this way. Having already served their time or satisfied a civil judgment, the wrongdoers have paid their debt to society. And the debt having been paid, they are entitled to be judged on a clean slate. To use a previous conviction in a subsequent trial is to impose an additional penalty precisely because the evidence of the past wrong increases the probability of liability for this one. The legal system, in excluding these past acts as evidence, is sympathetic, refusing to allow past convictions or past wrongs to be used for the purpose of now attempting to prove that someone did something similar on a subsequent occasion.[13]

Perhaps recognizing that this justification for ignoring past acts tends to persuade neither insurance companies nor very many ordinary people, the legal system and the law of evidence have another and arguably stronger justification for refusing to infer subsequent behavior from previous acts. And this justification explains why the legal system's refusal to use previous acts as evidence for the existence of a subsequent act applies not only to crimes and other wrongs but also to behavior in general, criminal or not, good or bad. Yes, the law appears to say, previous acts are indeed relevant to making determinations about subsequent behavior. And perhaps in an ideal world those previous acts would be given some limited amount of weight as evidence. But this is not an ideal world, and "some" is not the same as "all." Giving previous acts some weight is not the same as treating the inferences from those past acts as indisputable. After all, people who have negligently caused accidents in the past are not negligent every time, and so they might not have been negligent this time. Just because some people have lied previously does not mean that every single statement they make is a lie. And similarly for people who have committed crimes in the past. So even if previous acts are relevant, they are typically not conclusive. "Once a liar, always a liar" overstates things, and "Once a liar, more likely than others to be lying now," even if less catchy, comes closer to reality.

Yet although past acts do not conclusively prove current behavior, the legal system worries that people think otherwise. Especially when the people who think otherwise are judges and members of juries. Accordingly, the legal system has long assumed that jurors, and even judges, actually do believe in the "Once a liar, always a liar" adage, and believe it literally, however exaggerated it may be. Or once a thief, always a thief. Or once a bad driver, always a bad driver. And so on. In other words, although past acts appear to have *some* value as evidence of subsequent behavior, the law of evidence worries that judges and juries will *overvalue* these past acts. The legal system fears that the person charged with burglary who has in the past been convicted of burglary will be presumed *of course* to have committed this burglary. Sarah Sanders, after all, wanted her audience to take Michael Cohen's past perjury as conclusively proving that he is not telling the truth now. But although Cohen's past perjury might give us some reason to be skeptical about the truth of what he is saying now, and although someone's past burglaries might give us some reason to doubt that person's claims of innocence when he is charged with committing a burglary now, these doubts are hardly conclusive. Consequently, the legal system, fearing that jurors and even judges will take past acts as conclusive proof of present behavior, excludes using those past acts as evidence. Better to give those past acts too little weight, the law says, than allow judges and jurors to give them too much.[14]

In addition to reflecting a fear of overvaluation, the legal system also tries to prevent juries, and perhaps also judges, from punishing people for what they have done in the past and not for what they are being charged with in the present. Although related to the additional penalty implicitly imposed when evidence of past acts increases the probability of conviction or liability for the act now being tried, the concern here is different. Here the concern is that people will be punished once again for the prior acts or even for acts for which they were not punished but that are not the subject of the current proceedings. Courts are supposed to try people only for the acts with which they are now charged, but there will always be the temptation to punish for something else, especially if the something else seems especially horrid, and especially if the something else has thus far escaped punishment. Fearing that judges and jurors will succumb to this temptation, the legal system compensates, and perhaps overcompensates, by using the law of evidence to keep jurors, especially, from even knowing about acts other than the one now being tried that might be thought by these jurors to deserve punishment, or to deserve additional punishment beyond whatever punishment was already imposed.[15] Indeed, the legal system's treatment of character and of past acts may reflect an important theme in the law of evidence—that more evidence is not necessarily better, and not even more relevant evidence, especially if juries or even judges will misuse or be misled by that evidence. Sometime in the law, less evidence is thought to produce greater accuracy, and this lesson may well be valuable, even if rare, outside of the legal system as well.

Character—Good and Bad

Consider again the provision of the *Federal Rules of Evidence* quoted above. The rule does not say simply that past acts cannot be used to prove current behavior. The rule takes the additional step of providing that past acts cannot be used to prove that someone has the kind of *character,* or disposition, that would lead them to commit acts of this kind. If someone has been found negligent in three previous automobile accidents, we might think that they are careless people, or at least careless drivers. And if they are careless drivers, they are more likely to be careless in the future, more likely carelessly to cause accidents, and more likely to have carelessly caused the accident that is now at issue. Sarah Sanders urged us to believe that Michael Cohen had the character trait of dishonesty—a trait, she insisted, that gives us reason to not believe anything he says.

Even with this additional step—from past acts to character to current acts, and not just from past acts to current acts—the law, in presumptively excluding the use of character as well as past acts, once again departs from what seems to be common sense. People are, most of us believe, careful or careless, honest or dishonest, punctual or tardy, sloppy or neat, selfish or considerate, rude or polite, and so on. "He's always late." "She can be trusted with money." "He's short-tempered." We make these judgments about people all the time, and we make them on the basis of their past acts. And having made these judgments of character or disposition, we use them predict what they are likely to do in the future and to reach conclusions about what else they might have done in the past. If I have been caught with my hand in the cookie jar on four previous occasions, I become the leading suspect for the current cookie theft because my past acts produce the inference that I have the disposition to steal cookies. It is not simply that I sometimes or frequently steal cookies. It is that I am a cookie stealer. Or maybe just a thief. Or just dishonest. That is my character. Those are my dispositions.

Such conclusions about a person's character are precisely what the legal system prohibits judges and juries from using. For the reasons just described, the law typically does not allow judges and juries to engage in what, technically, is called *propensity* reasoning.[16] Judges and juries are not permitted to conclude that a person's past bank robberies or past negligent driving show them to have a propensity for robbing banks or a propensity for bad driving. Such propensities—however real they seem to be, however consistent with common sense they seem to be, and however much they are supported by empirical research—cannot be taken into account in deciding whether someone acted in a way that is consistent with that propensity on a particular occasion.

In worrying about the use of character in this way, or, more accurately, about the overuse of character, the legal system tracks some of the central themes of modern academic experimental psychology.[17] In particular, psychologists have long been concerned with the relative importance of *dispositions,* or *traits,* on the one hand, and *situations,* on the other, in determining how people act. Dispositions are deep-seated characteristics of personality or character, and include such things as introversion and extraversion, selfishness and altruism, honesty and deceptiveness, conscientiousness and laziness, and so on. And for a long time many psychologists believed, along with many (most?) ordinary people, that such dispositions are the chief determinants of human actions.[18] There are dishonest people who are inclined to lie and steal, so it was said, just as there are aggressive people who are likely to cut you off on the highway, egoistic people who will talk about themselves all the time, amoral people who will engage in selfish behavior, and cautious people who will never take chances. Accordingly, if one were looking for evidence about what happened on some occasion, it would be very useful to know about the dispositions—the characters, the traits, the personalities—of the people whose actions were under investigation. If two people were in a fight, and the police wanted to know who started it, then knowing that one of the combatants was generally aggressive and short-tempered while the other was shy, cautious, and tolerant would be good evidence about who was the likely aggressor—about who started the fight. The same goes for parents or teachers who are adjudicating competing claims of "He started it!" by the two combatants in a playground, backyard, or backseat scuffle. In such instances, knowing the traits of the participants would help decide what really happened. Or so the so-called dispositionists would have had us believe.

In the 1960s, Yale psychologist Stanley Milgram famously conducted a series of experiments in which seemingly normal people were induced to commit seemingly abnormal acts—applying increasingly painful electric shocks, in the most notorious of these experiments—because of group pressure or a desire to please an authority figure.[19] Psychologists then became increasingly committed to the view that it was the situation rather than the dispositions of the people involved that was the principal determinant of human action. If you wanted to know who started the fight, you would want to know what the disagreement was about, whether the combatants had a history with each other, whether there were other people present or involved, and much more. All of these things would be part of the situation in which the fight started, and such facts could provide much better evidence of who started the fight than merely knowing the character or dispositions or traits of the fighters. And to ignore all of these, it was said, was to commit the *fundamental attribution error*—to attribute far too much explanation for an action to dispositions and far too little to the situation.[20]

These days most psychologists recognize that explaining behavior is not only a matter of understanding dispositions or traits, and not only a matter of understanding the situation. Instead, human behavior is a function of the *interaction* between dispositions and situations.[21] Different people react to the same situations in different ways, and thus it is a mistake to think that it is all about the situation. There really are aggressive people who will start a fight under the same circumstances (the same situation) in which others, with less aggressive personalities, will walk away. But even people with more or less the same dispositions (or traits, or personality) react in different ways to different situations. If you wanted to know who started the fight, therefore, you would want to learn as much as you could about the personalities of the fighters, but you would also want to learn as much as possible about the full situation in which the fight started. Knowing all of this, or at least much of it, would provide better evidence of who probably started the fight than would the evidence provided by dispositions alone, or by the situation alone.[22]

A good example of the issue, in the context of just this common question of who started the fight, comes from a widely publicized 2003 Massachusetts event. A Harvard graduate student named Alexander Pring-Wilson was walking home very late one evening after having consumed a considerable quantity of alcohol with several friends. As he was walking home, he was spotted in Cambridge by several local individuals, who also were drinking, and who were sitting in a car while waiting outside a pizza shop for their pizza to be ready. Words were exchanged, including the loud observation by one of the individuals in the car that Pring-Wilson was "shit-faced." Pring-Wilson took umbrage at this apparently accurate observation, which was accompanied by other expletives. Tempers flared, a fight ensued, and one of the individuals in the car, Michael Colono, wound up being stabbed by Pring-Wilson. The stab wounds turned out to be fatal, and Colono, the victim of the stabbing, died in the hospital shortly thereafter.

At this point the stories diverge. Samuel Rodriguez and Giselle Abreu, companions of the deceased Michael Colono, testified that Pring-Wilson came over to the car, pulled one of the individuals out of the car, and started the fight. Pring-Wilson, however, claimed that two of the people in the car jumped out of the car and attacked him, leading him to take out a knife for use in self-defense. And thus, with tragic consequences, the question was the familiar one of who started the fight. If Pring-Wilson's story was true, then he acted in self-defense and had committed no crime. But if the deceased's companions' story was true, then Pring-Wilson, as the instigator, was guilty of murder, and he was indeed so charged and tried in the Middlesex County Superior Court.

At the trial Pring-Wilson's lawyer attempted to present evidence of the victim's character—specifically that the victim, Michael Colono, was, and was well known to be, a volatile hothead who was the kind of person who would start a fight. The trial judge, relying on the law's traditional aversion to character evidence, initially refused to allow the evidence of the victim's character to be heard by the jury, and the jury, knowing nothing of Colono's character, then convicted Pring-Wilson of voluntary manslaughter. Pring-Wilson thereafter moved to have the verdict set aside, arguing that an intervening decision of the Massachusetts Supreme Judicial Court required the trial judge to admit evidence of Colono's character.[23] The trial judge agreed and set aside the conviction, a decision which was upheld, against the Commonwealth's appeal, by the Supreme Judicial Court. The court concluded that a victim's character could indeed be offered as evidence to show who was the likely first aggressor, a conclusion that is now an explicit exception to the federal rule quoted above, although that rule is not directly applicable to a Massachusetts state court prosecution.[24] At a second trial, the jury was unable to reach a verdict, and, Pring-Wilson eventually pled guilty to the lesser charge of involuntary manslaughter and served several years in prison. But this anticlimactic denouement is less important to us, if not to Pring-Wilson, than the way in which the case clearly presents the question of the extent to which someone's character is relevant in the determination, under conditions of uncertainty, of what actually happened.

The issue in *Commonwealth v. Pring-Wilson,* the technicalities of the law apart, is a relatively straightforward question of evidence. We don't know who started the fight, and there are two conflicting stories. It would seem useful, therefore, to know something about the characters and past activities of the fighters, not because we are interested in those activities themselves, but because those past activities provide evidence as to what might have happened now, just as Sarah Sanders wanted us to believe that Michael Cohen's past untruthfulness provides evidence about whether he is being untruthful now. As a result of Pring-Wilson's case, and the earlier one that had led the trial judge to grant the new trial, it is now the law in Massachusetts, as it is in federal courts and in states whose rules of evidence are modeled after the federal rules, that where the question is one of identifying the first aggressor, the character of the victim is deemed admissible, and so too, in response, is evidence about the character of the alleged perpetrator. But although the events of this case provide a useful and vivid laboratory for considering the extent to which character and past behavior (which is, after all, what people use in attributing some character to a person) should be used to reach conclusions about what likely happened now, it is important to bear in mind that this case and the treatment of "victim character" present an exception to the general rule. And the general rule, at least in the courts, is that past acts cannot ordinarily be used be used to try to prove what someone did or did not do or did or did not know.

Outside the Courts

What makes the law interesting here is precisely the way in which the judicial system's general aversion to past act evidence and character evidence seems so at odds with common sense and with how people make decisions in everyday life. Sarah Sanders knew that the best way to cast doubt on Michael Cohen's story was to call attention to his proved past acts showing him to be someone with a less than scrupulous concern for the truth. And in doing so, Sanders recognized that people do not follow the *Federal Rules of Evidence* in making their normal and everyday decisions. If you contract food poisoning after eating at Sammy's Steakhouse, you are likely to think that Sammy's concern for restaurant cleanliness is lacking, even though it is of course possible that this was a onetime consequence that could not be attributable to any of Sammy's practices. And if you read on Yelp or Tripadvisor or any other such site that three other customers have complained about food poisoning at Sammy's, you would likely conclude that Sammy has an unsanitary and thus unsafe kitchen, even though such past reports and past complaints would likely not be admissible in court were someone to sue Sammy's for negligently serving a contaminated salad.

In this and many other non-courtroom settings, the question is more about predicting future behavior than it is about discovering the truth about some past act. But the evidentiary question of what happened in the past is similar in this regard to the question of what will happen in the future. Even those aspects of the law that are concerned with prediction will use past acts to predict future behavior. Judge Richard Berman of the US District Court in New York denied bail to then-accused and now-deceased child molester Jeffrey Epstein because Epstein's past acts, while on bail, indicated to the judge that he would do the same thing were he to be released on bail this time. And outside the law the reasoning process involved in prediction of future events is similar to the reasoning process of trying to determine what happened in the past. Past food poisonings at Sammy's Steakhouse will lead most of us to predict a greater likelihood of food poisoning in the future—or tonight, when we are deciding where to eat—than for restaurants with a "cleaner" history. But those same past food poisonings will also lead us to point the finger at Sammy's if someone who contracts food poisoning today ate at three different restaurants yesterday, one of which is Sammy's and two of which have never been known to serve contaminated food. Or consider the common situation, the far milder version of the Pring-Wilson case, in which two squabbling siblings each protest to their parents that the other started it. Most parents will be more inclined to believe the child known to be less aggressive, or known to be more truthful, even as they recognize that this fundamentally evidentiary determination based on character or past acts might be mistaken on this occasion. And those same parents will also treat the same past acts as relevant for prediction of future behavior, as when they must decide the age at which the respective children will be allowed to have something that can be used as a weapon—a penknife, say—or the age at which the children will be allowed to go unaccompanied to concerts or parties.

As these examples suggest, it is unrealistic to suppose that, outside of the courtroom, people will or should ignore past acts in trying to determine what happened, or what will happen. And it is not just that refraining from using past acts in this way—by citizens, by politicians, and by insurance companies, among many others—is unrealistic. It is irrational as well. Past acts and the character they reveal are genuinely relevant in a vast number of instances aimed at determining what happened, as the barrage of examples offered above is designed to show. And they are relevant in the same way and to the same effect as they are in the legal system and, for that matter, in most of our everyday evidential reasoning.[25] That is, past acts typically make our belief in the existence of some act more likely if we know about the past acts than if we do not. Consider, for example, the recent accusations that three sitting United States senators—Senator Richard Burr of North Carolina, Senator Dianne Feinstein of California, and then-senator Kelly Loeffler of Georgia—had unlawfully sold securities based on information received in confidential briefings about the effect of Covid-19 on the economy. With respect to Senator Burr, however, although not to the other two, the accusations come against the background of his previously having traded securities of companies connected with his senatorial responsibilities, although these latter trades were plainly lawful.[26] The question, then, is whether these prior acts, somewhat different from but also somewhat similar to the acts for which Senator Burr is now being investigated, are relevant in determining the truth of Burr's denial that his recent and suspect trades were based on inside information. There is a good chance that those prior acts would not be admissible as evidence in a trial charging Burr with criminal or civil violations.[27] But they might well have been "admissible" for voters deciding whether to vote for Burr in an election, for the Senate in deciding whether internal discipline is appropriate, for a president considering whether to nominate Burr to an appointive office, or for a corporation considering whether to put Burr on its board of directors. All of which is to say that the legal system's common exclusion of past acts, and the character they manifest, need not be determinative of the relevance of those acts and that character as evidence of the truth or falsity of Burr's denial of culpable knowledge, or of many other questions of disputed fact, in a wide range of contexts with a wide range of consequences outside of the legal system.

Although the evidentiary relevance of past acts and inferences about character from those acts is as obvious as it is ubiquitous, the cautions embodied in the legal system's approach should not be lightly dismissed, for they are applicable outside of the legal system as well. Most importantly, the tendency of people to overvalue past acts is real, and thus the need to counterbalance that overvaluation is real as well. Sarah Sanders wants us to take Michael Cohen's past plagiarism as conclusively establishing that he is lying now, but that is too simple. Yes, there are reasons to be more skeptical of what Cohen says now than there would be of what the modern-day George Washington—he of the almost-certainly-apocryphal unwillingness to lie about chopping down the cherry tree—would say, but that skepticism should only go so far. This skepticism based on past acts is properly understood as a veracity discount, but it is not a discount to zero. If we are rational, we will recognize, Sarah Sanders's urgings notwithstanding, that we might be inclined to make too much of past acts, and not enough of the possibility that people can change their ways, and not enough of potentially relevant differences between the past acts and our current concerns.

So too with the legal system's concern that we not punish again those who have already been punished. A common complaint among those who have been through bankruptcy is that bankruptcy is not the fresh start that it is billed as being because the stigma of having been in bankruptcy follows post-bankruptcy efforts to obtain loans, mortgages, and often employment. Much the same might be said about having been held liable for causing an automobile accident, engaging in medical malpractice, or committing any number of other acts that might produce what at first seems like onetime civil liability, but that in fact stick to the originally liable individual like barnacles on the bottom of a ship—permanently annoying and all but impossible to remove.

None of this is to suggest that in making our daily decisions about who did what to whom, or about what happened, we should ignore the genuine relevance of similar past acts. Nor should we ignore the dispositionist side of the psychological debate between the dispositionists and the situationists. Dispositions, traits, characters—whatever we choose to call them—are real, and so is their value in helping us make decisions under circumstances of uncertain knowledge, just as knowing of Michael Colono's traits helps us to reach conclusions about the actual facts of his fatal altercation with Alexander Pring-Wilson. Indeed, Pring-Wilson's own traits and prior acts might have provided similar assistance had there not finally been a plea bargain.

Still, the legal system's seeming reluctance—a reluctance admittedly softened by many exceptions—to allow past acts to be used to prove subsequent conduct should not easily be dismissed. At first it appears that the legal system is acting irrationally, and that its sharp departure from common sense is a good reason to ignore its approach when we make decisions in our nonlegal lives. But dismissing the law's approach is too easy. As we have seen, there are sound reasons behind the law's reluctance to use what so many of us use in our daily lives. And if it seems a bit much to go as far as the law goes when we have to decide which child started the fight in the backseat of the car seems, remembering why the law does what it does can often provide a useful corrective to making too much of past acts. As Sarah Sanders seemingly recognized, there is a strong appeal to using past acts or past wrongs to make decisions about who or what to believe now. Sarah Sanders implored us to recognize why the past matters. But she intentionally did not tell us why it might not.

Another Note on Profiling

All of the examples in this chapter share a focus on the past acts of an identifiable individual. What is the evidentiary import of what Michael Cohen, Martha Stewart, Michael Colono, and all of the others have done before? But it is worth signaling again, as I did in Chapter 10, the close connection between the questions raised in this chapter and the larger issue of profiling based on group characteristics, where some of the evidentiary inferences from group characteristics to individual acts are accurate but many are not, and where some of these inferences are benign and many are pernicious.

Consider again the malingering tennis pro. The question, for the match referee or for the doctor, is whether this tennis pro's past acts of faking or exaggerating injuries should be relevant in determining whether *this* claim of injury is real. The evidence for the claim being accurate—for the injury being real—might come from what the player is now saying, from the way the player walks or runs, from the expression on the player's face, and much else. And the evidence against the injury being real might include the fact that this very player has in the past faked injuries under circumstances very similar to the current one.

But now let us change things slightly. Suppose that this player has no prior history of faking injuries. Still, both the referee and the doctor know that tennis players in situations like these often do fake their injuries. In evaluating the player's claim of injury, and the consequences that might flow from an injury, should the referee or the doctor take account of the fact that professional tennis players in situations like these often—or at least more often than other people—claim injuries that do not exist, or claim that their injuries are far more serious than they actually are? In other words, is it evidence against the existence of an injury, as claimed by this particular tennis player, that professional tennis players in general often fabricate injuries in similar circumstances?

Once we move beyond individuals and their past individual acts, the evidentiary weight to be given to evidence of this sort will plainly vary with the size of the class within which we place this particular person or event. If the particular tennis player, the legitimacy of whose injury we are trying to evaluate, is a thirty-eight-year-old male from some particular country, then statistics indicating that tennis players with these exact characteristics and from that country have a high incidence of fabricated injuries would seem to have a great deal of evidentiary weight, whereas statistics indicating that men have a higher rate of injury fabrication than do all players, regardless of gender, would be less weighty.

All of this is familiar to most people who have visited the doctor in recent years. More and more, physicians are interested in basing, or at least assisting, their diagnoses by this very kind of statistical data, often in the name of the so-called evidence-based medicine discussed in Chapter 2. Of course, all medicine is evidence-based, and has been for millennia. When physicians listen to their patient's heartbeats, or test their reflexes, or look into their ears, they are using their observations as evidence of some condition. What makes this kind of evidence-based medicine different is that here the evidence, as with our example of the potentially malingering tennis player, comes not only from the individual, but from what we know about some class of which the individual is a member.

The crucial point here is that class-based evidence is still evidence. Doctors know it. Captain Renault knew it. We all know it. If a child comes home crying that he has been bitten by a neighborhood dog, and if one of the dogs in the neighborhood is a pit bull, the greater incidence of aggressiveness for pit bulls than for many other breeds will be some evidence, although hardly conclusive, that it was the neighborhood pit bull and not the neighborhood golden retriever that was responsible.[28]

Although class-based evidence is evidence, there is another side of the story. The other side of the story is about the dangers, commonly associated with racial profiling, of too easily attributing to all members of a class the attributes that are possessed by the class on average, even if not by every member of the class. There is little harm if we take the class-based reliability statistics of certain models of cars—the Yugo from the former Yugoslavia and the Trabant from former East Germany come to mind—as evidence of the likely unreliability of a particular car. But when we do the same not for cars but for humans who are members of groups defined by race, religion, gender, age, sexual orientation, and much else, the issue becomes far more complex, and there are often sound reasons for refusing to use as evidence even the class-based characteristics that have some statistical basis. These and related complexities have been widely discussed and analyzed, but it is worth noting here that both the virtues of evidence-based medicine and the vices of racial and ethnic profiling emerge from the way in which, at times, the class characteristics of a class of which some individual is a member can provide some evidence about what that individual has done in the past, or is likely to do in the future. Indeed, and again recalling the discussion of evidentiary inference in Chapter 2, there is a sense in which all evidence is of this variety. When we believe that the person wearing a ski mask and running out of the bank with a bag has just robbed that bank, we do so because of what we know, or think we know, about the class of people wearing ski masks and running out of banks with bags, a class of which this particular person is a member. And when we side with Sarah Sanders and against Bernie Sanders in supposing that past acts are at least some evidence of current and future behavior, we are also, as with our masked and bag-carrying bank robber, engaged in class-based evidentiary inference. We worry about John Henry Wigmore's published belief, discussed in Chapter 8, that women are less reliable witnesses than men because it is empirically unfounded and because it would be unjust even if not, but that cannot be a general worry about drawing inferences from classes of acts or events to individual acts or events. Doing so is what evidentiary inference is all about, and doing so for the inference from past to present is little different from the kinds of inference that evidence demands, even if, as with the use of past acts in courts of law, there may sometimes or even often be sound reasons for refusing to take into consideration what the evidence seems to suggest.

Chapter 13

Seeing What We Want to See

AS CHAPTER I EMPHASIZED, this is a book about facts. Obviously some facts are clearer than others. And equally obviously there are often disagreements about facts. Sometimes those disagreements arise when there is evidence leading to opposing conclusions, such as the evidence leading to, but occasionally challenging, the conclusion that Thomas Jefferson was the biological father of the six children of Sally Hemings, as discussed in Chapter 2. There is similar disagreement about the conflicting evidence that Leonardo Da Vinci was, or perhaps was not, the painter of a painting known as *Salvator Mundi*.[1] But even when all or most of the evidence points in the same direction, there is often, and perhaps surprisingly, still disagreement. And at least on the surface these disagreements appear not to be about values or goals or high principles, but about facts. Plain, hard facts.

Many of these disagreements about facts, and about clear facts as well as unclear ones, are influenced by preferences. In theory, preferences should not matter about hard concrete physical facts. I wish I were taller and thinner and younger, but I am what I am, regardless of my preferences. And although I wish that the days were as long in December as they are in June, what I wish matters not a bit.

Although most of the factual world successfully resists adapting to our preferences, often, and perhaps surprisingly, our *perception* of that factual world does conform to our preferences. This phenomenon is especially familiar to participants and spectators at sporting events. Tennis balls are in or out, and even the close ones are either slightly in or slightly out. Nevertheless, the typical tennis court argument involves—or at least did involve prior to electronic line calling—the player who hit the shot insisting that the ball was in while his or her opponent insists with equal vehemence that it was out. And when the question is whether a soccer ball (or the hockey puck) did or did not cross the line to count as a goal, whether a baseball was fair or foul, or whether the football receiver was in bounds or out when he caught the ball, it is tediously familiar that both players and fans will loudly see these entirely factual matters in the way that aligns with their outcome preferences.

And so too with things that matter more than tennis, soccer, hockey, baseball, or football. Elections, for example. Although the 2020 presidential election was noteworthy in part for the admirable willingness of election officials in Georgia, most prominently, and elsewhere to make factual decisions about vote counts that departed from their party affiliations and presidential electoral preferences, the behavior of the Georgia officials was, regrettably, more the exception than the rule.[2] In the extremely close election between Frank McCloskey and Richard McIntyre for the US House of Representatives in Indiana's Eighth Congressional District in 1984, for example, both election officials and members of the House of Representatives made decisions that closely tracked their party affiliations.[3] History provides many other examples of the same phenomenon.[4] The 2020 election, in more ways than one, was far more exceptional than representative. And we should not forget the millions of people who believe that former president Barack Obama was born in Kenya, which he was not; that former president George W. Bush knew in advance of the September 11, 2001 attacks, which he did not; and that the AIDS epidemic was the product of a government and pharmaceutical industry conspiracy, which it was not.[5]

Whether it be football, tennis, elections, or anything else, the phenomenon of seeing the factual world in ways that reflect preferences for how that world *ought* to be, rather than how it actually is, has been amply documented by psychologists for generations, typically under the label "motivated reasoning," and sometimes with the catchier label "myside bias." The basic idea—we can think of it as fallaciously deriving is from ought—was first developed in the research of the social psychologist Ziva Kunda.[6] Subsequently a broad and deep research program has followed.[7] And although most of primary research has been done by experimental psychologists, more recently we have seen political scientists, academic lawyers, and others adapting (and sometimes relabeling) the basic idea to fit their own domain-specific interests and purposes.[8] But throughout the domains of application, the basic idea is that the receipt and evaluation of evidence, and the evaluation of that evidence, is heavily influenced by normative preferences about what it would be good for the evidence to show. And that is so even when the evidence is about a matter of hard fact—where Barack Obama was born, for example—and as to which the evidence is overwhelmingly clear.

The Mechanisms of Motivation

Understanding motivated reasoning is crucial for understanding when and how evidence matters in the world, and when and how it does not. The "motivated" part of motivated reasoning is straightforward, even if lamentable, but the "reasoning" part mixes together four different phenomena, which it is important to separate. All four are about the world of evidence, and we can label them *motivated production, motivated transmission, motivated retrieval,* and *motivated processing.*

Motivated production is about the way in which evidence is generated—produced—in the first place. The Sherlock-Holmes-with-his-magnifying-glass image notwithstanding, much of the evidence we use is not just sitting there waiting to be found. Rather, the evidence is produced—or created—often by motivated parties with a preference for a particular seemingly evidence-based outcome. This is most obvious in a trial in court, where all of the evidence is supplied by advocates for one side or another. But the phenomenon also exists outside of court. An especially vivid example, documented by Naomi Oreskes and Erik Conway, comes from the story of how the tobacco industry *created*—and did not simply find and did not simply present—the great bulk of the evidence purporting to demonstrate the safety of smoking.[9] By funding research and by funding and hiring researchers, the industry was able to stock (and thus stack) the pool of evidence with a large amount of data, and a large number of studies and conclusions, that supported their preferred outcome. Oreskes and Conway also reveal, not surprisingly, the fossil fuel industry's role in creating much of the evidentiary foundation for climate-change skepticism and denial.

The phenomenon of creating a skewed pool of evidence is not principally about fabricating evidence for false conclusions. Nor is it about funding bogus studies purporting to demonstrate something like the effectiveness of phrenology or the empirical soundness of astrology. Instead, the phenomenon of motivated production starts from the premise that for many issues there is potentially at least some evidence supporting both sides of a contested conclusion regarding the facts. There is evidence for and against the conclusion that Leonardo himself painted *Salvator Mundi,* and there is at least some evidence downplaying the harmfulness of cigarettes and the dangers of climate change. In these latter cases, there is vastly more evidence for the opposite conclusion—that cigarettes are very harmful and that climate change is heading toward catastrophe—but the ratio of evidence for one conclusion rather than its negation can be upset if sponsorship, funding, and much else aims at inflating that proportion of the evidentiary universe on some question occupied by the minority position. Things that are not even close can be made to appear close if motivated, resourceful, and resourced actors can make a minority position look far more respectable than it actually is.

A good example of this phenomenon comes from the process of litigation, as documented and theorized by Sheila Jasanoff.[10] The typical lawsuit, including lawsuits claiming liability for the manufacture and distribution of harmful products, involves two parties. One is the plaintiff, or the class of plaintiffs. The other is the defendant. And each is given the opportunity to present evidence. It is in the nature of the litigation process, however, that each side is given roughly the same opportunity to present evidence, regardless of the actual state of the evidence or the judge's view of it. Judges are not permitted to say that the plaintiff will get to present four times as many witnesses as the defendant because of the judge's belief that the plaintiff's evidence is four times stronger than the defendants. As a result, the structure of litigation is amenable to making an unequally sound array of evidence appear more equally sound than it actually is. The same thing happens with congressional hearings, newspaper coverage, and any other setting in which the design of that setting, or the norms of the domain in which the setting exists, demands and allows evidence to be produced and presented in a proportion that diverges from the intrinsic soundness of the evidence.

On a wide range of tissues, therefore, motivated parties—especially motivated parties with financial resources, social cachet, and political power—can populate the field of available evidence by sponsoring, in the broadest sense, the creation of evidence in support of their preferred outcome. In so doing, these motivated parties have engaged in the process of motivated production, a process that influences the makeup of the array of evidence available to anyone seeking evidence on some question.

Not only can evidence be created, it must also be communicated or transmitted to those who might use it. And communication—what is communicated, what is not communicated, and how what is communicated is communicated—is also influenced by those with particular values and goals. We can label this as *motivated transmission*. Here the motivated parties are not only the usual suspects—tobacco companies with advertising agencies, oil refiners with public relations firms, lifestyle purveyors with their influencers, advocacy organizations with their own publications and press releases, for example—but also the seemingly disinterested media itself. Think again of horses and zebras. Horses in the neighborhood are not newsworthy, but zebras are. And so the statistically unlikely presence of zebras makes news. And whether it be "man bites dog" or "if it bleeds, it leads," a host of venerable canards of the news business supports the conclusion that the facts of which we are made aware, and the evidence for those facts, are not only often provided by motivated actors, but are filtered and transmitted by other actors with motivations of their own. The field of evidence is mediated by motivated mediators, and the stock of evidence that is "out there" comes to us, and to anyone interested in consulting or following the evidence, in a way that bears the influence of all of those with interests of one form or another.

Often the motivations of motivated transmitters will incline in opposed directions, and the effects may be salutary. The dangers of GMOs may appeal to some of the mainstream press and to various advocacy groups, but the producers of genetically modified products are hardly without resources or power of their own. Evidence about acts of police brutality will be transmitted by victims, their lawyers, and activists, but the police possess their own communicative resources. With respect to at least some topics and controversies, the clash of slants may help the consumers of evidence appreciate and evaluate the actual weight of the evidence. But hardly always.

Here is an uncontroversial fact about evidence: There is a lot of it. And much more with the rise of the internet and social media. This observation might seem as silly as it is true, but it exposes an important way in which motivated reasoning manifests itself. When we are faced with an overwhelming barrage of evidence—as if we were drinking from a fire hose, to cite a common metaphor—we are of necessity forced to select some but not all of even the relevant evidence. The limitations of time, effort, and mental space compel us to be selective, and the well-documented lesson from the motivated reasoning research program is that not only do we often engage in *biased perception,* but we also just as frequently engage in *biased assimilation*—selecting the evidence that reinforces our existing beliefs, and our preferences—and ignoring or at least slighting the evidence that goes the other way.[11] In the typology I have offered here, we can call this *motivated retrieval.*

Philosophers of science, especially those of a more skeptical bent, have long recognized a related phenomenon, usually labeled *theory-laden observation.*[12] Because it is impossible simply to observe every fact about the world, we observe that world through the lens of our theories and our explanations. And thus, it is argued, not only how we observe but also what we observe is determined by our background theories or presuppositions. Moreover, and more relevantly here, it is but a short step from theory-laden observation to value-laden observation.[13] There are active debates about whether observation is *necessarily* value-laden.[14] But the far more modest claim, and one that is sufficient for our purposes here, is that observation, especially outside of the world of science, is often value-laden even if it is not necessarily so. And this modest claim warns us that the selection of evidence from all of the evidence available is commonly heavily influenced by the values and preferences of the selector and the evaluator.

Sometimes this selectivity manifests itself in people selecting evidence that reinforces their prior beliefs and ignoring evidence that challenges those beliefs. This is the well-known and well-researched phenomenon of *confirmation bias,* and it is not always a matter of first-order preferences.[15] The physician who initially diagnoses a set of symptoms as indicating Lyme disease, to take an example from Chapter 2, might then discover another symptom or other indication that would be inconsistent with Lyme disease. Although we would hope that the physician would be willing to revise the initial diagnosis in light of new evidence, this would be inconsistent, regrettably, with how people often behave. Commonly, although by no means universally, people resist new evidence that challenges their earlier conclusions, while at the same time they welcome or even search for new evidence that confirms what they have already concluded. As a result, the process of receiving new evidence turns out to be systematically skewed in the direction of confirmatory evidence and against refuting evidence. It might be nice if we were able to say, "The evidence says that . . . ," but it turns out that all too often what the evidence says is partial in two senses: in the sense that it is not all of the evidence, and in the sense that the evidence we see as relevant tilts in a direction that less-partially-selected evidence might not.

A powerful example of motivated retrieval comes from studies focusing on political and ideological polarization. Cass Sunstein, for example, has documented and analyzed the way in which providing information to polarized parties increases polarization.[16] People will pick the evidence that supports their own pole of the polarization, and thus the provision of additional evidence often increases rather than decreases polarization as people select—cherry-pick—only the evidence that supports what they had previously believed, and ignore the remainder.[17] An even more depressing version of this phenomenon comes from research on the effects of attempting to counteract false beliefs with evidence of true ones. It would be nice if such counteracting efforts were effective, and they may well be, but there are also studies indicating that the counteracting evidence, by accentuating the salience of the evidence to be counteracted, actually turns out often to have exactly the opposite of its intended effect.[18]

Finally, we have *motivated processing,* which comes closest to the traditional idea of motivated reasoning. Even when confronted with all of the relevant evidence, people will often see that evidence in a way that reinforces their own prior beliefs. Sometimes they will simply reject whatever challenges those beliefs, and sometimes they will spin the data—no matter how unspinnable it might appear to an unbiased observer—in ways that do not force them to reject what they had previously believed or accept conclusions that are inconsistent with their preferred outcomes.

The motivated production of evidence, then filtered through the motivated transmission of evidence, then selectively retrieved in light of the retriever's motivations and preferences, and then evaluated in light of those preferences, makes for an alarming picture. But we should not let that alarm cause us to fall into the trap that the trap is about. If we believe in the importance and power of evidence, we can use that belief as a potential antidote to the motivation that leads us to look in a motivated, and thus skewed, way at that evidence. But we also have evidence of the pervasive phenomenon of motivated reasoning. So if, again, we believe in the importance and power of evidence, then we should recognize the evidence of motivated reasoning. And we should not discard our belief in the importance and power of evidence when it is time to examine the evidence of how evidence is actually used by real people making real decisions.

A Porous but Useful Distinction

It may be helpful to distinguish two forms of motivated reasoning, even while recognizing that the border between the two is both fuzzy and porous. There is a distinction between motivated reasoning when there is evidence both supporting and refuting some factual proposition, on the one hand, and the motivated rejection of evidence when all or almost all of the evidence points in one direction. The former occurs when, in more or less good faith, and with more or less of an open mind, we look at the evidence for and against some conclusion and discover that the evidence, even when filtered through the applicable burden of proof, leaves us genuinely uncertain. Under those circumstances what we can call "soft" motivated reasoning kicks in to lead us to choose the option that pleases us rather than the one that does not, even if there is some evidence for both, and even if the evidence is somewhat in equipoise. Soft motivated reasoning, by definition, is at work only when there is what we might think of as decent evidence both supporting and rejecting some conclusion, and it is perhaps too much to imagine that it could ever be otherwise.

By contrast, "hard" motivated reasoning occurs when strong or overwhelming evidence in favor of some proposition is rejected by those who do not like the implications of the evidence. These days the claim that there was widespread fraud in the 2020 presidential election is the most salient example; the claim that global warming is not real runs a close second. In these cases, a hypothetical neutral observer would see all or almost all of the evidence going in one direction. But there are people who, for reasons of outcome preference, simply reject the evidence. We should lament the existence of hard motivated reasoning—and societies, by education or otherwise, should do much more than they now do to diminish its frequency and consequences. But at the end of the day the analysis of evidence is not going to do very much, if anything, for those for whom evidence does not matter in the first instance. We can wish that evidence would persuade people to relinquish their beliefs that the Parkland school shootings were a "false flag" plot by the political left or that no airplane crashed into the Pentagon on September 11, 2001, to take two of the claims of Representative Marjorie Taylor Greene.[19] But it is unlikely that more evidence can persuade people who from the outset are simply uninterested in the evidence.

Enter Dr. Pangloss

The most memorable character in Voltaire's 1759 satirical novel *Candide* is Dr. Pangloss, who almost three centuries later survives as the character who gave us the adjective "Panglossian." Dr. Pangloss was an eternal optimist, and to be Panglossian now is to see the world and the future through rose-colored glasses. Even more particularly, to be Panglossian in a world of conflicting facts, competing goals, and inconsistent principles is to suppose that all of these conflicts are illusory, and that what seem to be inconsistent facts, goals, and principles can all fit together such that no conflict exists.[20] Some people might suppose, for example, that freedom of speech and public order are inconsistent, forcing us to choose between them in particular contexts. Not so for the Panglossian. The threat to public order is not really an exercise of free speech, or the exercise of free speech does not really threaten public order. Either way, the conflict disappears.

Dr. Pangloss is highly relevant to questions of evidence, and in particular to the questions of motivated reasoning we are considering in this chapter. If the evidence appears to point to one conclusion, but that conclusion is in tension with someone's values, aspirations, or preferences, Panglossianism counsels the person so conflicted to adapt their preferences to fit the evidence, or to adapt the evidence to fit their preferences. Either strategy eliminates the conflict, but we know that it is difficult for people to change their values and their preferences. They can avoid having to do this by adapting the evidence, or at least their perception of the evidence, and then, for them, the conflict disappears.[21]

This phenomenon has been documented by psychologists who have identified the human desire for *cognitive consistency*.[22] The failure to achieve cognitive consistency—so familiar that the label has penetrated popular consciousness—is *cognitive dissonance*.[23] Although this latter label is often tossed about by those who know a little, but only a little, about psychology, cognitive dissonance is the carefully documented phenomenon by which people tend to avoid having to negotiate incompatible ideas, principles, goals, desires, and even facts. It is no surprise that people have a "need to see the world as structured, consistent, and orderly."[24] And this is not only about how people see the world. It is about how people see much of what exists within and about their lives. If I would like to lose weight and I like ice cream, I can convince myself that ice cream is not all that fattening, or that I am not really that fat. Either way the consistency has evaporated, even if it took some revision of my view of the facts to produce that outcome.

In much the same way, motivated reasoning, which has as many causes as it has effects, is, at least in part, a product of this kind of dissonance avoidance. Insofar as one aspect of reasoning is reaching factual conclusions, then reaching factual conclusions that are consistent with our factual preferences is a good way of doing it. Motivated reasoning, we might say, is inconsistent with evidentiary honesty, with following the evidence where it leads. But the existence of motivated reasoning is itself the product of an evidentiary inquiry about human behavior, and if we think that motivated reasoning is something to be avoided, which it is, then we should make sure that we are not engaged in motivated reasoning when we downplay the extent or the consequences of motivated reasoning.

Coda

On February 6, 2021, on the eve of the second impeachment trial of by-then-former-president Donald Trump, Brian Schatz, a Democratic senator from Hawaii, observed, "It's not clear to me that there is any evidence that will change anyone's mind."[25] In the context of an impeachment trial—which might not ever be very much about evidence, and which is especially not about evidence in a situation in which the decision makers, the members of the Senate, believe they have first-person experiences flowing from having themselves been on the premises during the January 6, 2021, invasion of the Capitol building—Senator Schatz's observation seems depressingly self-evident. Impeachment trials are not now and never have been, at least at the presidential level, events in which evidence is presented and carefully considered.

Somewhat more disturbing, however, is the fact that Schatz's statement may not only be about impeachment, and it may not only be about proceedings in the United States Senate. What Schatz said may, regrettably, characterize much of human behavior and human decision making, processes in which making up one's mind all too often either precedes or precludes consultation of the evidence, or distorts the process of selecting and evaluating that evidence. There is some indication that those who are more politically sophisticated are more likely—not less likely—to engage in politically motivated reasoning and evidence selection, perhaps because they are more attuned to looking for flaws in the arguments or positions with which they disagree, but less willing to search for or recognize the flaws in their own positions, their own arguments, and their own evidence.[26]

In an important way, this final chapter on motivated reasoning could have been part of every chapter of this book—a qualification of every chapter of this book. Every chapter of this book has been premised on the view that for some people, at some times, and on some issues, evidence matters. This book has been written for those for whom evidence matters, and for when it matters to them. For those for whom evidence does not matter, no amount of evidence, and no amount of the analysis of evidence, is going to make a difference.

Notes

Index

Notes

Chapter 1. As a Matter of Fact

1. Especially in Chapter 13, addressing what psychologists call "motivated reasoning."

2. Those of us who know little about either vaccination or autism can assert that vaccination does not cause autism because experts who *do* know about vaccination and autism have concluded that vaccination does not cause autism. My evidence is the fact of the conclusion of the experts, even though *their* evidence comes from controlled experiments, data analysis, systematic observation, and other methods of scientific inquiry. See Frank DeStefano, Cristofer S. Price, and Eric S. Weintraub, "Increasing Exposure to Antibody-Stimulating Proteins and Polysaccharides in Vaccines Is Not Associated with Rise of Autism," *Journal of Pediatrics* 163 (2013): 561–567; Dennis K. Flaherty, "The Vaccine-Autism Connection: A Public Health Crisis Caused by Unethical Medical Practices and Fraudulent Science," *Annals of Pharmacotherapy* 45 (2011): 1302–1304. Treating expert conclusions as evidence is the focus of Chapters 9, 10, and 11, and the vaccination–autism example reappears in Chapter 9.

3. See "FDA Cautions against Use of Hydroxychloroquine or Chloroquine for COVID-19 Outside of the Hospital Setting or a Clinical Trial Due to Risk of Heart Rhythm Problems," at www.fda.gov (July 1, 2020), referencing Pharmacovigilance Memorandum of May 19, 2020, prepared by the Office of Surveillance and Epidemiology, Center for Drug Evaluation and Research, Food and Drug Administration, at www.accessdata.fda.gov; Recovery Collaborative Group, "Effect of Hydroxychloroquine in Hospitalized Patients with Covid-19," *New England Journal of Medicine* 383 (Nov. 2020): 2030–2040; Adam Clark Estes, "Hydroxychloroquine Conspiracies Are Back, but Trump's the Patient Now," at www.vox.com (Oct. 7, 2020).

4. Daniel P. Moynihan, "More than Social Security Was at Stake," *Washington Post,* Jan. 18, 1983, A17. The phrase and the idea are now associated with Moynihan, but the website Quote Investigator (www.quoteinvestigator.com) reports that much the same phrase was first used by the financier Bernard Baruch in the 1940s and by then–secretary of defense James Schlesinger in the 1970s.

5. David Hume, *A Treatise of Human Nature,* ed. L. A. Selby-Bigge, 2nd ed., revised by P. H. Nidditch (Oxford: Clarendon Press, 1975) (orig. pub. 1739), bk. 3, pt. 1, sec. 1, par. 27. Ironically, questions of evidence now surround Hume himself. The University of Edinburgh recently renamed (to 40 George Square) what was previously the David Hume Tower, basing the renaming on racist statements Hume made in some of his writings, especially in a footnote in "Of National Characters," in David Hume, *Essays Moral, Political Literary,* ed. Eugene F. Miller (Indianapolis: Liberty Fund, 1987) (orig. pub. 1777), 197–215, at 207n10. As a result of the renaming, questions of evidence *about* Hume, and not just *in* the Hume *oeuvre,* are now prominent. Although questions whether to rename buildings or take down statues are normative, lurking behind the normative questions are a host of preliminary factual ones. For Hume, such factual questions—questions whose answers demand evidence—include questions such as what Hume did or did not write, what opinions Hume did or did not hold, what actions Hume did or did not take, and what beliefs Hume's contemporaries did or did not possess. As long as we accept some version of Hume's distinction between the is and the ought, these factual questions are unavoidable prerequisites to any decision about whether and how to celebrate Hume and whether, how, and how much to condemn him.

6. More accurately, yellowish-appearing skin is evidence of jaundice, and jaundice is evidence of hepatitis. Although it may be more difficult to detect the change of skin tone for many African Americans than for most whites, the same phenomenon exists for both.

7. See Adam Liptak, "Amy Coney Barrett, Trump's Supreme Court Pick, Signed Anti-Abortion Ad," *New York Times,* Oct. 1, 2020, A1. The link from a judge's current policy or moral beliefs to that judge's current judicial decision making is uniformly resisted by nominees themselves, as it was by Justice Barrett in her confirmation hearings in October 2020. And it is typically resisted by many—perhaps most—legal professionals. At least with respect to Supreme Court justices, however, the conclusion that current moral and policy views are strong evidence of likely votes as a justice is supported by decades of research by empirical political scientists. See Saul Brenner and Harold J. Spaeth, *Stare Indecisis: The Alteration of Precedent on the Supreme Court, 1946–1992* (New York: Cambridge University Press, 1995); Jeffrey J. Segal and Harold J. Spaeth, *The Supreme Court and the Attitudinal Model Revisited* (New York: Cambridge University Press, 2002). The attitudinal model exemplified in these books has been challenged and refined in recent years, but the basic idea that pre-legal attitudes are the chief (but not the only) determinant of Supreme Court votes remains the "holy grail" of empirical research about Supreme Court

decision making. Nancy Scherer, "Testing the Court: Decision Making under the Microscope," *Tulsa Law Review* 50 (2015): 659–668, at 661.

8. See CNN Opinion, "Who Won the Debate," www.cnn.com, Oct. 23, 2020; Jennifer Agiesta, CNN Poll, "Biden Wins Final Presidential Debate," www.cnn.com, Oct. 23, 2020.

9. Admirably and fortunately, not always. See Dave Boucher, "Michigan Board Votes to Certify Election Results despite GOP Calls to Delay," *Detroit Free Press,* Nov. 23, 2020; Brad Raffensperger, "I Have Fought to Uphold the Integrity of Elections in Georgia. It Doesn't Matter if the Attacks Come from the Guy I Voted For," *USA Today,* Nov. 25, 2020.

10. "Sir, I had rather be right than president," speech in the United States Senate, Feb. 7, 1839. See Robert Seager III, "Henry Clay and the Politics of Compromise and Non-Compromise," *Register of the Kentucky Historical Society* 85 (1987): 1–28.

11. Philippa Foot, "Moral Arguments," *Mind* 67 (1958): 502–513. A valuable overview is Pekka Väyrynen, "Thick Ethical Concepts," *Stanford Encyclopedia of Philosophy,* www.plato.stanford.edu (2016); Bernard Williams, *Ethics and the Limits of Philosophy* (Cambridge: Cambridge University Press, 1985), 141–144.

12. For background see John Hooper, *Fatal Voyage: The Wrecking of the Costa Concordia* (Amazon / Kindle, 2015); Marco Imarisio and Fiorenza Sarzanini, *Concordia: The True Story* (Milan: Corriere Della Sera, 2012); Edward Jones, *Reckless Abandon: The Costa Concordia Disaster* (Amazon / Kindle, 2012); "Captain of Ship That Capsized off Italy in '12 Is Convicted," *New York Times,* Feb. 12, 2015, A4.

13. See Gregory Korte, "'Crooks' Versus 'Socialists': Ads Frame Georgia Bitter Run-offs," Bloomberg News, Dec. 31, 2020, www.bloomberg.com.

14. See Dan Berman, "Barrett Ducks Questions on Presidential Power and Systemic Racism in New Answers to Senate," *CNN Politics,* at www.cnn.com (Oct. 21, 2020).

15. One of the first to treat evidence as a legal subject in its own right was Lord Geoffrey Gilbert, whose treatise *The Law of Evidence* was first published in London in 1754, twenty-eight years after Gilbert's death. On the origins of evidence law in the common-law world generally, see John H. Langbein, "Historical Foundations of the Law of Evidence: A View from the Ryder Sources," *Columbia Law Review* 96 (1996): 1168–1202.

16. This is not to suggest that common-law legal systems, which emerged from English law, are more valuable sources of enlightenment than the legal systems of the civil-law world. Rather, the contrast arises because most civil-law jurisdictions have traditionally employed something resembling a "free proof" approach tending to avoid much use of rules and instead evaluating evidence on a case-by-case basis in the same way that ordinary people evaluate evidence in their everyday lives. See Mirjan R. Damaška, *Evidence Law Adrift* (New Haven, CT: Yale University Press, 1997); Damaška, "Free Proof and Its Detractors," *American Journal of Comparative Law* 43 (1995): 343–357; Frederick Schauer, "The Role of Rules in the Law of Evidence," in *Philosophical Foundations of the Law of Evidence,* ed. Christian Dahlman, Alex Stein, and Giovanni Tuzet (Oxford: Oxford University Press, forthcoming

2021). There may be much to be said for the free-proof idea, and Jeremy Bentham, although living and writing in a common-law country, said a great deal of it with characteristic vitriol. Jeremy Bentham, *Rationale of Judicial Evidence*, in *The Works of Jeremy Bentham*, vol. 6, ed. John Bowring (Edinburgh: William Tait, 1843). But the nonsystematic approach of the free-proof model as compared to the rule-based common-law approach that makes the former less incrementally valuable in contributing to how we might think about evidence.

17. Oliver Wendell Holmes, "The Path of the Law," *Harvard Law Review* 10 (1897) 457–476, at 459, written when Holmes, not yet on the Supreme Court, was a justice of the Massachusetts Supreme Judicial Court.

18. Letter from Oliver Wendell Holmes Jr. to Harold J. Laski (Jan. 5, 1921), in *The Holmes-Laski Letters*, vol. 1, ed. Mark De Wolfe Howe (Cambridge, MA: Harvard University Press, 1953), 300.

19. Steven Brint, *In an Age of Experts: The Changing Role of Professionals in Politics and Public Life* (Princeton, NJ: Princeton University Press, 1994).

Chapter 2. Zebras, Horses, and the Nature of Inference

1. In fact, Dr. Woodward was nominated for (but did not win) a Nobel prize in 1948, but for his work on a cure for typhoid fever and not for the "horses, not zebras" maxim.

2. Nassim Nicholas Taleb, *The Black Swan: The Impact of the Highly Improbable* (New York: Random House, 2007).

3. Barbara Spellman reminds me that the problem with the "great minds think alike" adage is that it is wrong. Great minds are great precisely because they depart from the crowd (or the herd, as Aristotle put it) and from each other.

4. See Centers for Disease Control and Prevention, "Lyme Disease," at www.cdc.gov.

5. Just how those probabilities come into play implicates long-standing debates about "inference to the best explanation," Bayesian updating, and so-called probabilism, all to be addressed later in this chapter.

6. Ian Hacking, *An Introduction to Probability and Inductive Logic* (Cambridge: Cambridge University Press, 2001), 11.

7. See D. J. Friedland et al., *Evidence-Based Medicine: A Framework for Clinical Practice* (New York: McGraw-Hill / Lange, 1998); David M. Eddy, "Evidence-Based Medicine: A Unified Approach," *Health Affairs* 24 (2005), 9–17; Evidence-Based Medicine Working Group, "Evidence-Based Medicine: A New Approach to Teaching the Practice of Medicine," *Journal of the American Medical Association* 268 (1992): 2420–2425.

8. Evidence-based medicine is explicitly described as a "movement" in Desmond J. Sheridan and Desmond G. Julian, "Achievements and Limitations of Evidence-Based Medicine," *Journal of the American College of Cardiology* 68 (2016): 204–213, at 205.

9. D. L. Sackett, W. M. Rosenberg, and J. A. Gray, et al., "Evidence Based Medicine: What It Is and What It Isn't," *British Medical Journal* 312 (1996): 71–72.

10. See the summary in Matthew Herper and Helen Branswell, "Moderna Covid-19 Vaccine Is Strongly Effective, Early Look at Data Shows," www.statnews.com (Nov. 16, 2020). Pfizer's similarly designed study used 43,000 participants and yielded a 95 percent effectiveness rate; www.cnn.com (Nov. 18, 2020). For the full protocols of the Moderna and Pfizer tests, see https://www.modernatx.com/sites /default/files/mRNA-1273-p301-Protocol.pdf, and https://pfe-pfizercom-d8-prod.s3 .amazonaws.com/2020-09/C4591001_clinical_protocol.pdf. Obviously much depends on the "otherwise identical" configuration of the placebo and treatment groups. If we are dealing with humans, it is easy to grasp that no two groups are truly identical. But so too with lab mice, for no two groups of mice are identical, although the differences among mice may be less apparent to us. Still, the larger the treatment and control (placebo) groups, the more likely it is that the array of characteristics in one group will be highly similar to the array in another group drawn at random from the same population and selected in the same way.

11. On how qualitative or case-based inquiry can be (and should be) as theoretically informed and rigorous as quantitative inquiry using large data sets, see Gary King, Robert O. Keohane, and Sidney Verba, *Designing Social Inquiry: Scientific Inference in Qualitative Research* (Princeton, NJ: Princeton University Press, 1994).

12. "Wants us to believe . . ." is not a claim about the motivations of the evidence-based medicine movement. It is a claim about language, based on the idea that assertions are made only when there is some point in doing the asserting. And that point is usually the plausibility of the assertion's negation. As the philosopher John Searle puts it, "no remark without remarkableness." John R. Searle, *Speech Acts: An Essay in the Philosophy of Language* (Cambridge: Cambridge University Press, 1969), 144. If I observe, correctly, that my colleague Sam is sober today, I have raised the inference that there are days on which he is not, just as the signs on the Massachusetts Turnpike warning drivers not to back up on the high-speed limited access highway if they have missed their exit suggest, alarmingly, that there are Massachusetts drivers who would actually do that. So too with "evidence-based medicine," a practice whose label raises the inference that there is another kind of medicine, one not based on evidence.

13. This is especially true when an experiment is designed and conducted (or supervised) by researchers with no financial interest in the outcome. To minimize this risk, both Moderna and Pfizer took pains to stress that their tests were conducted in conjunction with health-focused government agencies such as the National Institute of Allergy and Infectious Diseases, a part of the National Institutes for Health.

14. On the QAnon conspiracy theory, see Kevin Roose, "What Is QAnon, the Viral Pro-Trump Conspiracy Theory?," *New York Times,* Oct. 19, 2020.

15. Donald J. Trump for President, Inc. v. Boockvar, Case 4:20-cv-02078-MWB (M.D. Pa., Nov. 21, 2020).

16. On circumstantial evidence, see Zechariah Chafee Jr., "La Critique du Témoignage" (book review), *Harvard Law Review* 42 (1929): 839–843, at 840, describing but not

endorsing the "widely prevalent belief" that there is something wrong with circumstantial evidence. But the law wisely knows no such category. That a defendant with motive to kill the victim was in the vicinity at the time and place of the murder may be stronger evidence than an eyewitness identification by a witness with poor eyesight from a great distance on a foggy night, and stronger than a partial fingerprint taken by an inexperienced police investigator. Evidence can be stronger or weaker, but the strong–weak scale maps poorly onto one that puts eyewitness identification or physical evidence at one pole and everything else, including circumstantial evidence, at the other. It was earlier argued that the direct / circumstantial distinction reflects the difference between evidence that is itself evidence of something that matters in some trial, and evidence that requires an additional inferential step, the latter being systematically weaker. Arthur P. Will, *A Treatise on the Law of Circumstantial Evidence* (Philadelphia: T and J. W. Johnson, 1896). Under this view, there is a difference between the direct evidence offered by someone standing nearby when the defendant says "Hand over the money or I'll shoot you" and the circumstantial evidence of someone who did not see the robbery but saw the defendant running out of the bank carrying a bag just after the robbery was alleged to have taken place. But the strength of the inference from the circumstantial evidence is often, as here, very strong, which is why the law refuses to treat the category of circumstantial evidence as categorically less valuable just because it is circumstantial. See, among thousands of decisions, State v. Quinet 752 A.2d 490 (Conn. 2000); State v. Jenks, 574 N.E.2d 492 (Ohio, 1991); State v. Derouchie, 440 A.2d 146 (Vt. 1981).

17. In *The Adventures of Silver Blaze* (1892), Sherlock Holmes inferred from the absence of a dog's barking the non-occurrence of an event that would have been expected to cause the dog to bark. And although on November 4, 2020, the day after the presidential election, the charges of electoral fraud made by President Trump and his allies were properly labeled as having been made without evidence, the subsequent failure over the ensuing months by those alleging fraud to provide documentary, statistical, testimonial, or circumstantial evidence of such fraud can be understood as evidence of the absence of fraud. With every day that passed without evidence having been offered by those with an interest in there being such evidence, what started as no evidence of fraud increasingly turned into evidence of no fraud.

18. A valuable book by Beth A. Bechky about crime labs and forensic evidence is entitled *Blood, Powder, and Residue: How Crime Labs Translate Evidence into Proof* (Princeton, NJ: Princeton University Press, 2021). The title implies that at some point individual pieces of evidence *prove* some conclusion. This usage is common, but it risks suggesting, misleadingly, that evidence is useful only when it is sufficient to establish criminal guilt beyond a reasonable doubt.

19. I say "typically" in order to leave to philosophers—and maybe neuroscientists—questions about what, if anything, we can know *a priori* (that is, without evidence). It is important to recognize, though, that even the things we understand as direct

perceptions—what we see, smell, hear, taste, and touch—are themselves based on evidence. That I think that something I am eating is salty, for example, is based on my having a sensation on my tongue that I have come to learn is produced by sodium chloride contacting certain of my taste buds.

20. See https://www.monticello.org/site/blog-and-community/monticello-affirms -thomas-jefferson-fathered-children-sally-hemings#footnoteref1-m550xjt. See also Annette Gordon-Reed, *Thomas Jefferson and Sally Hemings: An American Controversy* (Charlottesville: University of Virginia Press, 1997); Annette Gordon-Reed, *The Hemingses of Monticello: An American Family* (New York: W. W. Norton, 2008). For a dissenting view, see the claims of the Thomas Jefferson Heritage Society, www .tjheritage.org, and Robert F. Turner, ed., *The Jefferson-Hemings Controversy: Report of the Scholars Commission* (Durham, NC: Carolina Academic Press, 2011). Although the Thomas Jefferson Foundation admirably relied explicitly on Bayes' theorem to support the conclusions they reached from multiple and successive items of evidence, it is important to recognize that the .50 figure that the Foundation used as its prior probability—prior to its statistical analysis of the likelihood that Jefferson was the father of all six of Hemings's children—is itself a qualitative rough estimate of the evidence available prior to the statistical analysis. The .50 figure seems reasonable, but attaching a hard number to an impressionistic assumption, albeit one based on evidence, suggests greater accuracy than in fact exists. It is also worth noting that a common error, although not one that the Foundation commits, is setting the prior probability at .50 in the absence of any evidence. Doing so is often based on the assumption that in the absence of evidence, one could reach either of two opposing conclusions. But a proper assessment of prior probability comes from either evidence or a plausible assumption, and it would hardly have been plausible to assume a 50 percent probability that a slave owner named Thomas Jefferson impregnated an enslaved person in his household named Sally Hemings. So the true prior probability was very low. According to the Foundation's report, the DNA evidence and various pieces of documentary evidence then raised the posterior probability to .50. Then that posterior probability was used as the prior probability for the further evidence supplied by the statistical analysis.

21. Evidence that "merely" confirms what we already knew will ordinarily still be evidence whenever the probability prior to receiving the confirming evidence is less than 100 percent. If three witnesses observed a red Buick at the corner of First Avenue and Elm Street at 11 a.m. on October 6, then the observation of a car with the same description on the same day at the same time by a fourth witness makes the previously highly probably conclusion that that car was in that place at that time even more highly probable.

22. See Rudolf Carnap, *Logical Foundations of Probability,* 2nd ed. (Chicago: University of Chicago Press, 1962), 463; Mary Hesse, *The Structure of Scientific Evidence* (Berkeley: University of California Press, 1974), 134.

23. One example is Peter Achinstein, "Concepts of Evidence," *Mind* 87 (1978): 22–45.

24. Van Meegeren's forgeries have been the subject of several books, including Edward Dolnick, *The Forger's Spell: The True Story of Vermeer, Nazis, and the Greatest Art Hoax of the Twentieth Century* (New York: HarperCollins, 2008). Those taken in by van Meegeren's forgeries included prominent art experts, prominent museums, and Hermann Goering, which undoubtedly contributes to the continuing fascination.

25. After the end of the Second World War, van Meegeren was charged with collaborating with the Nazis for having sold several important paintings, including a Vermeer, to Hermann Goering, whose eagerness to "acquire" great art was without limit. Van Meegeren wisely preferred to be punished as a forger than as a traitor, and his confession to the forgery resulted in the dropping of charges against him for selling part of the Dutch patrimony to the Nazis. But van Meegeren died in 1947, within a month of his confession, and he never served any of his eventual one-year sentence for forgery. For the full story, see Dolnick, *The Forger's Spell;* Jonathan Janson, "Essential Vermeer 3.0," www.essentialvermeer.com (2020); Beneditta Ricca, "The Art of Forgery—Art Forgers Who Duped the World," *Artland,* April 17, 2020, https://magazine.artland.com/the-art-of-forgery-art-forgers-duped-world/.

    It is worth noting that confessions, although ordinarily strong evidence of what the confessor has confessed to, are still only evidence of that conclusion, and in some contexts may be less than reliable. For various reasons, people sometimes confess to doing things they did not do, even when the confession exposes them to criminal punishment. So although a confession is evidence, it is not conclusive. Saul M. Kassin, "False Confessions: Causes, Consequences, and Implications for Reform," *Current Directions in Psychological Science* 17 (2008): 249–253; Saul Kassin and Katherine L. Kiechel, "The Social Psychology of False Confessions: Compliance, Internalization, and Confabulation," *Psychological Science* 7 (1996): 125–128; Richard A. Leo, "False Confessions: Causes, Consequences, and Implications," *Journal of the American Academy of Psychiatry and Law* 37 (2009): 332–343.

26. A recent overview is Nick Chater et al., "Probabilistic Biases Meet the Bayesian Brain," *Current Directions in Psychological Science* 29 (2020): 506–512.

27. For "beliefs come in degrees," see Edward Elliott, "'Ramseyfying' Probabilistic Comparison," *Philosophy of Science* 87 (2020): 727–754.

28. On the use (and misuse) of generalizations in various contexts, see Frederick Schauer, *Profiles, Probabilities, and Stereotypes* (Cambridge, MA: Harvard University Press, 2003). On the concept of a generalization as being central to the idea of a *rule,* see Schauer, *Playing by the Rules: A Philosophical Examination of Rule-Based Decision-Making in Law and in Life* (Oxford: Clarendon Press, 1991). Also relevant is the idea of a *generic,* as theorized prominently by the philosopher Sarah-Jane Leslie. See Sarah-Jane Leslie, "Generics: Cognition and Acquisition," *Philosophical Review* 117 (2008): 1–47; Leslie, "Generics and the Structure of the Mind," *Philosophical Perspectives* 21 (2007): 375–403; Sarah-Jane Leslie and Adam Lerner, "Generic Generalizations," *Stanford Encyclopedia of Philosophy,* https://plato.stanford.edu/archives/win2016/entries/generics/ (2016). "Volvos are reliable" is a generic statement because most Volvos are reliable, but "ticks cause Lyme disease," to use one of Les-

lie's examples, is also a generic even though only about 1 percent of ticks cause Lyme disease. And some of why this is so depends on the category with which the generic is being compared, making the idea of a meaningful generic statement very close to the idea of incremental relevance as discussed in the text.

29. One accessible analysis applicable beyond the law is George F. James, "Relevancy, Probability, and the Law," *California Law Review* 29 (1941): 688–705.

30. "The Examination (Audit) Process," FS-2006-10 (Jan. 2006), at www.irs.gov.

31. See Karen Hube, "Game of Chance?," *Wall Street Journal*, Apr. 19, 1999.

32. Gilbert Harman, "The Inference to the Best Explanation," *Philosophical Review* 74 (1965): 88–95; Peter Lipton, *Inference to the Best Explanation*, 2nd ed. (London: Routledge, 2004).

33. The most comprehensive discussion of holistic reasoning, both in the legal system and generally, is Amalia Amaya, *The Tapestry of Reason: An Inquiry into the Nature of Coherence and Its Role in Legal Argument* (Oxford: Hart, 2015). As Amaya makes clear, inference to the best explanation is closely related (but not identical) to the idea of *abduction* as developed in the nineteenth century by the pragmatist philosopher Charles Sanders Peirce. On the differences between abduction in the modern sense (inference to best explanation) and abduction as understood by Peirce, see Igor Douven, "Abduction," *Stanford Encyclopedia of Philosophy,* at www.plato.stanford.edu (2017). On inference to the best explanation generally, see also Gloria Hon and Sam S. Rakover, eds., *Explanation: Theoretical Approaches and Applications* (Dordrecht: Springer, 2001); Peter Achinstein, "Inference to the Best Explanation: Or, Who Won the Mill-Whewell Debate?," *Studies in the History and Philosophy of Science* 23 (1992): 349–364; Philip Kitcher, "Explanatory Unification and the Causal Structure of the World," in *Scientific Explanation,* ed. Philip Kitcher and Wesley Salmon (Minneapolis: University of Minnesota Press, 1989), 410–505; Bas C. van Fraassen, *Laws and Symmetry* (Oxford: Oxford University Press, 1989).

34. In addition to sources cited earlier, see Stathis Psillos, "Inference to the Best Explanation and Bayesianism," in *Induction and Deduction in the Sciences,* ed. Friedrich Stadler (vol. 11 of the Institute of the Vienna Circle Yearbook) (Dordrecht: Springer, 2004), 83–92; Samir Okasha, "Van Fraassen's Critique of Inference to the Best Explanation," *Studies in the History and Philosophy of Science* 31 (2000): 691–710.

35. See Ronald J. Allen, "Factual Ambiguity and the Theory of Evidence," *Northwestern University Law Review* 88 (1994): 604–640; Ronald J. Allen and Michael S. Pardo, "Relative Plausibility and Its Critics," *International Journal of Evidence and Proof* 23 (2019): 5–59; Michael S. Pardo and Ronald J. Allen, "Judicial Proof and the Best Explanation," *Law and Philosophy* 27 (2008): 223–268; Nancy Pennington and Reid Hastie, "Explaining the Evidence: Tests of the Story Model for Juror Decision Making," *Journal of Personality and Social Psychology* 62 (1992): 189–206; Pennington and Hastie, "A Cognitive Theory of Juror Decision Making: The Story Model," *Cardozo Law Review* 13 (1991): 519–558; Pennington and Hastie, "Explanation-Based Decision Making: Effects of Memory Structure on Judgment," *Journal of Experimental Psychology: Learning, Memory, and Cognition* 14 (1988): 521–533.

36. Susan Haack, "Proving Causation: The Holism of Warrant and the Atomism of *Daubert*," *Journal of Health and Biomedical Law* 4 (2008): 253–289.

37. Lipton, *Inference to the Best Explanation*, at 1.

Chapter 3. The Burden of Proof

1. To the contrary is Richard H. Gaskins, *Burdens of Proof in Modern Discourse* (New Haven, CT: Yale University Press, 1992), 1–6, 108–114, equating ignorance with uncertainty.

2. For some philosophers, to know something is to be in such a state of confidence that it would be redundant to say "know for certain," precisely because "know" just *means* "know for certain." You only know something, under this view, if it would be inconceivable for it to be otherwise—if all contrary possibilities can be definitively ruled out. Descartes is the canonical source, and generations of philosophy students have been schooled in this absolutist conception of knowledge. See John Hospers, *An Introduction to Philosophical Analysis*, rev. 2nd ed. (London: Routledge and Kegan Paul, 1967), 153; Matthias Steup and Ram Neta, "Epistemology," *Stanford Encyclopedia of Philosophy*, https://plato.stanford.edu/archves/fall2020/entries/epistemology/ (2020). This conception pervades the professional philosophical landscape—see Alvin I. Goldman, *Knowledge in a Social World* (Oxford: Clarendon Press, 1999), 23, who describes this as knowledge in a "strong" sense—but it is not dominant in nonphilosophical discourse, and is not the conception I use in this book. Rather, references to knowledge here and in most of the world are to what Goldman sensibly calls W-knowledge (knowledge in the "weak" sense), and which Goldman uses in his book. I know that it is usually cold in Vermont in January, that my car is a 2019 Subaru Impreza, that my class meets at 10:10 a.m. on Mondays and Wednesdays, that I was born on January 15, and that Kamala Harris is now vice president of the United States. Such knowledge may not count as knowledge for some philosophers for some philosophical purposes, but it is noteworthy that experimental research has found that the philosophers' conception of knowledge differs not only from that of laypeople, but also from the usage in most other academic disciplines. Nat Hansen, J. D. Porter and Kathryn Francis, "A Corpus Study of 'Know': On the Verification of Philosophers' Frequency Claims about Language," *Episteme* 18 (2021): 242–268; Christina Starmans and Ori Friedman, "Expert or Esoteric? Philosophers Attribute Knowledge Differently than All Other Academics," *Cognitive Science* 44 (2020). See also Michael S. Pardo, "Epistemology, Psychology, and Standards of Proof: An Essay on Risinger's 'Surprise' Theory," *Seton Hall Law Review* 48 (2018): 1039–1055; Pardo, "The Gettier Problem and Legal Proof," *Legal Theory* 16 (2010): 37–58.

3. The legal system's historical aversion to using numbers to portray or operationalize "beyond a reasonable doubt" is defended in United States v. Hall, 854 F.2d 1036, 1043 (7th Cir. 1988) (Richard A. Posner J.); Ronald J. Allen and Alex Stein, "Evidence, Probability, and the Burden of Proof," *Arizona Law Review* 55 (2013): 557–

602; Laurence H. Tribe, "Trial by Mathematics: Precision and Ritual in the Legal Process," *Harvard Law Review* 84 (1971): 1329–1393. Contrary arguments, favoring translating such imprecise ideas into more precise formulas, whether in the legal system or otherwise, include Jennifer Rose Carr, "Imprecise Evidence without Imprecise Credences," *Philosophical Studies* 177 (2020): 2735–2758; Joe Fore, "'A Court Would Probably Find . . .': Defining Probability Expressions in Predictive Legal Analysis," *Legal Communication and Rhetoric: JALWD* 16 (2019): 49–84; Frederick Mosteller and Cleo Youtz, "Quantifying Probabilistic Assessments," *Statistical Science* 5 (1990): 2–12; Peter Tillers and Jonathan Gottfried, "United States v. Copeland: A Collateral Attack on the Legal Maxim That Proof Beyond a Reasonable Doubt Is Unquantifiable," *Law, Probability and Risk* 5 (2006): 135–157; [Judge] Jon O. Newman, "Taking 'Beyond a Reasonable Doubt' Seriously," *Judicature* 103, no. 2 (2019). And see *Judgment by the Numbers: Converting Qualitative to Quantitative Judgments in Law,* special issue of *Journal of Empirical Legal Studies* 8 (2011): 1–97.

4. Whether instructions to juries in criminal cases should include numerical percentages is a very different question, implicating the psychology of communication and the psychology of jury deliberation. I leave that question aside here.

5. See Georgi Gardner, "In Defence of Reasonable Doubt," *Journal of Applied Philosophy* 34 (2017): 221–241; David Kaye, "Laws of Probability and the Law of the Land," *University of Chicago Law Review* 47 (1979): 34–56; C. M. A. McCauliff, "Burdens of Proof: Degrees of Belief, Quanta of Evidence, or Constitutional Guarantees?," *Vanderbilt Law Review* 35 (1982): 1293–1336; Anne W. Martin and David A. Schum, "Quantifying Burdens of Proof: A Likelihood Ratio Approach," *Jurimetrics* 27 (1987): 383–401; [Judge] Jack B. Weinstein and Ian Dewsbury, "Comment on the Meaning of 'Proof Beyond a Reasonable Doubt,'" *Law, Probability and Risk* 5 (2006): 167–173. An influential critique of some implications of the beyond-a-reasonable-doubt standard is Larry Laudan, *Truth, Error, and Criminal Law: An Essay in Legal Epistemology* (Cambridge: Cambridge University Press, 2006). A critique of that critique is Raphael M. Goldman and Alvin I. Goldman, "Review of *Truth, Error, and Criminal Law: An Essay in Legal Epistemology,* by Larry Laudan," *Legal Theory* 15 (2009): 55–66.

6. Not all. See Rita James Simon and Linda Mahan, "Quantifying Burdens of Proof: A View from the Bench, the Jury, and the Classroom," *Law and Society Review* 5 (1971): 319–330, finding lower estimates based on surveys.

7. As we will see in Chapter 4, things are not quite this simple. To recover against Jill, Jack must prove (1) that Jill was negligent, (2) that Jack was injured, and (3) that Jill's negligence caused Jack's injuries; and if Jack must prove *each* of these by a preponderance of the evidence, then Jack's burden turns out to be greater than a bare preponderance of the evidence because Jack will lose if he fails to prove any one of these three elements. Conversely, if Jack need only prove that the conjunction of these three elements is true by a preponderance of the evidence, then his burden—for any one of the three can be lower than a preponderance. This is the *conjunction problem,* and it has been well-massaged by scholars of the law of evidence. See Dale A. Nance, *The Burden of Proof: Discriminatory Power, Weight of Evidence,*

and the Tenacity of Belief (Cambridge: Cambridge University Press, 2016), 75–77; David S. Schwartz and Elliott R. Sober, "The Conjunction Problem and the Logic of Jury Findings," *William and Mary Law Review* 59 (2017): 619–692; Mark Spottswood, "Unraveling the Conjunction Paradox," *Law, Probability and Risk* 15 (2016): 259–296; Bartosz W. Wojciechowski and Emmanuel M. Pothos, "Is There a Conjunction Fallacy in Legal Probabilistic Decision Making?," *Frontiers in Psychology* 9 (2018): 391–401.

8. The trial inspired an outpouring of books, most of them dreadful. Two of the more reliable accounts are Darnell M. Hunt, *O.J. Simpson Facts and Fictions: News Ritual in the Construction of Reality* (Cambridge: Cambridge University Press, 1999), and Jeffrey Toobin, *The Run of His Life: The People v. O.J. Simpson* (New York: Random House, 1996).

9. See B. Drummond Ayres Jr., "Civil Jury Finds Simpson Liable in Pair of Killings," *New York Times*, Feb. 5, 1997, A1; Richard Winton, "Kim Goldman's Crusade: Make O.J. Simpson Pay and Never Forget," *Los Angeles Times*, June 12, 2019.

10. Although the civil jury and not the criminal jury was told about threatening statements O.J. Simpson had made to Nicole Brown Simpson, there is little indication that admitting such statements in the criminal trial would have changed the outcome.

11. On the Scottish option and its effect, see Rachel Ormston et al., *Scottish Government, Scottish Jury Research: Findings from a Large Scale Mock Jury Study*, at www.gov .scot (Oct. 9, 2019).

12. In Bostock v. Clayton County, Georgia, 140 S. Ct. 1731 (2019), the Supreme Court ruled that Title VI's prohibition on sex discrimination in employment prohibited discrimination on the basis of sexual orientation regardless of the sex of the victim. Presumably the same applies to Title IX as well.

13. For accounts of the background law and the issues described here, see SurvJustice Inc. v. DeVos, 2019 WL5684522 (N.D. Cal., Nov. 1, 2019); Ilana Frier, "Campus Sexual Assault and Due Process," *Duke Journal of Constitutional Law and Public Policy Sidebar* 15 (2020): 117–143; William C. Kidder, "(En)Forcing a Foolish Consistency? A Critique and Comparative Analysis of the Trump Administration's Proposed Standard of Evidence Regulation for Campus Title IX Proceedings," *Journal of College and University Law* 45 (2020): 1–47; Sarah Swan, "Discriminatory Dualism in Process: Title IX, Reverse Title IX, and Campus Sexual Assault," *Oklahoma Law Review* 73 (2020): 69–99.

14. See United States v. Comstock, 560 U.S. 126 (2010); Addington v. Texas, 441 U.S. 418 (1979).

15. The phrase the Supreme Court used was "convincing clarity," which says the same thing with a slightly different grammatical structure. New York Times Co. v. Sullivan, 376 U.S. 254 (1964). The same burden of proof applies when the plaintiff seeks to prove, not actual knowledge of falsity, but "reckless disregard" of the truth, the latter requiring a failure to investigate in the face of demonstrated "serious doubts" about the truth of the publication. St. Amant v. Thompson, 379 U.S. 64 (1968).

16. William Blackstone, *Commentaries on the Laws of England* (London: 1769), as published in facsimile by University of Chicago Press (1979), 352.

17. Many of these other ratios are collected in Daniel Pi, Francesco Parisi, and Barbara Luppi, "Quantifying Reasonable Doubt," *Rutgers University Law Review* 72 (2020): 455–508; Frederick Schauer and Richard Zeckhauser, "On the Degree of Confidence for Adverse Decisions," *Journal of Legal Studies* 25 (1996): 27–52, at 34n11; Alexander Volokh, "*n* Guilty Men," *University of Pennsylvania Law Review* 146 (1997): 173–212.

18. Recent years have seen efforts to identify mistaken convictions and provide after-the-fact exoneration. See Brandon L. Garrett, *Convicting the Innocent: Where Criminal Prosecutions Go Wrong* (Cambridge, MA: Harvard University Press, 2011). But a mistaken conviction is not necessarily a product of mistaken institutional design. Changing the procedures to lessen the number of mistaken convictions will likely increase the number of mistaken acquittals, and then we are back to the Blackstonian task of determining how many mistaken acquittals we are willing to tolerate in order to achieve how much of a reduction in the number of mistaken convictions. For Blackstone, that determination did not involve any question of racially disproportionate effects, a question that now properly pervades the contemporary application of the Blackstonian calculus. Moreover, accepting the inevitability of some number of mistaken convictions does not preclude compensation or other redress when those mistakes become apparent in individual cases. See Erik Encarnacion, "Why and How to Compensate Exonerees," *Michigan Law Review First Impressions* 114 (2016): 139–154.

19. Ramos v. Louisiana, 140 S. Ct. 1390 (2020).

20. See Laudan, *Truth, Error, and the Criminal Law.* Moreover, Laudan argues that we should include in our calculus not only the mistakes. A proper analysis, he insists, would also include the benefits of accurate convictions and accurate acquittals, and these benefits should be weighed against the costs of mistaken acquittals and mistaken convictions. In expanding our understanding of the consequences of both correct and incorrect decisions in this way, he concludes, we would wind up with a more socially beneficial assessment of the proper burden of proof. Moreover, it would be a burden of proof that properly varies with the nature (and thus severity) of the crime charged, unlike the uniform approach now in force.

21. See Sarah Brown, "6 Things to Know About the New Title IX Guidance," *Chronicle of Higher Education,* July 21, 2021; Alexis Gravely, "Thoughts from the Public on Title IX," *Inside Higher Ed,* June 8, 2021, www.insidehighered.com. The entire issue remains in flux, however, largely because the Senate Committee on Health, Education, Labor, and Pensions refused, on August 3, 2021, to advance the nomination of Catherine Lhamon to be Assistant Secretary of the Office of Civil Rights of the Department of Education, the office in charge of Title IX enforcement. The burden of proof for Title IX proceedings was prominent in Lhamon's hearings, with the Committee's tie vote along partisan lines, leaving the issue open as of this writing.

22. An extensive historical and constitutional analysis is Thomas B. Ripy, "Standard of Proof in Senate Impeachment Proceedings," Congressional Research Service Report 98-990 (Jan. 7 1999), available at https://crs.reports.congress.gov. More recent, but dealing less with the standard of proof, is Jared P. Cole and Todd Garvey, "Impeachment and the Constitution" (Nov. 20, 2019), https://crs.reports.congress .gov..

23. Compare the book by an international player so accused, Terence Reese, *Story of an Accusation* (New York: Simon and Schuster, 1966), with the book about the same episode by the accuser, Alan Truscott, *The Great Bridge Scandal: The Most Famous Cheating Case in the History of the Game* (New York: Exposition Press, 1969). The decision-making body applied a high standard of proof, close but not identical to "beyond a reasonable doubt," and concluded, in the style of the Scottish "not proven" verdict, that the accusation had not been "supported."

24. In American professional football, the standard for reversing an on-the-field call by a referee is "unmistakable visual evidence," which seems analogous to "beyond a reasonable doubt."

25. See Andrew Ashworth and Lucia Zedner, *Preventive Justice* (Oxford: Oxford University Press, 2014), 200–203.

26. For the view that a presupposed moral and political right to liberty raises the burden of proof for such restrictions, see Eric Winsberg, Jason Brennan, and Chris W. Surprenant, "How Government Leaders Violated Their Epistemic Duties during the SARS-CoV-2 Crisis," *Kennedy Institute of Ethics Journal* 30 (2020): 215–242. But note that Winsberg et al.'s burden-raising right to general freedom of movement is not a right recognized in existing American legal doctrine. See Carmichael v. Ige, 470 F.3d 1133 (D. Haw. 2020).

27. See Roger Przybylski, *Recidivism of Adult Sexual Offenders,* published by the Office of Sex Offender Sentencing, Monitoring, Apprehending, Registering, and Tracking, US Department of Justice, Office of Justice Programs (2015), available at www .smart.ojop.gov.

28. One reason for not fully exploring the issues here is to avoid repeating what is in Frederick Schauer, *Profiles, Probabilities, and Stereotypes* (Cambridge, MA: Harvard University Press, 2003).

29. In addition to Ashworth and Zedner, *Preventive Justice,* see the various perspectives reflected in Andrew Ashworth, Lucia Zedner, and Patrick Tomlin, eds., *Prevention and the Limits of the Criminal Law* (Oxford: Oxford University Press, 2013), and also in Sandra G. Mayson, "In Defense of Consequentialist Prevention," *Criminal Law and Philosophy* 15, no. 1 (April 2021).

30. See Jennifer Carlson, "Gun Studies and the Politics of Evidence," *Annual Review of Law and Social Science* 16 (2020): 183–202.

31. The evidentiary dimensions of violent interactive videogames were debated in the Supreme Court. Brown v. Entertainment Merchants Ass'n, 564 U.S. 786 (2011). Because restrictions on such games implicate freedom of speech under the First Amendment, the Supreme Court presupposed that the burden of proof necessary

to justify a restriction was higher than it would have been to justify a more typical (and not constitutionally problematic) restriction of personal liberty. Differently put, but consistent with the decision theory of the burden of proof, the First Amendment commanded that the mistake of an unwarranted restriction be treated as worse than the mistake of an unwarranted nonrestriction. And the First Amendment also commanded that the mistake of an unwarranted restriction be treated as worse than an unwarranted restriction on activity not implicating the First Amendment (or other constitutional rights).

32. When we seek to attribute responsibility for a particular past act, whether that attribution takes place in the legal system or otherwise, we often use a deterministic conception of causation. Under this view, event *C* is a cause of consequence (effect) *E* if and only if *E* would not have happened but for *C*, and only if *C* always produces *E*. But when we are making policy about future acts, as with making policy about cigarettes or guns or opioids, such deterministic conceptions of causation are of little assistance, and probabilistic causation is the almost universal understanding. See Frederick Schauer and Barbara A. Spellman, "Probabilistic Causation and the Law," *Journal of Institutional and Theoretical Economics* 176 (2020): 4–17. The philosophical literature on probabilistic causation includes Patrick Suppes, *A Probabilistic Theory of Causality* (Amsterdam: North Holland, 1970); Nancy Cartwright, "Causal Laws and Effective Strategies," *Noûs* 13 (1979): 419–437; Ellery Eels, "Probabilistic Causal Interaction," *Philosophy of Science* 53 (1986): 52–64; I. J. Good, "A Causal Calculus I–II," *British Journal for the Philosophy of Science* 11 (1961): 305–318; David Papineau, "Probabilities and Causes," *Journal of Philosophy* 82 (1985): 57–74; Wesley Salmon, "Probabilistic Causality," *Pacific Philosophical Quarterly* 31 (1980): 50–74; Deborah Rosen, "In Defence of a Probabilistic Theory of Causality," *Philosophy of Science* 45 (1978): 604–613. A comprehensive and accessible statistical analysis is A. Philip Dawid, "Statistical Risk," *Synthese* 194 (2017): 3445–3474.

33. In the environmental context, the principle holds that "where there are threats of serious or irreversible damage, lack of full scientific certainty shall not be used as a reason for postponing cost-effective measures." Principle 15 of the UN Rio Declaration on Environment and Development, available at http://www.un.org/documents/ga/conf151/aconf15126-1annex1.htm. See Jane Holder and Maria Lee, *Environmental Protection, Law and Policy*, 2nd ed. (Cambridge: Cambridge University Press, 2008), 15–34; Marco Martuzzi and Joel A. Tickner, *The Precautionary Principle: Protecting Public Health, the Environment and the Future of Our Children* (Copenhagen: World Health Organization, 2004); Elizabeth Fisher, "Precaution, Precaution Everywhere: Developing a 'Common Understanding' of the Precautionary Principle in the European Community," *Maastricht Journal of European and Comparative Law* 9 (2002): 7–28. Skeptical analyses include Cass R. Sunstein, *Laws of Fear: Beyond the Precautionary Principle* (Cambridge: Cambridge University Press, 2005); Aaron Wildavsky, *But Is It True? A Citizen's Guide to Environmental Health and Safety Issues* (Cambridge, MA: Harvard University Press, 1997).

34. For an extensively referenced overview of the controversies, see Daniel Steel, "The Precautionary Principle and the Dilemma Objection," *Ethics, Policy and Environment* 16 (2013): 321–340.

35. See Klaus Messerschmidt, "COVID-19 Legislation in the Light of the Precautionary Principle," *Theory and Practice of Legislation* 8 (2020): 267–292.

36. A sampling of the more than fifty lawsuits, all dismissed, would include Texas v. Pennsylvania, No. 155, Orig. (Sup. Ct., Dec. 11, 2020); Trump for President, Inc. v. Secretary of Commonwealth of Pennsylvania, 2020 WL 7012522 (3d Cir., Nov. 27, 2020); Trump v. Wisconsin Elections Commission, 2020 WL 7318940 (E.D. Wis., Dec. 12, 2020); Bowyer v. Ducey, 2020 WL 7238261 (D. Ariz., Dec. 9, 2020); King v. Whitmer, 2020 WL 7134198 (E.D. Mich., Dec. 7, 2020); Wood v. Raffensperger, 2020 WL 6817153 (N.D. Ga. Nov. 20, 2020).

37. An example of the common view—that "proof" is in some unspecified way stronger than evidence, perhaps by being strong enough to justify a legal judgment—is a 1956 how-to-do-it book by Marshall Houts entitled *From Evidence to Proof: A Searching Analysis of Methods to Establish Fact* (Springfield, IL: Charles Thomas, 1956). More recently, see Beth A. Bechky, *Blood, Power, and Residue: How Crime Labs Translate Evidence into Proof* (Princeton, NJ: Princeton University Press, 2021).

38. See Naomi Oreskes and Erik M. Conway, *Merchants of Doubt: How a Handful of Scientists Obscured the Truth on Issues from Tobacco Smoke to Climate Change* (New York: Bloomsbury USA, 2010).

39. Diane Caruana, "Latest Study Finds No Conclusive Evidence that Vaping Leads to Smoking," Apr. 21, 2020, www.vapingpost.com.

40. See M. R. Avery et al., "Mechanisms of Influence: Alcohol Industry Submissions to the Inquiry into Fetal Alcohol Disorders," *Drug and Alcohol Review* 35 (2016): 665–672; International Alliance for Responsible Drinking, "No Conclusive Evidence of Link between Occasional, Light, or Moderate Drinking and Fetal Alcohol Spectrum Disorders," www.iard.org.

41. "No Definitive Proof of Effect of Video Games on Work Time," at www.nintendoenthusiast.com.

42. Brown v. Entertainment Merchants Ass'n, 564 U.S. 786 (2011). In most of the world, the idea that free speech concerns are even relevant to violent video games would be considered bizarre. But the United States is a protective outlier on free speech issues compared to the rest of the world, even the rest of the liberal democratic industrialized world. See Frederick Schauer, "The Exceptional First Amendment," in *American Exceptionalism and Human Rights,* ed. Michael Ignatieff (Princeton, NJ: Princeton University Press, 2005), 29–56. The view that regulation of such games must satisfy a First Amendment–elevated burden of justification was common ground even among the justices who disagreed about the evidence. On the effects of violent video games generally, compare American Psychological Association, "APA Task Force on Violent Media: Technical Report on the Review of the Violent Video Game Literature," https://www.apa.org/pi/families/review-video-ga,es

.pdf (2015), with Christopher F. Ferguson, Allen Copenhaver, and Patrick Markey, "Reexamining the Findings of the American Psychological Association's 2015 Task Force on Violent Media: A Meta-Analysis," *Perspectives on Psychological Science* 15 (2020): 1423–1443.

43. To be clear, there is no claim here that measures of statistical significance map easily onto measures of the burden of proof. See Michelle M. Burtis, Jonah B. Gelbach, and Bruce H. Kobayashi, "Error Costs, Legal Standards of Proof, and Statistical Significance," *Supreme Court Economic Review* 25 (2017): 1–58; Michael S. Pardo, "A Comment on Statistical Significance and Standards of Proof," *Supreme Court Economic Review* 25 (2017): 59–63.

44. See Valentin Amrhein, Sander Greenland, and Blake McShane, "Scientists Rise Up against Statistical Significance," www.nature.com (March 20, 2019), reporting on Blakey B. McShane, David Gal, Andrew Gelman, Christian Robert, and Jennifer L. Tackett, "Abandon Statistical Significance," *American Statistician* 73 (2019): 235–245.

Chapter 4. How to Tell the Truth with Statistics

1. Darrell Huff, *How to Lie with Statistics* (New York: W. W. Norton, 1954).

2. The assumptions are added in order to avoid the worst forms of the so-called reference class problem. If the reliability assessments for Subarus for a particular model year are based on the average of various different models, some of which are especially reliable and others of which are not, then using the all-models average for an inference about the especially unreliable model, or even about an unspecified model, is unwarranted. But if all Subarus are relevantly similar, then the reference class problem of moving from this class to a representative member of this class is substantially eliminated. See Edward K. Cheng, "A Practical Solution to the Reference Class Problem," *Columbia Law Review* 109 (2009): 2081–2105; Alan Hájek, "The Reference Class Problem Is Your Problem Too," *Synthese* 156 (2007): 563–585; Christian Wallman and Jon Williamson, "Four Approaches to the Reference Class Problem," in *Making It Formally Explicit: Probability, Causality and Indeterminism,* ed. Gábor Hofer-Szabó and Leszek Wronski (Cham, Switzerland: Springer, 2017), 61–81.

3. For the moment we are talking about individual attributes—solid or striped—and not about causation, relationships, or behavior. Things get more complicated when we are talking about causation: Is the fact that 90 percent of cases of lung cancer are caused by cigarette smoking evidence that this particular case of lung cancer, about which we know nothing more, was caused by cigarette smoking? And even more complications arise when the class that produces the aggregate data has nonidentical subclasses. This is the *ecological inference problem,* and statisticians and others have long debated whether individual-level causation or other individual-level relationships or patterns of behavior can be inferred from group-level data about those relationships and behavior. An important overview and proposed solution are in Gary King, *A Solution to the Ecological Inference Problem: Reconstructing*

Individual Behavior from Aggregate Data (Princeton, NJ: Princeton University Press, 1997). See also Gary King, Ori Rosen, and Martin A. Tanners, eds., *Ecological Inference: New Methodological Strategies* (Cambridge: Cambridge University Press, 2010); Nancy Cleave, Philip J. Brown, and Clive D. Payne, "Evaluation of Methods for Ecological Inference," *Journal of the Royal Statistical Society* 158 (1995): 55–72; Lutz Erbring, "Individual Writ Large: An Epilogue on the 'Ecological Fallacy,'" *Political Analysis* 1 (1989): 235–269; D. James Greiner, "Causal Inference in Civil Rights Litigation," *Harvard Law Review* 122 (2008): 533–598; Jon Wakefield, "Ecological Inference in the Social Sciences," *Statistical Methodology* 7 (2010): 307–322. The ecological inference problem aside, the use in the legal system of aggregate (statistical) data as evidence of specific causation is both common and defensible. See Susan Haack, "Risky Business: Statistical Proof of Specific Causation," *in Evidence Matters: Science, Proof, and Truth in the Law* (Cambridge: Cambridge University Press, 2014), 264–293.

4. As Laurence Tribe, who objects to the use of quantified statistical evidence in trials, puts it, "*All* factual evidence is ultimately 'statistical,' and all legal proof ultimately 'probabilistic,' in the epistemological sense that no conclusion can ever be drawn from empirical data without some step of inductive inference—even if only an inference that things are usually what they are perceived to be." Laurence H. Tribe, "Trial by Mathematics: Precision and Ritual in the Legal Process," *Harvard Law Review* 84 (1971): 1329–1393, at 1330. And note, consistent with Tribe's view, that saying that evidence is probabilistic says nothing about whether those probabilities can or should be reduced to, or expressed in terms of, numbers.

5. People v. Collins, 438 P.2d 33 (Cal. 1968).

6. Smith v. Rapid Transit, 58 N.E.2d 754 (Mass. 1945); Tribe, "Trial by Mathematics," at 1340–1341, 1346–1350.

7. See Emily Berman, "Individualized Suspicion in the Age of Big Data," *Iowa Law Review* 105 (2020): 463–506, at 475–476; Edward K. Cheng, "Reconceptualizing the Burden of Proof," *Yale Law Journal* 122 (2013): 1254–1279; David Enoch, Levi Spectre, and Talia Fisher, "Statistical Evidence, Sensitivity, and the Legal Value of Knowledge," *Philosophy and Public Affairs* 40 (2012): 197–224; Michael S. Pardo, "The Paradoxes of Legal Proof: A Critical Guide," *Boston University Law Review* 99 (2019): 233–290. A good overview of the literature is Enrique Guerra-Pujol, "Visualizing Probabilistic Proof," *Washington University Jurisprudence Review* 7 (2014): 39–75. To the same effect as *Smith v. Rapid Transit*, but on more complex facts, is Day v. Boston & Me. R.R., 52 A. 771 (Me. 1902), mysteriously distinguishing probabilistic from "real" evidence.

8. L. Jonathan Cohen, *The Probable and the Provable* (Oxford: Clarendon Press, 1977), 73–76.

9. See, in addition to the above references, Martin Smith, "When Does Evidence Suffice for Conviction?," *Mind* 127 (2018): 1193–1218; Gary L. Wells, "Naked Statistical Evidence of Liability: Is Subjective Probability Enough?," *Journal of Personality and Social Psychology* 62 (1992): 739–752.

10. Charles R. Nesson, "Reasonable Doubt and Permissive Inferences: The Value of Complexity," *Harvard Law Review* 92 (1979): 1187–1225, at 1192–1196.

11. In addition to references already cited, see Michael Blome-Tillman, "Statistical Evidence, Normalcy, and the Gatecrasher Paradox," *Mind* 129 (2020): 563–577; Marcello Di Bello, "Trial by Statistics: Is a High Probability of Guilt Enough to Convict?," *Mind* 128 (2019): 1045–1084; David Enoch and Talia Fisher, "Sense and 'Sensitivity': Epistemic and Instrumental Approaches to Statistical Evidence," *Stanford Law Review* 67 (2015): 557–611; Georgi Gardiner, "Legal Burdens of Proof and Statistical Evidence," in *Routledge Handbook of Applied Epistemology,* ed. David Coady and James Chase (London: Routledge, 2018), 179–195; David Kaye, "The Paradox of the Gatecrasher and Other Stories," *Arizona State Law Journal* 1979 (1979): 101–143; Sarah Moss, "A Knowledge Account of Legal Proof," in *Oxford Studies in Epistemology,* vol. 7 (Oxford: Oxford University Press, 2021); Mike Redmayne, "Exploring the Proof Paradoxes," *Legal Theory* 14 (2008): 281–309.

12. This example was suggested to me by David Enoch and Levi Spectre.

13. It is worth noting, again, that the alleged paradox does not depend on the use or non-use of actual numbers. If, as in the real *Smith v. Rapid Transit* case, the evidence was only that the vast majority of the buses operating on that route were operated by a specific company, that would still, for some people, create a problem, as it did for the court, because the intuition is that the problem is created by the lack of individuation and not by the presence of statistics in numerical form.

14. In the case on which the Blue Bus hypothetical is based, the absence of any other evidence that this was Rapid Transit's bus might be evidence that it was not. Most buses display their ownership quite prominently, and the failure to offer evidence about the bus's ownership might raise suspicion—which would be evidence—that it was not actually a Rapid Transit bus. See James Brook, "The Use of Statistical Evidence of Identification in Civil Litigation: Well-Worn Hypotheticals, Real Cases, and Controversy," *St. Louis University Law Journal* 29 (1985): 293–352, at 301–303.

15. One of the most rigorous defenses of a requirement for individualized evidence is Judith Jarvis Thomson, "Liability and Individualized Evidence," in *Rights, Restitution, and Risk: Essays in Moral Theory,* ed. William Parent (Cambridge, MA: Harvard University Press, 1986), 225–250.

16. This generalization not only is apparently true, but also is a staple of popular culture, as exemplified by Michelle Wolf's satirical "The Husband Did It" routine and a novel entitled *It's Always the Husband,* by Michelle Campbell (New York: St. Martin's Press, 2017).

17. See Michael J. Saks and Robert F. Kidd, "Human Information Processing and Adjudication: Trial by Heuristics," *Law and Society Review* 15 (1981): 123–160.

18. The most prominent reference is Daniel Kahneman, *Thinking, Fast and Slow* (New York: Farrar, Strauss and Giroux 2011). See also Maya Bar-Hillel, "The Base-Rate Fallacy in Probability Judgments," *Acta Psychologica* 44 (1980): 211–233.

19. See Alex Broadbent, "Epidemiological Evidence in Proof of Specific Causation," *Legal Theory* 17 (2011): 237–278; Melissa Moore Thompson, "Causal Inference in

Epidemiology: Implications for Toxic Tort Litigation," *North Carolina Law Review* 71 (1992): 247–291.

20. The case on which the Blue Bus hypothetical is based was real, but some complain that the made-up examples in the statistical evidence literature are without value because they could never arise in real life. Ronald J. Allen, "Naturalized Epistemology and the Law of Evidence," *Quaestio Facti* 2 (2021): 253–284. But that worry is misguided. A controlled scientific experiment seeks knowledge by varying a single attribute in order to determine if that attribute makes a difference, and, outside the laboratory, analytic isolation does the same in a more qualitative context. Barbara A. Spellman, "In Defense of Weird Hypotheticals," *Quaestio Facti* 2 (2021): 325–337. The fictional examples in the evidence literature are designed to isolate the factor of statistical probability and the permissible (or not) use of the characteristics of a class to support inferences about individual members of that class. Analytic isolation fosters close examination of how much difference, if any, this one factor makes, even if that factor—here, statistical likelihood—rarely appears alone, without other evidence, in the so-called real world. And so we use these artificial examples to learn about our non-artificial world in the way that an epidemiological experiment uses laboratory experiments to identify disease-causing or disease-curing agents that also might never appear alone outside of the laboratory.

21. This better-evidence-forcing view, applied to a wide range of evidentiary rules, is the central theme of Dale Nance, "The Best Evidence Principle," *Iowa Law Review* 73 (1988): 227–298.

22. The literature on the base-rate fallacy includes Aron K. Barbey and Steven A. Sloman, "Base-Rate Respect: From Ecological Rationality to Dual Processes," *Behavioral and Brain Sciences* 30 (2007): 241–254; Bar-Hillel, "The Base-Rate Fallacy"; Eugene Borgida and Richard Nisbett, "The Differential Impact of Abstract versus Concrete Information on Decisions," *Journal of Applied Social Psychology* 7 (1977): 258–271; Baruch Fischhoff and Maya Bar-Hillel, "Diagnosticity and the Base-Rate Effect," *Memory and Cognition* 12 (1984): 402–410; Keith J. Holyoak and Barbara A. Spellman, "Thinking," *Annual Review of Psychology* 44 (1993): 265–315; Daniel Kahneman and Amos Tversky, "Subjective Probability: A Judgment of Representativeness," *Cognitive Psychology* 3 (1972): 430–454.

23. The statement in the text is a slight overstatement. If in fact Henry committed these acts against these four accusers, then the four accusation are not truly statistically independent, because the existence of a common cause defeats independence. At the point at which we do not know of this common cause, however, the fact that the accusers do not know each other and do not know of the others' accusations is sufficient independence for our purposes.

24. For a qualified defense of a qualified aggregation principle, see Alon Harel and Ariel Porat, "Aggregating Probabilities across Cases: Criminal Responsibility for Unspecified Offenses," *Minnesota Law Review* 94 (2009): 261–308; Ariel Porat and Eric A. Posner, "Aggregation and Law," *Yale Law Journal* 122 (2012): 2–68. An even

more qualified defense is Frederick Schauer and Richard Zeckhauser, "On the Degree of Confidence for Adverse Decisions," *Journal of Legal Studies* 25 (1996): 27–52. On the related puzzles where one act can violate multiple prohibitions, see Larry Alexander, "The Aggregation / Culpability Puzzle," San Diego Legal Studies Paper 2-474, https://ssrn.com/abstract=3720171 (Dec. 18, 2020).

25. This issue differs from that in the infamous "Brides in the Bath" English case from 1915. There, George Joseph Smith had been prosecuted for murdering his wife by drowning her in a bathtub, and there was evidence that two of Smith's previous wives had died under very similar circumstances. R. v. Smith, 11 Cr. App. 229, 84 L.J.K.B. 2153 (1915). The evidence was admitted on the theory that it was extraordinarily unlikely that three wives of the same man would die in such similar fashion, and thus that Smith likely committed all three of these murders, and not just one unspecified. In this respect the issues in *Smith* are similar to those in the Pennsylvania conviction of Bill Cosby, subsequently reversed on other grounds. Commonwealth v. Cosby, 252 A.3d 1092 (Pa. 2021). At least one of the claims in the Cosby case, a claim resembling the prosecution claims in *Smith*, was that the method that Cosby used to drug and then sexually assault multiple women were so unusual that one person—Cosby—must have committed all of them. Because the Pennsylvania Supreme Court reversed Cosby's conviction on the grounds that he testified in a civil deposition in reliance on the prosecutor's commitment not to prosecute criminally, a commitment the state did not honor, the court never reached any of the issues regarding the evidence of other acts.

26. Kevin Clermont finds such a possibility "startling" and "astounding." Kevin M. Clermont, "Aggregation of Probabilities and Illogic," *Georgia Law Review* 47 (2012): 165–180.

27. This section is a highly abbreviated version of the main themes in Frederick Schauer, *Profiles, Probabilities, and Stereotypes* (Cambridge, MA: Harvard University Press, 2003). Further reflection over almost twenty years would lead me to a few different conclusions, a few different arguments, and more than a few more felicitous ways of expressing those conclusions and arguments. But the principal claims still strike me as correct, and are summarized here.

28. Department of Commerce v. New York, 139 S. Ct. 2551 (2019).

29. Utah v. Evans, 536 U.S. 452 (2002); Department of Commerce v. United States House of Representatives, 525 U.S. 316 (1999).

Chapter 5. Testimony, and Not Only in Court

1. R. F. Atkinson, *Knowledge and Explanation in History: An Introduction to the Philosophy of History* (Ithaca, NY: Cornell University Press, 1978), 42.

2. On the language-based nature of testimony, and how language distinguishes testimonial from observational, perceptual, experiential knowledge, see Elizabeth Fricker, "The Epistemology of Testimony," *Proceedings of the Aristotelian Society*, suppl. 61 (1987): 57–83.

3. Only recently in the history of philosophy have philosophers treated testimony as being of distinct philosophical interest, as opposed to being the philosophically uninteresting way in which philosophically interesting knowledge is transmitted. Fortunately, that neglect has been remedied. See, among other important treatments, C. A. J. Coady, *Testimony: A Philosophical Study* (Oxford: Oxford University Press, 1992); Jennifer Lackey, *Learning from Words: Testimony as a Source of Knowledge* (Oxford: Oxford University Press, 2008); Jennifer Lackey and Ernest Sosa, eds., *The Epistemology of Testimony* (Oxford: Oxford University Press, 2006); Richard Moran, *The Exchange of Words* (Oxford: Oxford University Press, 2018); Steven Shapin, *A Social History of Truth* (Chicago: University of Chicago Press, 1994); Jonathan Adler, "Epistemological Problems of Testimony," *Stanford Encyclopedia of Philosophy,* https://plato.stanford.edu/entries/testimony-episprob/; Robert Audi, "The Place of Testimony in the Fabric of Knowledge and Justification," *American Philosophical Quarterly* 34 (1997): 405–422; Elizabeth Fricker, "'Believing the Speaker' versus Believing on Evidence: A Critique of Moran," *European Journal of Philosophy* 27 (2019): 267–276; Fricker, "The Epistemology of Testimony," *Proceedings of the Aristotelian Society,* suppl. 61 (1987): 57–83; Peter Lipton, "The Epistemology of Testimony," *Studies in the History and Philosophy of Science* 29 (1998): 1–31; Angus Ross, "Why Do We Believe What We Are Told?," *Ratio* 28 (1986): 69–88.

4. See Jay A. Soled, "Exploring and (Re)Defining the Boundaries of the Cohan Rule," *Temple Law Review* 79 (2006): 939–970.

5. Cohan v. Commissioner of Internal Revenue, 39 F.2d 540 (2d Cir. 1930).

6. Prior to becoming an appellate judge, Hand had spent fifteen years as a federal trial judge. We can speculate that these fifteen years of listening to oral testimony as the principal form of courtroom evidence made Hand particularly attuned to the way in which oral testimony can count as evidence.

7. 26 U.S.C. §274 (2018).

8. See, more recently than *Cohan,* and more recently than the 1962 changes, La Forge v. Commissioner of Internal Revenue, 434 F.2d 370 (2d Cir. 1970); Baker v. Commissioner of Internal Revenue, T.C. Memo. 2014-122 (2014); *Mertens Law of Federal Income Taxation* §25F:12 (Dec. 2020 update).

9. Sometimes, trusting the testimony of another is based on personal commitments that have little to do with truth and little to do with reliance on the veracity of the testifier. See Philip J. Nickel, "Trust and Testimony," *Pacific Philosophical Quarterly* 93 (2012): 301–316. I trust my often-dissembling friend, and thus take his word for something, only because he is my friend and not because his saying something provides very good evidence for its truth. But here we are dealing with epistemic trust—actual belief in the truth of what someone has said just because of the knowledge that we assume lies behind their testimony. Epistemic trust is to be distinguished from what we can think of as social or moral trust.

10. The qualification in the text is an oblique reference to the theory of speech acts, which recognizes that much speech does not assert anything, and therefore does not make the kind of statement that there can be evidence for, or that is evidence

for something else. To take an example from J. L. Austin, the founder of modern speech act theory, saying "I do" at a wedding ceremony is to engage in an act for which the very idea of evidence is inapt. Once two people each say "I do" under appropriately specified circumstances, they are married by virtue of the saying, and nothing about that saying can be true or false. Just saying it makes it so. J. L. Austin, *How to Do Things with Words*, ed. J. O. Urmson and Marina Sbisà, 2nd ed. (Cambridge, MA: Harvard University Press, 1975).

11. See Nicholas Fandos, "Herrera Beutler Says McCarthy Told Her Trump Sided with Capitol Mob," *New York Times*, Feb. 13, 2021.

12. Maggie Haberman, "First Lady Stayed in N.Y.C. to Get New Deal, Book Says," *New York Times*, June 14, 2020, A29.

13. The hearsay rule retains considerable vitality in criminal cases as a result of the requirement in the Sixth Amendment that defendants have the opportunity to "confront" the witnesses against them. As a result, some out-of-court statements that might be admissible under some exception to the hearsay rule are excluded by application of the Sixth Amendment. The modern reinvigoration of this aspect of the confrontation clause began with Crawford v. Washington, 541 U.S. 36 (2004), and has generated considerable litigation and numerous Supreme Court decisions since.

14. The figure of thirty-one is derived by adding the twenty-three unqualified exceptions in Rule 803 to the six exceptions in Rule 804 that require that the maker of the original statement (declarant) be unavailable to the two in Rule 801 that are treated as not being hearsay at all even though they were so treated traditionally and historically.

15. See Frederick Schauer, "On the Supposed Jury-Dependence of Evidence Law," *University of Pennsylvania Law Review* 155 (2006): 165–202.

16. Were this an actual question in an actual court, or even if anything turned on it outside of a court hearing, there might well be reasons to doubt the article's message that Melania Trump does *not* speak French. For one thing, there is little reason to believe that either the book author or the *Times* reporter are sympathetic to the Trump family. As a result, their lack of sympathy might color their interpretations of what others have said. Moreover, the photographers might be French, and thus might embody the typical French attitude about the Francophone abilities of nonnative speakers who believe they speak French. Furthermore, there might be evidence inclining against the tenor of the *Times* article and the Jordan book. Even if the hearsay evidence of what the photographers believed is evidence against the proposition that she speaks French, other evidence might support that proposition. For example, someone from Slovenia, a country whose language is not widely spoken outside of its borders, and who operates professionally in international circles, as Ms. Trump did in her earlier years, is perhaps especially likely to have some competence in the major European languages. And although this statistical likelihood is hardly conclusive on the question of the linguistic abilities of a particular Slovene, it is still a piece of evidence for that conclusion.

17. Traditionally the example is of someone saying "I am Napoleon." Commonwealth v. Whitman, 901 N.E.2d 1206 (Mass. 2009); Edward W. Hinton, "States of Mind and the Hearsay Rule," *University of Chicago Law Review* 1 (1934): 394–423, at 397.

18. Austin, *How to Do Things with Words*, 5.

19. James Surowiecki, *The Wisdom of Crowds: Why the Many Are Smarter than the Few and How Collective Wisdom Shapes Business, Economics, Societies and Nations* (New York: Anchor Books, 2004).

20. The research inclining against the wisdom of crowds hypothesis includes Irving L. Janis, *Victims of Groupthink: A Psychological Study of Foreign-Policy Decisions and Fiascoes*, 2nd ed. (Boston: Wasdsworth, 1982); Norbert Kerr, Robert MacCoun, and Geoffrey P. Kramer, "Bias in Judgment: Comparing Individuals and Groups," *Psychological Review* 103 (1996): 687–719; Jan Lorenz, Heiko Rauhut, Frank Schweitzer, and Dirk Helbing, "How Social Influence Can Undermine the Wisdom of Crowds Effect," *Proceedings of the National Academy of Sciences* 108 (2011): 9020–9025; Garold Stasser and William Titus, "Pooling of Unshared Information in Group Decision Making: Biased Information Sampling during Discussion," *Journal of Personality and Social Psychology* 48 (1985): 1467–1478.

21. For overviews of the research, see Thomas W. Malone and Michael S. Bernstein, *Handbook of Collective Intelligence* (Cambridge, MA: Harvard University Press, 2015); Anita Williams Woolley, Ishani Aggarwal, and Thomas W. Malone, "Collective Intelligence and Group Performance," *Current Directions in Psychological Science* 24 (2015): 420–424.

22. Among many accounts including the quoted words, see Anne Gearan and Josh Dawsey, "Trump Issued a Call to Arms. Then He Urged His Followers to 'Remember This Day Forever,'" *Washington Post*, Jan. 6, 2021.

23. John Milton, *Areopagitica: A Speech for the Liberty of Unlicensed Printing, to the Parliament of England* (1644), in John Milton, *Prose Writings*, Everyman's Library (New York: Dutton, 1958).

24. John Stuart Mill, *On Liberty*, ed. David Spitz (New York: W. W. Norton, 1975) (orig. pub. 1859), chap. 2; Abrams v. United States, 250 U.S. 616, 630 (1919) (Holmes, J., dissenting). For illuminating background, see Thomas Healy, *The Great Dissent: How Oliver Wendell Holmes Changed His Mind—and Changed the History of Free Speech in America* (New York: Henry Holt, 2013).

25. Anthony Lewis, *Freedom for the Thought We Hate: A Biography of the First Amendment* (New York: Basic Book, 2007), as quoted in Timothy Garton Ash, *Free Speech: Ten Principles for a Connected World* (New Haven, CT: Yale University Press, 2016), 76.

26. See Christine Smallwood, "Astrology in the Age of Uncertainty," *New Yorker*, Oct. 28, 2019.

27. Of course there are genuine conspiracies. But the phrase "conspiracy theory," as commonly used, describes a false belief in the kind of conspiracy that explains a large amount of a set of behaviors, the unifying explanation satisfying some psychological need in the believer for much of what the believer dislikes all to be part of some master plan concocted by some evil force. See Karen M. Douglas,

Robbie M. Sutton, and Aleksandra Cichocka, "The Psychology of Conspiracy Theories," *Current Directions in Psychological Science* 26 (2017): 538–542. Why people have such beliefs is beyond the scope of this book, but what is relevant here is that a conspiracy theory is one way in which various psychological and sociological mechanisms may produce the acceptance of falsity despite evidence of its falsity.

28. For my own thoughts on this question—the explanatory force of the truth of a proposition in determining whether the proposition will be accepted, see Frederick Schauer, "Free Speech, the Search for Truth, and the Problem of Collective Knowledge," *SMU Law Review* 70 (2017): 231–252.

29. It would provide nice support for the skeptical point made here if it were true that lemmings follow each other to their death in an act of collective suicide. Alas, it is not, providing still another example of the fact that what "everyone knows" is often incorrect. See N. C. Stenseth and R. A. Ims, eds., *The Biology of Lemmings* (London: Academic Press, 1993).

30. See Federal Rule of Evidence 608(a); Michelson v. United States, 335 U.S. 469 (1948); Julia Simon-Kerr, "Credibility by Proxy," *George Washington Law Review* 85 (2017): 152–225, at 177–183.

Chapter 6. Testing Testimony

1. For a comprehensive comparative and historical study of the oath, see Helen Silving, "The Oath: I," *Yale Law Journal* 68 (1959): 1329–1390; and Silving, "The Oath: II," *Yale Law Journal* 68 (1959): 1552–1577. See also Nadine Farid, "Oath and Affirmation in the Court: Thoughts on the Power of a Sworn Promise," *New England Law Review* 40 (2006): 555–561; Ian Gallacher, "'Swear Not at All': Time to Abandon the Testimonial Oath," *New England Law Review* 52 (2018): 247–299.

2. On the difficulty and consequent rarity of criminal prosecutions for perjury, see, among many sources, Barbara A. Babcock, "Taking the Stand," *William and Mary Law Review* 35 (1993): 1–19, at 9; I. Bennett Capers, "Crime, Legitimacy, and Testilying," *Indiana Law Journal* 83 (2008): 835–880; Roberto Suro and Bill Miller, "Perjury: A Tough Case to Make," *Washington Post,* Sept. 24, 1998.

3. See Eugene Kiely, "Roger Stone's Crimes," at www.factcheck.org (Feb. 20, 2020).

4. Daniels Fund Ethics Initiative, "Martha Stewart's Insider Trading Scandal," at www.danielsethics.mgt.unm.edu (2011); Gerald Walpin, "Clinton's Future: Can He Polish His Image and Keep His License to Practice Law?," *Hofstra Law Review* 28 (1999): 473–491.

5. On exaggerating the probability of low-probability negative events, see Amos Tversky and Daniel Kahneman, "Judgment under Uncertainty: Heuristics and Biases," *Science* 185 (1974): 1124–1131; Tversky and Kahneman, "Advances in Prospect Theory: Cumulative Representation of Uncertainty," *Journal of Risk and Uncertainty* 5 (1992): 297–323. See also Daniel Kahneman, Paul Slovic, and Amos Tversky, eds., *Judgment under Uncertainty: Heuristics and Biases* (Cambridge: Cambridge University Press, 1982); Petko Kusev, Paul van Schaik, Pater Ayton, and John Dent,

"Exaggerated Risk: Prospect Theory and Probability Weighting in Risky Choice," *Journal of Experimental Psychology: Learning, Memory, and Cognition* 35 (2009): 1487–1505; W. J. Wouter Botzen, Howard Kunreuther, and Erwann Michel-Kerjan, "Divergence between Individual Perceptions and Objective Indicators of Tail Risks: Evidence from Floodplain Residents in New York City," *Judgment and Decision Making* 10 (2015): 365–385.

6. See Michael J. Saks and Barbara A. Spellman, *The Psychological Foundations of Evidence Law* (New York: NYU Press, 2016), 118–119.

7. For a similar categorization, see Stephen Mark Rosenbaum, Stephan Billinger, and Nils Stieglitz, "Let's Be Honest: A Review of Experimental Evidence of Honesty and Truth-Telling," *Journal of Economic Psychology* 45 (2014): 181–196.

8. See Nina Mazar, On Amir, and Dan Ariely, "The Dishonesty of Honest People: A Theory of Self-Concept Maintenance," *Journal of Marketing Research* 45 (2008): 633–644. But compare Bruno Verschuere et al., "Registered Replication Report on Mazar, Amir, and Ariely (2008)," *Advances in Methods and Practices in Psychological Science* 1 (2018): 299–317. More generally, see Dan Ariely, *The Honest Truth about Dishonesty: How We Lie to Everyone—Especially Ourselves* (New York: HarperCollins, 2012).

9. United States v. Turner, 558 F.2d 46, 50 (2d Cir. 1977); Mazar et al., "Dishonesty of Honest People."

10. In the wee hours of January 7, 2020, Democratic representative Conor Lamb of Pennsylvania provoked extraordinary and almost physical anger from some Republican colleagues for asserting that those colleagues had "lied" in alleging (or agreeing with others' allegations) that there was substantial evidence of fraud in the 2020 presidential election. The anger of these Republican colleagues was apparently based on Lamb's violation of a congressional norm against accusing one's colleagues of lying, a norm that might be understood as based on a further underlying norm, akin to an oath, against intentional falsity on the floor of the House. So Lamb stood accused of accusing others of violating the equivalent of an oath, and things went downhill from there. See Timothy Bella and Lasteshia Beachum (*Washington Post*), "'Sit Down!' 'No, You Sit Down!' Democrat's Speech Nearly Triggers Fistfight on House Floor," *Seattle Times*, Jan. 7, 2021.

11. The pledge quoted in the text is the one in force at the US Military Academy at West Point. The first college honor code was adopted by the College of William and Mary in 1736, but it, like most others these days apart from those of the military academies, does not contain an obligation, implicit or explicit, to report violators.

12. This observation is adapted from Antony Flew, who in commenting on the "Socratic method" of instruction widespread in the Socratic dialogues and in American law schools, observed that instructors "who have attempted to follow Socratic method will have been made aware of the importance of the fact that Plato was able to script the answers as well as the questions." Antony Flew, *A Dictionary of Philosophy* (New York: St. Martin's Press, 1979), 306.

13. John Henry Wigmore, *Evidence in Trials at Common Law,* rev. J. H. Chadbourn (Boston: Little, Brown, 1974), §1367, at 32.

14. And even Wigmore, just a few sentences later, added that a "skillful" cross-examiner may "make the truth appear like a falsehood."

15. The problem is (at least) twofold. First, a multipart question, typically coupled with a set of multipart assumptions and assertions, allows the responder to choose which questions to answer or which assumptions to accept and which to challenge, thus making evasion easier. And, second, the questioners at press conferences, unwilling to share their minute in the limelight, rarely ask follow-up questions to someone else's question. Good cross-examination is the art of the follow-up, making evasion more difficult. But if the questioners at press conferences refuse to build on previous questions by other questioners, and refuse to pressure the respondent at the podium to answer the question the responder is insistent on avoiding when the question happens to have come from someone else, the virtues of cross-examination, such as they are, are substantially diluted.

16. A classic work, still valuable, is Francis Lewis Welllman, *The Art of Cross-Examination,* 4th ed. (New York: Touchstone / Simon and Schuster, 1997) (orig. pub. 1903).

17. See Tom Lininger, "Bearing the Cross," *Fordham Law Review* 74 (2005): 1353–1423.

18. See Barbara A. Spellman and Elizabeth R. Tenney, "Credible Testimony in and out of Court," *Psychonomic Bulletin and Review* 17 (2010): 168–173.

19. It is often believed that British university hiring committees do this with letters of recommendation coming from Americans.

20. On calibration in law generally, see Frederick Schauer and Barbara A. Spellman, "Calibrating Legal Judgments," *Journal of Legal Analysis* 9 (2017): 125–151. Because courts reviewing the decisions of administrative agencies, and appellate courts reviewing the decisions of lower courts, might benefit from calibrating the decisions of the decision makers below in just this way, it would seem useful for the practice of calibration to have more of a presence in law than it actually does. Officially, such calibration is rarely available, and we do not see appellate judges explicitly scrutinizing more carefully the decisions of trial judges they know to make mistakes or who are known to have biases of one sort or another. But unofficially, such calibration is more common than most reviewing courts or other institutions are willing to admit.

21. See Alfred Avins, "The Right to Be a Witness and the Fourteenth Amendment," *Missouri Law Review* 31 (1966): 471–504; Bennett Capers, "Evidence without Rules," *Notre Dame Law Review* 94 (2019): 867–908; Gabriel J. Chin, "'Chinaman's Chance' in Court: Asian Pacific Americans and Racial Rules of Evidence," *U.C. Irvine Law Review* 3 (2013): 965–990; Sheri Lynn Johnson, "The Color of Truth: Race and the Assessment of Credibility," *Michigan Journal of Race and Law* 1 (1996): 261–346.

22. Jasmine B. Gonzalez Rose, "Toward a Critical Race Theory of Evidence," *Minnesota Law Review* 101 (2017): 2243–2308.

23. Miranda Fricker, *Epistemic Injustice: Power and the Ethics of Knowledge* (Oxford: Oxford University Press, 2007). For elaboration of Fricker's ideas, see Rae Langton,

Review [of Fricker], *Hypatia* 25 (2010): 459–464; Federico Luzzi, "Testimonial Injustice without Credibility Deficit (or Excess)," *Thought* 5 (2016): 203–211; Wade Munroe, "Testimonial Injustice and Prescriptive Credibility Deficits," *Canadian Journal of Philosophy* 46 (2016): 924–947.

24. So too for credibility enhancements, or boosts. In the United States, it rarely hurts one's credibility to have a British accent, and in the United Kingdom, as Professor Henry Higgins reminded us in *My Fair Lady,* regional or class accents can greatly influence a person's credibility and much else.

25. See E. Paige Lloyd, Kurt Hugenberg, Allen R. McConnell, Jonathan W. Kuntsman, and Jason C. Deska, "Black and White Lies: Race-Based Biases in Deception Judgments," *Psychological Science* 28 (2017): 1125–1136.

26. See the reports described in Catharine A. MacKinnon, "Reflections on Sex Equality under Law," *Yale Law Journal* 100 (1991): 1281–1328, at 1306n115.

27. John Henry Wigmore, *The Principles of Judicial Proof,* 2nd ed. (Boston: Little, Brown,1931), chap. 19, at 334, "updating" Wigmore's *The Principles of Judicial Proof, as Given by Logic, Psychology and General Experience and Illustrated in Judicial Trials* (Boston: Little, Brown, 1913), and as quoted and discussed in William Twining, *Theories of Evidence: Bentham and Wigmore* (London: Weidenfeld and Nicolson, 1985), at 138–139.

28. California Jury Instructions, Crim. No. 10.22 (3rd ed., 1970), as quoted and finally rejected in People v. Rincon-Pineda, 538 P.2d 247, 252 (Ca. 1975).

29. Casenote, *Fordham Urban Law Journal* 4 (1976): 419–430. Wigmore had views about the credibility of rape victims as well, favorably quoting Dr. Karl Menninger to the effect that the "psychic complexes" and "probably universal" "fantasies of being raped" of women and young girls led them to "contrive[e] false charges of sexual offenses by men." Wigmore, *Principles of Judicial Proof,* as quoted in Richard O. Lempert et al., *A Modern Approach to Evidence: Text, Problems, Transcripts and Cases,* 5th ed. (St. Paul, MN: West Academic, 2014), at 480.

30. Fricker, *Epistemic Injustice;* Ian James Kidd, José Medina, and Gaile Pohlhaus Jr., eds., *Routledge Handbook of Epistemic Injustice* (London: Routledge, 2017); Morten Fibieger Byskov, "What Makes Epistemic Injustice an 'Injustice'?," *Journal of Social Philosophy* 50 (2020): 1–18; David Coady, "Two Concept of Epistemic Injustice," *Episteme* 7 (2020): 101–113.

31. And thus some statistically nonspurious generalizations may still properly be rejected for use on moral or political grounds. Frederick Schauer, *Profiles, Probabilities, and Stereotypes* (Cambridge, MA: Harvard University Press, 2003).

32. See Selene Cansino et al., "The Rate of Source Memory Decline across the Adult Life Span," *Developmental Psychology* 49 (2013): 973–985; Trey Hedden and John D. E. Gabrieli, "Insights into the Aging Mind: A View from Cognitive Neuroscience," *Nature Reviews Neuroscience* 5 (2004): 87–96; Scott A. Small, "Age-Related Memory Decline: Current Concepts and Future Directions," *Archives of Neurology* 58 (2001): 360–364.

33. Federal Rule of Evidence 608 allows witnesses to testify as to their opinion of another witness's honesty, and as to another witness's reputation for honesty. And

Federal Rule of Evidence 609 allows evidence of the prior criminal convictions of a witness to be used to attack the credibility—to "impeach"—that witness. The empirical basis for this form of calibration is, to put it mildly, not well established, but it is nevertheless a long-standing feature of most common-law legal systems. See Andrea R. Spirn, "The Place for Prior Conviction Evidence in Civil Actions," *Columbia Law Review* 86 (1986): 1267–1282; Roger C. Park, "Impeachment with Evidence of Prior Convictions," *Southwestern University Law Review* 36 (2008): 793–817.

Chapter 7. Of Lies and Liars

1. A current version of the rule is Federal Rule of Evidence 803(2). For history and critique of the rule (as well as the related exception for "present sense impressions") in both its current and traditional versions, see Steven Baicker-McKee, "The Excited Utterance Paradox," *Seattle University Law Review* 41 (2017): 111–178; Aviva Orenstein, "'My God!': A Feminist Critique of the Excited Utterance Exception to the Hearsay Rule," *California Law Review* 85 (1997): 159–223; Jon Waltz, "The Present Sense Impression Exception to the Rule against Hearsay: Origins and Attributes," *Iowa Law Review* 66 (1981): 869–898.

2. See Michael J. Saks and Barbara A. Spellman, *The Psychological Foundations of Evidence Law* (New York: NYU Press, 2016), 192–196.

3. A now-canonical work is Sissela Bok, *Lying: Moral Choice in Public and Private Life* (New York: Vintage Books, 1978). More recently, see Brooke Harrington, ed., *Deception: From Ancient Empires to Internet Dating* (Stanford, CA: Stanford University Press, 2009); Seana Valentine Shiffrin, *Speech Matters: On Lying, Morality, and the Law* (Princeton, NJ: Princeton University Press, 2014); Cass R. Sunstein, *Liars: Falsehoods and Free Speech in an Age of Deception* (New York: Oxford University Press, 2021); Christine Korsgaard, "The Right to Lie: Kant on Dealing with Evil," *Philosophy and Public Affairs* 15 (1986): 325–349.

4. George Fisher, "The Jury's Rise as a Lie Detector," *Yale Law Journal* 107 (1997): 575–711, at 624–625.

5. Kenneth S. Abraham, "The Common Law Prohibition on Party Testimony and the Development of Tort Liability," *Virginia Law Review* 95 (2009): 489–515; John H. Langbein, "Historical Foundations of the Law of Evidence: A View from the Ryder Sources," *Columbia Law Review* 96 (1996): 1168–1202, at 1184–1186.

6. For Shiffrin (*Speech Matters*, 12), a lie is "an intentional assertion of A to B of a proposition P such that
   1. A does not believe P, and
   2. A is aware that A does not believe P, and
   3. A intentionally presents P in a manner or context that objectively manifests an intention that B is to take and treat P as an accurate representation of A's belief."

7. Donald Trump has taken, and even out of office is still taking, presidential lying to new heights, but it is worth remembering that it was Democratic senator Bob

Kerrey who observed that then-president Bill Clinton was an "unusually good liar." And that was even before most of the details about Jennifer Flowers, Paula Jones, Monica Lewinsky, and others became public. See Stephen Chapman, "Bill Clinton and the Boy Who Cried Wolf," *Chicago Tribune,* Jan. 25, 1998.

8. See Caroline Kitchener and Matt Thompson, "A Journalist's Guide to Presidential Lying," *Columbia Journalism Review,* June 6, 2018; James Fallows, "How to Deal with the Lies of Donald Trump: Guidelines for the Media," *The Atlantic,* Nov. 28, 2016; Matthew Ingram, "When Should Journalists Use the 'L' Word?," *Fortune,* Jan. 26, 2017; Pete Vernon, "Lie? Falsehood? What to Call the President's Words," *Columbia Journalism Review,* May 29, 2018; Gary Weiss, "Calling Trump a Liar Sets a Thorny Precedent," *Columbia Journalism Review,* Nov. 1, 2016.

9. Regarding the false claim to have been awarded the Medal of Honor: United States v. Alvarez, 567 U.S. 709 (2012), holds exactly such a statement to be protected by the First Amendment.

10. Yes, there is such a product. See Terry Dunkle, "Slim Slippers: A Precautionary Tale," at www.quackwatch.com (2002). And no, they do not work. Nor do diet earrings and diet soap, the latter allegedly washing off the fat. See Federal Trade Commission, Deception in Weight Loss Advertising Workshop, at www.ftc.gov/bcp/workshops/weightloss/transcripts/transscript-full.pdf (2002).

11. See Cameron McWhirter and Lindsay Wise, "Trump Pressured Georgia Secretary of State to 'Find' Votes," *Wall Street Journal,* Jan. 4, 2021.

12. 52 U.S.C. § 20511 (2018). See Eric Lipton, "Trump Call to Georgia Official Might Violate State and Federal Law," *New York Times,* Jan. 3, 2021.

13. See Frederick Schauer and Richard Zeckhauser, "Paltering," in Harrington, *Deception,* 38–54.

14. For the full and fascinating history, see Jill Lepore, *The Secret History of Wonder Woman* (New York: Knopf, 2014).

15. 293 F. 1013 (D.C. Cir. 1923).

16. See David Faigman et al., *Modern Scientific Evidence: The Law and Science of Expert Testimony* (St. Paul, MN: Thomson West, 2020), §§ 1:2–1:6.

17. See Ken Alder, *The Lie Detectors: The History of an American Obsession* (New York: Free Press, 2007); Kerry Segrave, *Lie Detectors: A Social History* (Jefferson, NC: McFarland, 2003); Allison Marsh, "A Brief History of the Lie Detector," *IEEE Spectrum,* August 2019; Philip Reichert and Louis F. Bishop Jr., "Sir James MacKenzie and His Polygraph: The Contributions of Louis Faugeres Bishop, Sr.," *American Journal of Cardiology* 24 (1969): 401–403; Paul V. Trovillo, "A History of Lie Detection," *Journal of Criminal Law and Criminology* 29 (1939): 848–881, and 30 (1939): 104–119.

18. See Don Grubin and Lars Mardin, "Lie Detection and the Polygraph: A Historical Review," *Journal of Forensic Psychiatry and Psychology* 16 (2005): 357–369; Martina Vicianova, "Historical Techniques of Lie-Detection," *European Journal of Psychology* 11 (2015): 522–534.

19. See Samatha Mann, Aldert Vrij, and Ray Bull, "Detecting True Lies: Police Officers' Ability to Detect Suspects' Lies," *Journal of Applied Psychology* 89 (2004): 137–

149; Miron Zuckerman, Richard Koestner, and Robert Drover, "Beliefs about Cues Associated with Deception," *Journal of Nonverbal Behavior* 6 (1981): 105–114.

20. See Bella M. DePaulo et al., "Cues to Deception," *Psychological Bulletin* 129 (2003): 74–118. See also DePaulo, *The Psychology of Lying and Detecting Lies* (Summerland, CA: Bella DePaulo, 2018); DePaulo, *The How and Whys of Lies* (Summerland, CA: Bella DePaulo, 2010); Charles F. Bond Jr. and Bella DePaulo, *Is Anyone Really Good at Detecting Lies? Professional Papers* (Summerland, CA: Bella DePaulo, 2011).

21. See Gary D. Bond, "Deception Detection Expertise," *Law and Human Behavior* 32 (2008): 339–351; Peter J. DePaulo and Bella M. DePaulo, "Can Deception by Salespersons and Customers Be Detected through Nonverbal Behavioral Cues?," *Journal of Applied Social Psychology* 19 (1989): 1552–1577. The use of multiple cues appears to help slightly, but even then the accuracy of lie detection by human observers is far less than commonly believed. Maria Hartwig and Charles F. Bond Jr., "Lie Detection from Multiple Cues: A Meta-Analysis," *Applied Cognitive Psychology* 28 (2014): 661–676.

22. See Karl Ask, Sofia Calderon, and Erik Mac Giolla, "Human Lie-Detection Performance: Does Random Assignment versus Self-Selection of Liars and Truth-Tellers Matter?," *Journal of Applied Research in Memory and Cognition* 9 (2020): 128–136; Tim Brennen and Svein Magnussen, "Research on Non-Verbal Signs of Lies and Deceit: A Blind Alley," *Frontiers in Psychology* 11 (2020); Maria Hartwig and Charles F. Bond Jr., "Why Do Lie-Catchers Fail? A Lens Model Meta-Analysis of Human Lie Judgments," *Psychological Bulletin* 137 (2011): 643–659.

23. For examples, see United States v. Sanchez, 118 F.3d 192, 197 (4th Cir. 1997); United States v. Nelson, 217 Fed. App'x 291 (4th Cir. 2006); State v. Jones, 753 N.W.2d 677, 690 (Minn. 2008); State v. Domicz, 907 A.2d 395 (N.J. 2006). Things are changing, albeit slowly. New Mexico now generally permits the use of lie-detection results in court (New Mexico Rule of Evidence 11-707; State v. Dorsey, 539 P.2d 204 (N.M. 1975), and some state and federal courts have eliminated the traditional blanket exclusion of polygraph evidence in favor of a more flexible approach that takes into account, among other factors, the proficiency of the examiner, the reliability of the particular device or method used, and the use to which the evidence is being put. See United States v. Benavidez-Benavidez, 217 F.3d 720 (9th Cir. 2000); State v. Porter, 698 A.2d 739, 769 (Conn. 1997); Commonwealth v. Duguay, 720 N.E.2d 458 (Mass. 1999). And see also United States v. Semrau, 693 F.3d 510 (6th Cir. 2012), rejecting defendant's attempt to use fMRI (brain scan) evidence to establish lack of criminal intent.

24. United States v. Scheffer, 523 U.S. 303, 313 (1998), quoting United States v. Barnard, 490 F.2d 907, 912 (9th Cir. 1974); Fisher, "The Jury's Rise as a Lie Detector." The *Scheffer* decision held that a defendant had no constitutional right to present polygraph evidence in his own defense but said nothing about whether using such evidence was permissible as a matter of nonconstitutional evidence law.

25. See National Research Council, *The Polygraph and Lie-Detection* (Washington, DC: US Government Printing Office, 2003); Madeleine Baran and Jennifer Vogel,

"Inconclusive: The Truth about Lie Detector Tests," *APM Reports*, Sep. 20, 2016, at www.apmreports.org; M. Raheel Bhutta, Melissa J. Hong, Yun-Hee Kim, and Keum-Shik Hing, "Single-Trial Lie Detection Using a Combined fNIRS-Polygraph System," *Frontiers in Psychology* (2015); John C. Kircher, Steven W. Horowitz, and David C. Raskin, "Meta-Analysis of Mock Crime Studies of the Control Question Polygraph Technique," *Law and Human Behavior* 12 (1988): 79–90; Ionnis Pavlidis, Norman Eberhardt, and James A. Levine, "Seeing Through the Face of Deception," *Nature* 415 (2002): 35; Runxin Yu et al., "Using Polygraph to Detect Passengers Carrying Illegal Items," *Frontiers in Psychology* (2019).

26. For descriptions of these various techniques, with references, see Frederick Schauer, "Lie-Detection, Neuroscience, and the Law of Evidence," in *Philosophical Foundations of Law and Neuroscience,* ed. Dennis Patterson and Michael S. Pardo (Oxford: Oxford University Press, 2016), 85–104.

27. Sebastian Bedoya-Echeverry et al., "Detection of Lies by Facial Thermal Imagery Analysis," *Revista Facultad de Inginiera* 26 (2017), http:/dx.doi.org/10.19053/01211129.v.26.v44.2017.5771; Maria Serena Panasiti et al., "Thermal Signatures of Voluntary Deception in Ecological Conditions," *Nature Science Reports* 6 (2016), art. 35174 (Oct. 13, 2016).

28. Xiao Pan Ding, Xiaoqing Gao, Genyue Fu, and Kang Lee, "Neural Correlates of Spontaneous Deception: A Functional Near Infrared Spectroscopy (fNIRD) Study," *Neuropsychologia* 51 (2013): 704–712; Febghua Tian, Vikrant Sharma, Frank Andrew Kozel, and Hanli Liu, "Functional Near Infrared Spectroscopy to Investigate Hemodynamic Responses in the Prefrontal Cortex," *Brain Research* 1303 (2009): 120–130.

29. Marzieh Daneshi Kohan, Ali Motie Nasrabadi, and Mohammad Bagher Shamsollahi, "Interview Based Connectivity Analysis of EEG in Order to Detect Deception," *Medical Hypotheses* 136 (2020), art. 109517; J. Peter Rosenfeld, "P300 in Detecting Concealed Information and Deception: A Review," *Psychophysiology* 57 (March 11, 2019), art. E13362.

30. See, among many sources, Qian Cui et al., "Detection of Deception Based on fMRI Activation Patterns Underlying the Production of a Deceptive Response and Receiving Feedback about the Success of the Deception after a Mock Murder Crime," *Social Cognitive and Affective Neuroscience* 9 (2014): 1472–1480; Daniel D. Langleben et al., "Polygraphy and Functional Magnetic Resonance Imaging in Lie Detection," *Journal of Clinical Psychiatry* 77 (2016): 1372–1380. A balanced critique and overview is Martha J. Farah,. J. Benjamin Hutchinson, Elizabeth A. Phelps, and Anthony D. Wagner, "Function MRI-Based Lie Detection: Scientific and Social Challenges," *Nature Reviews Neuroscience* 15 (2014): 312–319.

31. For an overview of the skepticism, and for my own skepticism about the skepticism, see Schauer, "Lie-Detection, Neuroscience"; Frederick Schauer, "Neuroscience, Lie-Detection, and the Law: A Contrarian View," *Trends in Cognitive Science* 14 (2010): 101–103; Schauer, "Can Bad Science Be Good Evidence? Neuroscience, Lie-Detection, and Beyond," *Cornell Law Review* 95 (2010): 1191–1220.

32. Indeed, use by a defendant in an attempt to raise a reasonable doubt was the original proposed (and rejected) use in the *Frye* case, and was the proposed (and rejected) use in the Supreme Court's *Scheffer* decision.

33. Deena Skolnick Weisberg et al., "The Seductive Allure of Neuroscience Explanations," *Journal of Cognitive Neuroscience* 20 (2008): 470–477; Martha J. Farah and Cayce J. Hook, "The Seductive Allure of 'Seductive Allure,'" *Perspectives on Psychological Science* 8 (2013): 88–90; Cayce Hook and Martha J. Farah, "Look Again: Effects of Brain Images and Mind-Brain Dualism on Lay Evaluations of Research," *Journal of Cognitive Neuroscience* 25 (2013): 1397–1405. Subsequent research has clarified that neuroscience *information* may be irrationally influential, but that nothing about the visual and seemingly photographic presentation of that information contributes to the effect. Diego Fernandez-Duque, Jessica Evans, Colton Christian, and Sara D. Hughes, "Superfluous Neuroscience Information Makes Explanations of Psychological Phenomena More Appealing," *Journal of Cognitive Neuroscience* 27 (2015): 926–944.

34. 29 U.S.C. §§ 2001 et seq. (2018).

35. Katie Galioto, "Justin Fairfax Releases Polygraph Test as He Fights Back against Accusers," *Politico,* Apr. 3, 2019.

36. John Walsh, "Here Is the Polygraph Test Christine Blasey Ford Took Following Her Sexual Assault Accusation against Brett Kavanaugh," *Business Insider,* Sept. 26, 2018.

37. www.converus.com.

38. www.discernscience.com. For description and critique of these and other recent developments, see Jake Bittle, "Lie Detectors Have Always Been Suspect. AI Has Made the Problem Worse," *APM Reports,* Sept. 20, 2016.

Chapter 8. Can We Believe Our Eyes and Ears?

1. The issue here is not the reliability, for any of the senses, of the sensation itself. It is of the reliability of sensation as evidence for what is sensed. If someone reports that they smelled rotten eggs, the question is not whether their smelling sensation is what they have reported, but whether that sensation was caused by actual rotten eggs, or, as is likely, by leaking natural gas.

2. See Thomas D. Albright, "Why Eyewitnesses Fail," *Proceedings of the National Academy of Sciences* 114 (2017): 7758–7764; Neil Brewer and Gary L. Wells, "Eyewitness Identification," *Current Directions in Psychological Science* 20 (2011): 24–27; Steven E. Clark, "Costs and Benefits of Eyewitness Identification Reform," *Perspectives on Psychological Science* 7 (2012): 238–259; Steven E. Clark and Ryan D. Godfrey, "Eyewitness Identification and Innocence Risk," *Psychonomic Bulletin and Review* 16 (2009): 22–42; Gary L. Wells, Amina Memon, and Steven D. Penrod, "Eyewitness Evidence: Improving Its Probative Value," *Psychological Science in the Public Interest* 7 (2006): 45–75; Gary L. Wells et al., "Policy and Procedure Recommendations for the Collection and Preservation of Eyewitness Identification Evidence,"

Law and Human Behavior 44 (2020): 3–36; John Wixted and Gary L. Wells, "The Relationship between Eyewitness Confidence and Eyewitness Accuracy: A New Synthesis," *Psychological Science in the Public Interest* 18 (2017): 10–65.

3. The law often calls this "factual innocence." Many wrongful convictions are wrongful because of the denial of a defendant's procedural rights—for example, the right to have an effective lawyer, to have illegally obtained evidence suppressed, to confront opposing witnesses, and to have a properly instructed jury. Convictions obtained when such rights have been violated are legally wrong and properly overturned, too often too late, but overturning convictions on those grounds says little about whether the defendant actually committed the deed that produced the conviction. By contrast, other overturnings—exonerations in a narrower sense—are based on witness recantation, subsequently uncovered evidence, someone else confessing to the crime that the defendant is alleged to have committed, and various other grounds for a post-conviction belief that the defendant simply did not do it. This latter basis for exoneration—factual innocence—is the principal concern here.

4. See especially C. J. Brainerd and V. F. Reyna, *The Science of False Memory* (New York: Oxford University Press, 2005); Elizabeth F. Loftus, *Eyewitness Testimony* (Cambridge, MA: Harvard University Press, 1979); Loftus, "Planting Misinformation in the Human Mind: A 30-Year Investigation of the Malleability of Memory," *Learning and Memory* 12 (2005): 361–366; Daniel L. Schachter, *The Seven Sins of Memory: How the Mind Forgets and Remembers* (Boston: Houghton Mifflin, 2001).

5. For a valuable philosophical analysis of such manipulation, see Jennifer Lackey, "Eyewitness Testimony and Epistemic Agency," *Noûs* (June 11, 2021).

6. State v. Henderson, 27 A.3d 872 (N.J. 2011); Elizabeth F. Loftus, "Eyewitness Science and the Legal System," *Annual Review of Law and Social Science* 14 (2018): 1–10.

7. The expression "with their own eyes" is common, but how someone could actually see something with someone else's eyes is not entirely clear. Presumably the expression is designed to distinguish the first-person observation from hearsay—what someone has heard someone else report.

8. A sampling of the extensive research includes Brainerd and Reyna, *Science of False Memory;* Daniel L. Schachter, *Seven Sins of Memory;* Michael C. Anderson and Barbara A. Spellman, "On the Status of Inhibitory Mechanisms in Cognition: Memory Retrieval as a Model Case," *Psychological Review* 102 (1995): 68–100; David A. Gallo, "False Memories and Fantastic Beliefs: 15 Years of the DRM Illusion," *Memory and Cognition* 38 (2010): 833–848; Simona Ghetti, "Memory for Nonoccurrences: The Role of Metacognition," *Journal of Memory and Language* 48 (2003): 722–739; Henry L. Roediger III, "Memory Illusions," *Memory and Language* 35 (1996): 76–100; Daniel L. Schachter and Scott D. Slotnick, "The Cognitive Neuroscience of Memory Distortion," *Neuron* 44 (2004): 149–160.

9. Clark, "Costs and Benefits," unconventionally, controversially, but wisely emphasizes the costs (in terms of an increase in the number of mistaken acquittals) as well as benefits of eyewitness identification reform. And see also the work of Larry

Laudan, who has repeatedly focused attention on how the devices of the criminal law—especially, in his view, the requirement of proof beyond a reasonable doubt—produce errors of false acquittal, possibly in greater numbers than is generally assumed. Larry Laudan, *Truth, Error, and the Criminal Law: An Essay in Legal Epistemology* (Cambridge: Cambridge University Press, 2006); Laudan, "The Rules of Trial, Political Morality, and the Costs of Error," *Oxford Studies in the Philosophy of Law* 1 (2011): 195–227; Laudan, "Is Reasonable Doubt Reasonable?," *Legal Theory* 9 (2003): 295–331. For a challenge to Laudan's empirical claims, see Diego del Vecchi, "Laudan's Error: Reasonable Doubt and Acquittals of Guilty People," *International Journal of Evidence and Proof* 24 (2020): 211–232.

10. A rich philosophical literature, largely from a feminist perspective, goes by the name of "standpoint epistemology." A valuable overview is Elizabeth Anderson, "Feminist Epistemology and the Philosophy of Science," *Stanford Encyclopedia of Philosophy*, https://plato.stanford.edu/archives/spr2020/entries/feminist-epistemology/ (2020). But we must distinguish three claims, one I embrace and two I resist. The claim I embrace, one falling under the heading of epistemic injustice, is that we have long ignored or discounted the accounts of marginalized groups, including women, racial and ethnic and religious minorities, and those with less traditional sexual orientations and identities. By ignoring those accounts, we make epistemic and evidentiary mistakes as well as perpetuate injustice generally. But two other claims are more controversial. One is that the perspective of the victim is better evidence because of that perspective. But here it depends on the question. Obviously a person denied a job because of her race or gender knows what that feels like in ways that no one else can. But if the question is about what happened, and not how it felt, what the victim knows is not necessarily better evidence than what the perpetrator knows. And most controversial of all is the claim that it is perspective all the way down, with the existence of multiple perspectives proving that there is no fact of the matter. Throughout this book I obviously resist this claim, but explaining why would take a book in itself.

11. Susan Sontag, *On Photography* (New York: Dell, 1973).

12. I am grateful to Bob Allison, Kevin Cullen, Larry DiCara, and Shaun O'Connell for sharing their recollections with me and correcting mine. The election itself is the subject of a still-important book by Murray B Levin, *The Alienated Voter: Politics in Boston* (New York: Holt, Rinehart and Winston, 1960).

13. Kendall Walton, "Transparent Pictures: On the Nature of Photographic Realism," *Critical Inquiry* 11 (1984): 246–277. And see also the discussion in Michael Morris, *Real Likenesses: Representation in Paintings, Photographs, and Novels* (Oxford: Oxford University Press, 2020).

14. Bhadra Sharma and Sameer Yasir, "Nepal Seeks to Ban 2 Climbers It Says Faked Everest Summit," *New York Times*, Feb. 1, 2021, A8.

15. The examples in the text are selected because Goya's *Disasters of War* and Manet's *Execution of Emperor Maximilian* are two of the most revered nonphotographic visual works about war of the nineteenth century, and of all time.

16. Simon Brann Thorpe, *Toy Soldiers* (London: Dewi Lewis, 2015). To be sure, Thorpe was making a point about war as well as about photography.
17. Among thousands of examples, see Kleveland v. United States, 345 F.2d 134 (2d. Cir. 1965); Moore v. Leaseway Transport Corp., 402 N.E.2d 1160 (N.Y. 1980).
18. United States v. Lubich, 2013 WL186675 (Ct. Mil. App. Armed Forces, May 3, 2013); Fisher v. State, 643 S.W.2d 571 (Ark. 1982).
19. On so-called Day in the Life videos, typically used to depict an injured person's life before the litigation-prompting accident, see Dempster v. Lamorak Insurance Co., 2020 WL5665172 (E.D. La., Sep. 23, 2020); Families Advocate. LLC v. Sanford Clinic North, 2019 WL10943310 (D.N. Dak., June 12, 2019).
20. In reality, Daguerre was preceded by the his countryman Joseph Nicéphore Niépce and the Englishman Thomas Wedgwood, but Daguerre's is the name that most endures. See Beaumont Newhall, *The History of Photography* (New York: Museum of Modern Art; Boston: Little, Brown, 1982), 13–26.

Chapter 9. Of Experts and Expertise

1. Conventionally, I date the transformation to all of the nominations subsequent to those of Judge Robert Bork in 1987.
2. See John Schwartz and Hiroko Tabuchi, "By Calling Climate Change 'Controversial,' Barrett Created Controversy," *New York Times,* Oct. 15, 2020 (updated Oct. 22, 2020), at https://www.nytimes.com/2020/10/15/climate/amy-coney-barrett-climate-change.html.
3. See Susan Haack, "Federal Philosophy of Science: A Deconstruction—and a Reconstruction," *NYU Journal of Law and Liberty* 5 (2010): 394–435; Haack, *Evidence Matters: Science, Proof, and Truth in the Law* (Cambridge: Cambridge University Press, 2014), 122–155.
4. A thorough examination of the problem of nonexpert evaluation of expertise is Scott Brewer, "Expert Testimony and Intellectual Due Process," *Yale Law Journal* 107 (1998): 1535–1681, esp. 1616–1647. In the philosophical literature, see Alvin I. Goldman, "Experts: Which Ones Should You Trust?," *Philosophy and Phenomenological Research* 63 (2001): 85–110; John Hardwig, "Epistemic Dependence," *Journal of Philosophy* 82 (1985): 335–349. Hardwig's influential article argues that to make a decision based on the knowledge or expertise of others is to make a decision without evidence, a conclusion with which I (and Goldman) disagree. Only by starting with the assumption that little other than first-person perception can qualify as evidence can we reject the testimony of others (including the testimony of experts) as evidence, an assumption that much of this book is committed to resisting.
5. On this problem in the context of the use or non-use of expertise by appellate judges, see Frederick Schauer, "The Dilemma of Ignorance: PGA Tour, Inc. v. Casey Martin," *Supreme Court Review 2001* (2002): 267–297.
6. The example is real, being an abbreviated reference to the case of Daryl Bem, a well-credentialed Cornell University social psychologist whose research on extra-

sensory perception (ESP) is commonly thought to have triggered the methodological concerns and debates in the field that are often described as the "replication crisis." For an overview, see Daniel Engber, "Daryl Bem Proves ESP Is Real," *Slate*, June 7, 2017. For a more detailed account and explanation, see Barbara A. Spellman, "A Short (Personal) Future History of Revolution 2.0," *Perspectives on Psychological Science* 10 (2015): 886–899.

7. See Roger Cooter, *The Cultural Meaning of Popular Science: Phrenology and the Organization of Consent in Nineteenth-Century Britain* (Cambridge: Cambridge University Press, 1984); John van Wyhe, *Phrenology and the Origins of Victorian Scientific Naturalism* (Burlington, VT: Ashgate, 2004); Minna Scherlinder Morse, "Facing a Bumpy History," *Smithsonian*, Oct. 1997; Pierre Schlag, "Law and Phrenology," *Harvard Law Review* 110 (1997): 877–921.

8. See the methodologically rigorous debunking of phrenology's main claims in Parker Jones, F. Alfaro-Almagro, and S. Jbabdi, "An Empirical 21st Century Evaluation of Phrenology," *Cortex* 106 (2018): 26–35.

9. Frighteningly, roughly 30 percent of the American people. See Sabrina Stierwalt, "Is Astrology Real? Here's What Science Says," *Scientific American*, June 25, 2020.

10. On the lack of scientific basis for astrology, see Alexander Boxer, *A Scheme of Heaven: The History of Astrology and the Search for Our Destiny* (New York: W. W. Norton, 2020); Richard A. Crowe, "Astrology and the Scientific Method," *Psychological Reports* 67 (1990): 163–191; I. W. Kelly, "Astrology and Science: A Critical Examination," *Psychological Reports* 44 (1979): 1231–1240; Jayant V. Narlikar, Sudhakar Kunte, Navendra Dabholkar, and Prakash Ghatpande, "A Statistical Test of Astrology," *Current Science* 96 (2009): 641–643; Bernie I. Silverman, "Studies of Astrology," *Journal of Psychology* 77 (1971): 141–149; G. A. Tyson, "An Empirical Test of the Astrological Theory of Personality," *Personality and Individual Differences* 5 (1984): 247–250. A quirky, seeming counterexample is provided by the so-called relative age effect. In youth sports, the age at which you begin, or the league in which you are placed, varies with birth month. So children born in, say, December, are placed with those who are generally younger, and those born in January are placed with those generally older. And because it turns out that when you start, and the level at which you start, is predictive of future athletic success, birth month is predictive of athletic success. And, of course, astrological sign is, for most days of the month, coincident with birth month. The conclusion, therefore, is that astrological sign is predictive of athletic success. Vittoria Addona and Philip A. Yates, "A Closer Look at the Relative Age Effect in the National Hockey League," *Journal of Quantitative Analysis of Sports* 6 (2010): 1017; William Hurley, Dan Lior, and Steven Tracze, "A Proposal to Reduce the Age Discrimination in Canadian Minor Hockey," *Canadian Public Policy* 27 (2001): 65–75. And on the relative age effect in educational achievement, see Joshua Angrist and Alan Krueger, "Does Compulsory School Attendance Affect Schooling and Earning?," *Quarterly Journal of Economics* 106 (1991): 979–1014.

11. See Federal Rules of Evidence 703, 704, 705; Christopher B. Mueller and Laird C. Kirkpatrick, *Evidence*, 4th ed. (New York: Aspen, 2009), §§ 7.8–7.13.

12. For a skeptical take on the view that expert evidence must meet a higher standard of reliability in order to be admitted as evidence in civil or criminal trials, see Frederick Schauer and Barbara A. Spellman, "Is Expert Evidence Really Different?," *Notre Dame Law Review* 88 (2013): 1–26. The bases for the skepticism, as argued there, are two. One is that the traditional view is premised on the worry that jurors, and perhaps even judges, will be so impressed by experts that their testimony will be given more weight than it intrinsically deserves. But research on jury evaluation of expert evidence indicates that this long-held assumption might not be true. Second, a corollary of the first and consistent with a running theme of this book, is that relatively weak expert evidence may still have some evidentiary value. If the worry about expert evidence being given too much evidentiary value is not supported by the relevant research, then there seems little reason to discard expert evidence when its evidentiary—probative—value is no less than the evidentiary value of the various other forms of inconclusive evidence that are routinely admitted.

13. Frye v. United States, 293 F. 1013 (D.C. Cir. 1923).

14. See Editors of Lingua Franca, *The Sokal Hoax: The Sham That Shook the Academy* (Lincoln: University of Nebraska Press, 2000).

15. Daubert v. Merrell Dow Pharmaceuticals, Inc., 509 U.S. 579 (1993). *Daubert,* along with Kumho Tire Co. v. Carmichael, 526 U.S. 137 (1999), and General Electric Co. v. Joiner, 522 U.S. 136 (1997), still represent the last word (from the Supreme Court) on the question.

16. See Shannon Hall, "Exxon Knew about Climate Change Almost 40 Years Ago," *Scientific American,* Oct. 26, 2015; Maxine Joselow, "GM, Ford Knew about Climate Change 50 Years Ago," *E and E News,* Oct. 26, 2020, at www.eenews.net. On the politics and incentives of climate change denial more generally, see, among hundreds of sources, Riley E. Dunlap, "Climate Change Skepticism and Denial: An Introduction," *American Behavioral Scientist* 57 (2013): 691–698; Ferenc Jankó et al., "Sources of Doubt: Actors, Forums, and Language of Climate Change Skepticism," *Scientometrics* 124 (2020): 2251–2277; Raul P. Lejano, "Ideology and the Narrative of Climate Skepticism," *Bulletin of the American Meteorological Society* 100 (2019): ES415–ES421; Charles W. Schmidt, "A Closer Look at Climate Change Skepticism," *Environmental Health Perspectives* 118 (2010): A536–A540.

17. Useful starting places include Hervé Le Treut et al., "Historical Origins of Climate Change Science," in *Climate Change 2007: The Physical Science Basis: Contribution of Working Group 1 to the Fourth Assessment Report of the Intergovernmental Panel on Climate Change,* ed. S. Solomon et al. (Cambridge: Cambridge University Press, 2007); IPCC 2013, *Climate Change 2013: The Physical Science Basis: Contribution of Working Group 1 to the Fifth Assessment Report of the Intergovernmental Panel on Climate Change* (Cambridge: Cambridge University Press, 2013). The IPCC process and reports have hardly been without challenge and controversy. See Eli Kintisch, "IPCC / Climategate Criticism Roundup," *Science,* Feb. 15, 2010.

18. On the nature of GMO opposition, see Edward B. Royzman, Corey Cusimano, Stephen Metas, and Robert F. Leeman, "Is Opposition to Genetically Modified Food

'Morally Absolutist'? A Consequence-Based Perspective," *Perspectives on Psychological Science* 15 (2020): 250–272.

19. See Nassim Nicholas Taleb, "The Precautionary Principle (with Application to the Genetic Modification of Organisms)," *ArXive* (2014).

20. In the United States, a 2016 report of the National Academies of Science is one of the principal sources of assurance on GMO safety. National Academies of Science, *Genetically Engineered Crops: Experience and Prospects* (Washington, DC: National Academies Press, 2016). To the same effect, and reporting on the similar conclusions of the American Academy for the Advancement of Science and other high-prestige scientific groups, see Jane E. Brody, "Are G.M.O. Foods Safe?," *New York Times,* Apr. 2, 2018, D5; Niras Chokshi, "Stop Bashing G.M.O. Foods, More than 100 Nobel Laureates Say," *New York Times,* June 30, 2016; Mark Lynas, "GMO Safety Debate Is Over," May 23, 2016, at www.allianceforscience.cornell.edu; William Saletan, "Unhealthy Fixation," *Slate,* July 15, 2015. But the "in the United States" modifier in the text is important, as the views outside the United States, and especially in western Europe, are very different and substantially more skeptical of GMO safety. See Angelika Hilbeck et al., "No Scientific Consensus on GMO Safety," *Environmental Sciences Europe* 27 (2015), art. 4.

21. On the difficult issue of how nonexperts are to evaluate expert opinion as evidence when there is genuine expert disagreement, see Ben Almassi, "Conflicting Expert Testimony and the Search for Gravitational Waves," *Philosophy of Science* 76 (2009): 570–584; David Christensen, "The Epistemology of Disagreement: The Good News," *Philosophical Review* 116 (2007): 187–217; Gideon Rosen. "Nominalism, Naturalism, Epistemic Relativism," *Philosophical Perspectives* 15 (2001): 69–91.

22. And see, with an admirable change of mind on this very issue, Gary Comstock, "Ethics and Genetically Modified Foods," in *The Philosophy of Food,* ed. David M. Kaplan (Berkeley: University of California Press, 2012), 122–139.

23. See Jelani Cobb, "African-American Resistance to the Covid-19 Vaccine Reflects a Broader Problem," *New Yorker,* Dec. 19, 2020; Amelia M. Jamison, Sandra Crouse Quinn, and Vicki S. Fellmuth, "'You Don't Trust a Government Vaccine': Narratives of Institutional Trust and Influenza Vaccination among African-American and White Adults," *Social Science and Medicine* 222 (2019): 87–94; Peng-jun Lu et al., "Racial and Ethnic Disparities in Vaccination Average among Adult Populations in the U.S.," *Vaccine* 33 (supp.) (2015): D83–D91.

24. See Jonathan M. Berman, *Anti-Vaxxers: How to Challenge a Misinformed Movement* (Cambridge, MA: MIT Press, 2020); Anna Kirkland, *Vaccine Court: The Law and Politics of Public Inquiry* (New York: NYU Press, 2016); Gregory A Poland and Robert M. Jacobson, "The Age-Old Struggle against the Antivaccinationists," *New England Journal of Medicine* 364 (2011): 97–99; Robert M. Wolfe and Lisa K. Sharp, "Anti-Vaccinationists Past and Present," *British Medical Journal* 325 (2002): 430–432.

25. In particular, see the federal Institute of Medicine's extensive study of all of the then-existing studies. Institute of Medicine, *Immunization Safety Review: Vaccines and Autism* (Washington, DC: National Academies Press, 2004).

26. Nathan Ballantyne, "Epistemic Trespassing," *Mind* 128 (2019): 367–395, revised as chapter 8 in Ballantyne, *Knowing Our Limits* (New York: Oxford University Press, 2019), 195–219.

27. See Atomic Heritage Foundation, "Leo Szilard's Fight to Stop the Bomb," at www .atomicheritage.org.

28. Wilson D. Miscamble, *The Most Controversial Decision: Truman, the Atomic Bomb, and the Defeat of Japan* (Cambridge: Cambridge University Press, 2005); Richard Rhodes, *The Making of the Atomic Bomb* (New York: Simon and Schuster, 1986).

Chapter 10. The Science of Crime

1. Daubert v. Merrell Dow Pharmaceuticals, Inc., 509 U.S. 579 (1993), followed, importantly, by General Electric Co. v. Joiner, 522 U.S. 136 (1997), and Kumho Tire Co. v. Carmichael, 526 U.S. 137 (1999). The Supreme Court's decisions on expert evidence are interpretations of the *Federal Rules of Evidence* and are not based on the US Constitution. Accordingly, they are not binding on state courts, although most (but not all) states have followed the Supreme Court's lead. See Paul C. Giannelli, "*Daubert* in the States," *Criminal Law Bulletin* 34 (1998): 154–166. Although the Supreme Court's insistence that scientific and other expert evidence must be determined by the trial judge to be reliable before it can be admitted into evidence applies to all cases, the Court's decisions arose in civil cases involving tort liability and not criminal cases involving forensic identification.

2. See Brandon L. Garrett and Peter J. Neufeld, "Invalid Forensic Science Testimony and Wrongful Convictions," *Virginia Law Review* 95 (2009): 1–97; Jon B. Gould, Julia Carrano, Richard A. Leo, and Katie Hail-Jares, "Predicting Erroneous Convictions," *Iowa Law Review* 99 (2014): 471–517.

3. An early skeptic was US District Judge Louis Pollak, although he was subsequently skeptical of his own skepticism. United States v. Llera Plaza, 179 F. Supp. 2d 1192 (E.D. Pa. 2001), vacated at 188 F. Supp. 2d 549 (2002). More comprehensively, see American Association for the Advancement of Science, *Forensic Science Assessment: A Quality and Gap Analysis of Latent Fingerprint Examination* (Washington, DC: AAAS, 2017); Erica Beecher-Monas, *Evaluating Scientific Evidence: An Interdisciplinary Framework for Intellectual Due Process* (New York: Cambridge University Press, 2007), 104–109; Brandon L. Garrett and Gregory Mitchell, "How Jurors Evaluate Fingerprint Evidence: The Relative Importance of Match Language, Method Information and Error Acknowledgment," *Journal of Empirical Legal Studies* 10 (2013): 484–511; Garrett and Mitchell, "The Proficiency of Experts," *University of Pennsylvania Law Review* 166 (2018): 901–960; Jonathan J. Koehler, "Fingerprint Error Rates and Proficiency Tests: What They Are and Why They Matter," *Hastings Law Journal* 59 (2008): 1077–1100; Gregory Mitchell and Brandon L. Garrett, "The Impact of Proficiency Testing Information and Error Aversions on the Weight Given to Fingerprint Evidence," *Behavioral Science and Law* 37 (2019):195–210; Jennifer L. Mnookin, "Fingerprints: Not a Gold Standard," *Issues in Science and Technology* 20 (2003): 47–

54; Jason M. Tangen, Matthew B. Thompson, and Duncan J. McCarthy, "Identifying Fingerprint Expertise," *Psychological Science* 22 (2011): 995–997.

4. National Research Council, *Strengthening Forensic Science in the United States: A Path Forward* (Washington, DC: National Academies Press, 2009). A more recent report, somewhat narrower in focus, largely but not completely confirms much of the 2009 report's skepticism. President's Council of Advisors on Science and Technology (PCAST), *Forensic Science in Criminal Courts: Ensuring Scientific Validity of Feature-Comparison Methods,* available at https://obamawhitehouse.archives.gov/sites/default/files/microsites/ostp/PCAST/pcast_forensic_science_report_final_pdf (2016). And for an extensive and revealing account of how the forensics community reacted and adapted to the 2009 National Research Council report, see Beth A. Bechky, *Blood, Powder, and Residue: How Crime Labs Translate Evidence into Proof* (Princeton, NJ: Princeton University Press, 2021).

5. Itiel E. Dror and Nicholas Scurich, "(Mis)use of Scientific Measurements in Forensic Science," *Forensic Science International: Synergy* 2 (2020): 330–338; see, in the context of testimony by a ballistics expert, United States v. Glynn, 578 F. Supp. 2d 567 (S.D.N.Y. 2008); United States v. Montiero, 407 F. Supp. 2d 351 (D. Mass. 2006). For the views of a less skeptical judge, see United States v. Casey, 928 F. Supp. 2d 397 (D. Puerto Rico, 2013). And most recently, also less skeptical, see United States v. Johnson, 2019 WL1130258 (S.D.N.Y., Mar. 11, 2019).

6. United States v. Cantoni, 2019 WL1259630 (E.D.N.Y., Mar. 19, 2019).

7. See Nancy Ritter, "The Science behind Firearm and Tool Mark Examination," *National Institute of Justice Journal* 274 (Dec. 2014); John Song et al., "Estimating Error Rates for Firearm Identification in Forensic Science," *Forensic Science International* 284 (2018): 15–32.

8. United States v. Glynn. Other judges have been more willing to allow qualified experts to use less qualified language. United States v. Johnson.

9. See, famously, United States v. Spock, 416 F.2d 165 (1st Cir. 1969). Benjamin Spock, famous for his books on child rearing, was an active member of the Vietnam-era antiwar movement and had urged draft-eligible men to take various actions (including destroying their draft cards) in violation of Selective Service System regulations. Although Dr. Spock would have preferred to have had his conviction for counseling and abetting violation of the Selective Service Act reversed on the grounds of the unconstitutionality of the Act, the unconstitutionality of the Vietnam War, or his rights to freedom of speech under the First Amendment, in fact the appeals court overturned the jury verdict because the judge had required the jury to answer a series of questions—special questions, in the standard terminology—keyed to the particular elements of the offense, rather than permitting them simply to find the defendant guilty or not guilty.

10. See United States v. Harris, 2020 WL 6488714 (D.D.C., Nov. 4, 2020). In United States v. Tibbs, 2019 WL 4359486 (D.C. Super. Ct., Sept. 5, 2019), the judge also discussed the differences between genuine peer review and the kinds of review that preceded publication in a professional ballistics journal. For the latter, the reviewers

knew who had written the article, and the authors knew who the reviewers were, both facts casting doubt on the soundness of peer review in legitimating a method by virtue of its publication. Moreover, the publication was accessible only to members of the typically prosecution-employed and prosecution-aligned community of professional ballistics examiners, thus depriving the results of scrutiny by those most likely to identify defects in the methods.

11. Although the distinction between admissibility and weight is a technical legal one, it is applicable to all uses of evidence in all contexts. Outside of the courtroom, the counterpart of admissibility is the decision to treat some fact as evidence in the first place. And this is a decision that, in theory, is independent of the question of how much weight that single piece of evidence will have when considered alongside all of the other evidence we have.

12. Roy N. King and Derek J. Koehler, "Illusory Correlations in Graphological Inference," *Journal of Experimental Psychology: Applied* 6 (2000): 336–348; Carla Dazzi and Luigi Pedrabissi, "An Empirical Study of Handwriting Analysis," *Psychological Reports* 105 (2009): 1255–1268; Anne Trubek, "Sorry, Graphology Isn't Real Science," *JSTOR Daily,* May 17, 2017, at www.daily.jstor.org. Note the confusing use of the term "graphology" to refer to the use of handwriting to describe personality or even predict the future, which has no empirical basis, but also to describe the use of handwriting to identify the writer, a method that has at least some empirical basis, even though the questions of how much and how we know how much are exactly the matters at issue.

13. For a Federal Bureau of Investigation description of the methods, see Diana Harrison, Ted M. Burkes, and Danielle Seiger, "Handwriting Examination: Meeting the Challenges of Science and the Law," *Forensic Science Communications* 11, no. 4 (2009), available at www.archives.fbi.gov. And for a recent comprehensive description of the methods, but cited with the caution that the author makes his living by using those methods, see Ron Morris, *Forensic Handwriting Identification,* 2nd ed. (Cambridge, MA: Academic Press, 2021).

14. Almeciga v. Center for Investigative Reporting, Inc., 185 F. Supp. 3d 401 (S.D.N.Y. 2016) (Rakoff, J.); Samuel R. Gross, "Detection of Deception: The Case of Handwriting Expertise," *Virginia Law Review* 87 (2001): 1847–1855; Michael Risinger, Mark P. Denbeaux, and Michael J. Saks, "Exorcism of Ignorance as a Proxy for Rational Knowledge: The Lessons of Handwriting Identification Expertise," *University of Pennsylvania Law Review* 137 (1989): 731–792.

15. See Michael D. Risinger, "Cases Involving the Reliability of Handwriting Identification Evidence since the Decision in *Daubert,*" *Tulsa Law Review* 43 (2013): 477–596.

16. See Kristy Martire, Bethany Gowns, and Danielle Navarro, "What Do the Experts Know? Calibration, Precision, and the Wisdom of Crowds among Forensic Handwriting Experts," *Psychonomic Bulletin and Review* 25 (2018): 2346–2355. See also National Institute of Standards and Technology, Working Group on Human Factors in Handwriting Examination, *Forensic Handwriting Examination and Human Factors* (Washington, DC: US Department of Commerce, 2020).

17. Compare *Almeciga* with United States v. Pitts, 2018 WL1116550 (E.D.N.Y.. Feb. 26, 2018).
18. 880 F. Supp. 1027 (S.D.N.Y. 1995).
19. For the claim, consistent with *Starzecpyel* but going further, that the question should not be science or not science, but, instead, whether some approach, science or not, was empirically sound, see Susan Haack, "An Epistemologist in the Bramble Bush: At the Supreme Court with Mr. Joiner," *Journal of Health Politics, Policy and Law* 20 (2001): 217–248.
20. Kumho Tire Co. v. Carmichael. *Kumho Tire* involved a plaintiff's witness in a products liability tort case, the witness purporting to be an expert in tire failure analysis. The witness testified that the blowout on an old and practically bald tire that had been consistently poorly maintained and incorrectly inflated was nevertheless caused by defective manufacture. And because the witness's methods of visual and tactile examination of the tire had never been tested in any way, the Supreme Court appeared to treat this as just the kind of junk science or junk expertise that had inspired the Court's entry into the area in the first place.
21. If the correct degree of acknowledgment of the importance of avoiding false convictions is already built into the "proof beyond a reasonable doubt" standard, then is heightening the requirements even further for prosecution use of otherwise relevant and admissible evidence a type of "double counting"? Yes, suggests Larry Laudan in *Truth, Error and the Criminal Law: An Essay in Legal Epistemology* (Cambridge: Cambridge University Press, 2006).
22. See John T. Rago, "A Fine Line between Chaos and Creation: Lessons on Innocence Reform from the Pennsylvania Eight," *Widener Law Review* 12 (2006): 359–441.
23. A sensationalized and plainly ballistics-friendly account of the case is Colin Evans, *Slaughter on a Snowy Morn: A Tale of Murder, Corruption and the Death Penalty Case that Revolutionised the American Courtroom* (London: Icon Books, 2010).
24. For an extended and well-argued suggestion to just this effect, see Christopher Slobogin, *Proving the Unprovable: The Role of Law, Science, and Speculation in Adjudicating Culpability and Dangerousness* (New York: Oxford University Press, 2007), 131–144.
25. See, for example, United States v. Bell, 833 F.2d 272 (11th Cir. 1987); United States v. Lieberman, 637 F.2d 95 (2d Cir. 1980); United States v. Rich, 580 F.2d 929 (9th Cir. 1978).
26. See, for example, Brandon L. Garrett, *Autopsy of a Crime Lab: Exposing the Flaws in Forensics* (Berkeley: University of California Press, 2021).
27. Useful guides to DNA evidence include National Research Council, *The Evaluation of Forensic DNA Evidence* (Washington, DC: National Academies Press, 1996); David H. Kaye and George Sensabaugh, "Reference Guide on DNA Identification Evidence," in National Research Council / Federal Judicial Center, *Reference Manual of Scientific Evidence* (Washington, DC: National Academies Press, 2011), 129–210; William C. Thompson, "Forensic DNA Evidence: The Myth of Infallibility," in *Genetic Explanations: Sense and Nonsense,* ed. Sheldon Krimsky and Jeremy Gruber (Cambridge, MA: Harvard University Press, 2013), 227–255.
28. See David Faigman et al., *Modern Scientific Evidence,* 7th ed. (St. Paul, MN: Thomson / West, 2020), vol. 4, § 30:19. On the interrelationship between the ideal

statistical probability and the statistical probability of laboratory error, compare Margaret A. Berger, "Laboratory Error Seen through the Lens of Science and Policy," *U.C. Davis Law Review* 30 (1997): 1081–1111, with Jonathan J. Koehler, "Why DNA Likelihood Ratios Should Account for Error (Even When a National Research Council Report Says They Should Not)," *Jurimetrics* 37 (1997): 425–437.

29. Ex parte Perry v. State; 586 So.2d 242 (Ala. 1991); United States v. Beasley, 102 F.3d 1440 (8th Cir. 1996); People v. Venegas, 954 P.2d 525 (Cal. 1998).

30. Presenting DNA statistics in this way, and omitting the crucial "no other evidence" qualification, is an example of the "defense attorney's fallacy," no more and no less a fallacy than the prosecutor's fallacy of arguing that the existence of a very small probability of a single random match coming from anyone other than the defendant proves by itself that the defendant is guilty beyond a reasonable doubt. William C. Thompson and Edward L. Schumann, "Interpretation of Statistical Evidence in Criminal Trials: The Prosecutor's Fallacy and the Defense Attorney's Fallacy," *Law and Human Behavior* 11 (1987): 167–187. The DNA revolution has inspired a large literature on whether the statistics involved can be understood by jurors (and, for that matter, judges). See D. H. Kaye and Jonathan J. Koehler, "Can Jurors Understand Probabilistic Evidence?," *Journal of the Royal Statistical Society, Series A* 154 (1991): 75–81; Jonathan J. Koehler, "The Psychology of Numbers in the Courtroom: How to Make DNA Statistics Seem Impressive or Insufficient," *Southern California Law Review* 74 (2001): 1275–1306; Jason Schklar and Shari Seidman Diamond, "Juror Reactions to DNA Evidence: Errors and Expectancies," *Law and Human Behavior* 23 (1999): 159–184.

31. For a much more detailed (and sophisticated) analysis of the evidentiary force of DNA tests from a Bayesian perspective, see Ian Ayres and Barry Nalebuff, "The Rule of Probabilities: A Practical Approach for Applying Bayes' Rule to the Analysis of DNA Evidence," *Stanford Law Review* 67 (2015): 1447–1503. See also David J. Balding, *Weight-of-Evidence for Forensic DNA Profiles* (Chichester, UK: John Wiley, 2005); Bess Stiffelman, "No Longer the Gold Standard: Probabilistic Genotyping Is Changing the Nature of DNA Evidence in Criminal Trials," *Berkeley Journal of Criminal Law* 24 (2019): 110–146.

32. Greg Handikian, Emily West, and Olga Akselrod, "The Genetics of Innocence: Analysis of 194 U.S. DNA Exonerations," *Annual Review of Genomics and Human Genetics* 12 (2011): 97–120; Gerald LaPorte, "Wrongful Convictions and DNA Exonerations: Understanding the Role of Forensic Science," *National Institute of Justice Journal* 279 (Apr. 2018): 1–16.

Chapter 11. The Expanding Domain of Expertise

1. See https://www.iapcollege.com/program/lifestyle-expert-certificate-course-online/.

2. The philosopher Karl Popper famously refused to think of Freudian (or any form of) psychoanalysis as scientific. Karl R. Popper, *Conjectures and Refutations: The*

Growth of Scientific Knowledge, 4th ed. (London: Routledge and Kegan Paul, 1972), 33–65; Popper, Realism and the Aim of Science, ed. W. W. Bartley III (Totowa, NJ: Rowman and Littlefield, 1983), 159–193. Even after Daubert v. Merrell Dow Pharmaceuticals, Inc., 509 U.S. 579 (1993), however, courts have recognized Freudian psychology as legitimate expertise. United States v. Rouse, 100 F.3d 560 (8th Cir. 1996); Clark v. Edison, 881 F. Supp. 2d 192 (D. Mass. 2012).

3. The sentence in the text was written prior to the appearance of the 2021 movie Minari, in which chicken sexing plays a surprisingly large role.

4. See R. D. Martin, The Specialist Chick Sexer (Box Hill, Victoria, Australia: Bernal, 1994); Irving Biederman and Margaret M. Shiffrar, "Sexing Day-Old Chicks: A Case Study and Expert Systems Analysis of a Difficult Perceptual-Learning Task," Journal of Experimental Psychology: Learning, Memory and Cognition 13 (1987): 640–645; James McWilliams, "The Lucrative Art of Chicken Sexing," Pacific Standard, Sept. 8, 2018, at https://psmag.com/magazine/the-lucrative-art-of-chicken-sexing.

5. Taylor Dafoe, "A Deep-Pocketed Art Collector Just Dropped More than $92 Million at Sotheby's on This Pristine Botticelli Portrait," Artnet, Jan. 28, 2021.

6. These, in descending order of authenticity, historical importance, and, commonly, value, are the descriptions typically given by the major auction houses to the works they are offering at auction. The "best" description would contain none of these qualifiers, and thus a description of a painting as simply "Botticelli" would indicate the auction house's own opinion (presumably expert-certified) that Botticelli actually painted the work being offered.

7. For a good laugh, and references to other good laughs, see John Mariani, "The Uselessness of Winespeak," Forbes, July 2, 2019.

8. Denis Dutton calls this "nominal" authenticity, as distinguished from the more ephemeral "expressive" authenticity, the latter being the judgment about whether the work genuinely expresses what is important about the artist or about the genre in which the work is created. Denis Dutton, "Authenticity in Art," in The Oxford Handbook of Aesthetics, ed. Jerrold Levinson (New York: Oxford University Press, 2003), 258–274.

9. In addition to the references in Chapter 2, see John Godley, Van Meegeren: Master Forger (New York: Scribner's, 1967); Frederik H. Kreuger, Han van Meegeren Revisited: His Art and the List of His Works (Delft: Quantes, 2013). On July 7, 2004, Sotheby's sold Vermeer's A Young Woman Seated at the Virginal, which had taken ten years to authenticate to Sotheby's (and, presumably, the buyer's) satisfaction, for slightly over $30 million dollars. On November 2, 2020, an oil painting by van Meegeren sold at auction in The Hague, Netherlands, for $1,046, and on December 9, 2020, a van Meegeren chalk drawing sold in the same location for $641. Q.E.D. (www.artprice.com).

10. See Ronald Spencer, ed., The Expert versus the Object: Judging Fakes and False Attributions in the Visual Arts (New York: Oxford University Press, 2004). Also useful is Michael Findlay, The Value of Art: Money, Power, Beauty (New York: Prestel, 2014), at 42–43.

11. Daubert.

12. "The art world places little faith in signatures. An expert on Jackson Pollock once explained why. 'How long would it take you to learn to sign Pollock's signature' he asked, 'and how long would it take you to learn to *paint* like Pollock?'" Edward Dolnick, *The Forger's Spell: A True Story of Vermeer, Nazis, and the Greatest Arty Hoax of the Twentieth Century* (New York: HarperCollins, 2008), 151. Amusingly, one of the forgeries that brought about the demise of the art gallery Knoedler was an alleged Pollock with the signature misspelled as "Pollok." Patricia Cohen, "Note to Forgers: Don't Forget the Spell Check," *New York Times*, July 11, 2014.

13. An accessible discussion of such methods is Jehane Ragai, *The Scientist and the Forger: Insights into the Scientific Detection of Forgery in Paintings* (London: Imperial College Press, 2015). And for a practitioner's insight into how forgers might attempt to defeat those methods, see Eric Hebborn, *The Art Forger's Handbook* (Woodstock, NY: Overlook Press, 2004).

14. See Lluís Peñuelas I Reixach, "The Authentication of Artworks," *in The Authorship, Authentication and Falsification of Artworks* (Barcelona: Poligrafa, 2011), 124–153. This sense of subjective is to be distinguished from the sense in which taste is subjective. Monet's being a better painter than Guillaumin is a largely subjective judgment because there is no actual fact of the matter, but this painting being by Monet or not may be subjective in the different sense because the evidence is unclear and interpretation and judgment become essential.

15. Indeed, a common characteristic—or pathology—of many art authentication experts is that they take the evidence produced by their own "eye" as being better than the scientific evidence, even when the two forms of evidence are directly in conflict. See Dolnick, *The Forger's Spell,* and the various contributions in Spencer, *The Expert versus the Object.*

16. See Cedric Neumann and Hal Stern, "Forensic Examination of Fingerprints: Past, Present, and Future," *Chance* 29 (2016): 9–16. Modern methods have moved beyond counting points of similarity.

17. Moreover, the personal incentives of authenticators might lead them to have higher or lower personal burdens of proof. A past failure might lead one authenticator to use an elevated burden of proof in order to avoid another mistake, but a past failure might lead a different authenticator to have a lower burden of proof in an attempt at redemption, as with Abraham Bredius, the mistaken authenticator of the most famous Vermeer forgery. Dolnick, *The Forger's Spell.*

18. Sociological in the sense of the collective judgment of the community of experts themselves, and the collective judgment of the community of consumers of the expert opinions.

19. Susan Mulcahy, "Why Were So Many Stettheimer Art Works Up for Sale? Not All Were Real," *New York Times*, Feb. 7, 2021, C1.

20. This assumes that, at least for museums, one or two cases of display of inauthentic artworks would be less fatal to its reputation than would be the same number or percentage of instances of inauthenticity for an auction house or dealer. No one will stop going to the Louvre if they take down two or three paintings revealed to

be forgeries. At some point, of course, museums displaying a large number of works known to be inauthentic would lose their clientele as well.

21. Van Meegeren. Vermeer painted no such painting, although van Meegeren was able successfully to persuade many experts and museums otherwise. Dolnick, *The Forger's Spell.*

22. No, said the 1964 Commission on the Assassination of President Kennedy (the Warren Commission). Yes, say more than a half century of conspiracy theories, some of which are described and debunked in Sean Munger, "Oswald Acted Alone: Faith vs. Fact in the Assassination of John F. Kennedy," at www.SeanMunger.com (Nov. 22, 2020).

23. Yes, said a Norfolk County jury, which found them guilty, and yes, said Governor Alvan Fuller, who refused to commute their death sentences. No, said a large number of distinguished contemporary commentators, including then-professor and later-Supreme Court justice Felix Frankfurter. See Paul Avrich, *Sacco and Vanzetti: The Anarchist Background* (Princeton, NJ: Princeton University Press, 1980); Moshik Temkin, *The Sacco-Vanzetti Affair: America on Trial* (New Haven, CT: Yale University Press, 2009).

24. This question is the subject of active and occasionally heated debate. For an overview of the positions and of the evidence marshaled for various answers, see "When Was New Zealand First Settled?," in *Te Ara: The Encyclopedia of New Zealand,* at www .teara.govt.nz.

25. An account of the dispute can be found in Adam Serwer, "The Fight over the 1619 Project Is Not about the Facts," *The Atlantic,* Dec. 23, 2019. And although the article's title says that the dispute is not about the facts, the critics, as the article makes clear, claim the dispute is about "matters of verifiable fact." So there are two disputes. One dispute is about the facts. And the other dispute is about whether the dispute is about the facts.

26. Among literally scores—maybe hundreds—of books on the *Titanic,* the classic is Walter Lord, *A Night to Remember* (New York: Henry Holt, 2005) (orig. pub. 1955). Of the more recent comprehensive contributions, see Charles Pellegrino, *Farewell, Titanic: Her Final Legacy* (Hoboken, NJ: John Wiley, 2012). Regarding whether Garfield could have been saved if he had been treated by physicians who were not excessively self-confident, the answer is "probably yes." See Candice Millard, *Destiny of the Republic: A Tale of Madness, Medicine and the Murder of a President* (New York: Anchor Books, 2012).

27. They almost certainly were not. See "The Trouble with False Teeth," at www .mountvernon.org, providing strong support for the hippopotamus ivory hypothesis.

28. Plausibly yes. See G. W. Bernard, *Anne Boleyn: Fatal Attractions* (New Haven, CT: Yale University Press, 2010).

29. See Carolyn E. Holmes, *The Black and White Rainbow: Reconciliation, Opposition, and Nation-Building in Democratic South Africa* (Ann Arbor: University of Michigan Press, 2020).

30. See P. H. Nowell-Smith, *What Actually Happened* (Lawrence: University of Kansas Press, 1971); and, for example, R. F. Atkinson, *Knowledge and Explanation in History: An Introduction to the Philosophy of History* (Ithaca, NY: Cornell University Press, 1978), 39–68.

31. See, for overviews, Loren Haskins and Kirk Jeffrey, *Understanding Quantitative History* (Cambridge, MA: MIT Press, 1990); Konrad H. Jarausch and Kenneth A. Hardy, *Quantitative Methods for Historians: A Guide to Research, Data, and Statistics* (Chapel Hill: University of North Carolina Press, 1991). Several journals, especially *Cliodynamics: The Journal of Quantitative History and Cultural Evolution* and *Historical Methods: A Journal of Quantitative and Interdisciplinary History,* have the focus described in the text.

32. An interesting contrast is between the adjudication of guilt or liability in a legal proceeding and the adjudication of guilt by a referee in football, basketball, or hockey. In these and many other sports, and certainly before the confounding introduction of video replays, the referee would see something and immediately adjudicate it by calling a foul or some other sort of infraction. And although such determinations themselves involve evidence, typically they are the evidence of first-person and simultaneous observation, a form of evidence not available in legal proceedings and rarely available to the historian.

33. See Gilbert J. Garraghan, *A Guide to Historical Method* (New York: Fordham University Press, 1946); Martha Howell and Walter Prevenier, *From Reliable Sources: An Introduction to Historical Methods* (Ithaca, NY: Cornell University Press, 2001); R. J. Shafer, *A Guide to Historical Method,* 3rd ed. (Homewood, IL: Dorsey Press, 1977); Torstén Thuren, *Källkritik* (Stockholm: Almqvist & Wiksellm 1997).

34. See Margaret Sullivan, "How Do You Use an Anonymous Source? The Mysteries of Journalism Everyone Should Know," *Washington Post,* Dec. 10, 2017. As the title of Sullivan's article indicates, the use of anonymous sources as evidence has traditionally been discouraged, but the best description of that principle, even for the elite print press, is probably "soft and getting softer."

35. See Charles L. Barzun, "Rules of Weight," *Notre Dame Law Review* 83 (2008): 1957–2018; John H. Wigmore, "Required Numbers of Witnesses: A Brief History of the Numerical System in England," *Harvard Law Review* 15 (1901): 83–108.

Chapter 12. The Relevance of the Past to the Present

1. Arlette Saenz, "Neera Tanden to Keep Reaching Out to Senator Next Week as Confirmation Is in Jeopardy," www.cnn.com (Feb. 20, 2021). The nomination was subsequently withdrawn.

2. "White House Calls Cohen Liar Ahead of Testimony," *U.S. New and World Report,* Feb. 26, 2019.

3. Alan Blinder, "Was That Ralph Northam in Blackface? An Inquiry Ends without Answers," *New York Times,* May 22, 2019. Although there remains uncertainty about whether a picture showing one student in blackface and another in Ku Klux Klan

garb included Northam, he did acknowledge that he had appeared in blackface while a medical student.

4. E. J. Dionne Jr., "Biden Admits Plagiarism in School but Says It Was Not 'Malevolent,'" *New York Times,* September 18, 1987.

5. Constance L. Hays, "Martha Stewart's Sentence: The Overview; 5 Months in Jail, and Stewart Vows, 'I'll Be Back,'" *New York Times,* July 17, 2004.

6. Pritha Sarkar, "Tennis: Injury Cheats Should Be Shamed on Court, Says Veteran Physio," www.reuters.com, July 8, 2017.

7. Karen Crouse, "Patrick Reed's Club Hit the Sand: Now There's a Dust-Up," *New York Times,* December 12, 2019.

8. Indeed, a question arose at the Farmers Insurance Open in San Diego on January 30, 2021, about whether the Patrick Reed mentioned in Crouse, "Patrick Reed's Club," had improperly claimed relief from an "embedded" golf ball on a wet day. Although an official called to the scene determined that Reed had done nothing wrong, Reed felt aggrieved because the same issue on the same day involving another competitor, Rory McElroy, had received less scrutiny. But because Reed had more of a history with rules issues than McElroy, the closer scrutiny of the former than the latter was hardly surprising. See Bob Harig, "Even in a Win, Patrick Reed Can't Escape His Own History," at www.espn.com (Jan. 31, 2021).

9. Rick Reilly, *Commander in Cheat: How Golf Explains Trump* (New York: Hachette, 2019). Cheating at golf appears to be a bipartisan activity. See Don van Natta Jr., "Presidential Mulligans: Taking Second Chances, Par for Clinton's Course," *New York Times,* Aug. 29, 1999; Brian Viner, "Slick Willy and Tricky Dicky Prove That Golf's Ethics Can Land Us All in the Rough," *The Independent,* May 20, 2006.

10. N. R. Kleinfeld, "Motorman's Colleagues Say He Drank at Work," *New York Times,* August 30, 1991.

11. Federal Rule of Evidence 404(b). For commentary, see Christopher Mueller, Laird Kirkpatrick, and Liesa Richter, *Evidence,* 6th ed. (New York: Wolters Kluwer, 2018), § 4.15 at pp. 200–207; Glen Weissenberger, "Making Sense of Extrinsic Act Evidence: Federal Rule of Evidence 404(b)," *Iowa Law Review* 70 (1985): 579–614. The basic principle long precedes the *Federal Rules of Evidence.* See Fleming James Jr. and John J. Dickinson, "Accident Proneness and Accident Law," *Harvard Law Review* 63 (1950): 769–795.

12. Two recent offerings featuring the "paid his debt to society" theme are *Boy A* (2007) and *Debt to Society* (2015).

13. Good lawyers know that there are many ways around the rule as just stated. But although the rule has many exceptions and many methods of avoiding it, the basic principle remains that past acts cannot be used to show a propensity to commit acts of that type, and thus a greater likelihood of having committed such an act on the occasion in question.

14. See Michelson v. United States, 335 U.S. 469 (1948); United States v. Rubio-Estrada, 857 F.2d 845 (1st Cir. 1988); John H. Wigmore, *Evidence at Trials at Common Law,* rev. Peter Tillers (New York: Wolters Kluwer, 1983), § 58.2; Paul S. Milich, "The De-

grading Character Rule in American Criminal Trials," *Georgia Law Review* 47 (2013): 775–800.

15. Spencer v. Texas, 385 U.S. 554, 575 (1967) (opinion of Warren, C.J.).

16. See United States v. Green, 617 F.3d 233 (3d Cir. 2011). A good overview of the American law is in Richard O. Lempert et al., *A Modern Approach to Evidence,* 5th ed. (St. Paul, MN: West Academic, 2014), 347–357. See also Thomas J. Reed, "The Development of the Propensity Rule in Federal Criminal Cases, 1840–1975," *University of Cincinnati Law Review* 51 (1982): 299–325. An important exception can be found in the controversial Federal Rules of Evidence 413–415, which permit exactly the otherwise prohibited propensity evidence in cases charging sexual misconduct, based largely on the even more controversial assumption that sexual offenses are more the product of uncontrollable tendencies than are other criminal acts. See Katherine Baker, "Once a Rapist? Motivational Evidence and Relevancy in Rape Law," *Harvard Law Review* 110 (1997): 563–624; Christina E. Wells and Erin Elliott Motley, "Reinforcing the Myth of the Crazed Rapist: A Feminist Critique of Recent Rape Legislation," *Boston University Law Review* 81 (2001): 127–198.

17. For an overview of the debates and positions, often characterized as the "person-situation" debate, see David C. Funder, "Personality," *Annual Review of Psychology* 52 (2001): 197–221.

18. See especially Gordon W. Allport, *The Person in Psychology: Selected Essays* (Boston: Beacon Press, 1968); Allport, *Personality and Psychological Interpretation* (Oxford: Henry Holt, 1937). More recently, and responding to many challenges, see Willia Fleeson and Eranda Jayawickreme, "Whole Trait Theory," *Journal of Research on Personality* 56 (2015): 82–92.

19. Stanley Milgram, *Obedience to Authority: An Experimental View* (New York: Harper and Row, 1974); Milgram, "Some Conditions of Obedience and Disobedience to Authority," *Human Relations* 18 (1965): 57–76; Milgram, "Behavioral Study of Obedience," *Journal of Abnormal and Social Psychology* 67 (1963): 371–378. On the controversies arising out of the experiments, see Thomas Blass, *The Man Who Shocked the World: The Life and Legacy of Stanley Milgram* (New York: Basic Books, 2004); Arthur G. Miller, *The Obedience Experiments: A Case Study of Controversy in Social Science* (New York: Praeger, 1986).

20. On the "situationist" reaction to the dispositionists, see Walter Mischel, "Toward an Integrative Science of the Person," *Annual Review of Psychology* 55 (2004): 1–22; Mischel, *Personality and Assessment* (Hoboken, NJ: Wiley, 1968). See also, with varying degrees of commitment to situationism, Lee Ross and Richard E. Nisbett, *The Personality and the Situation: Perspectives of Social Psychology* (New York: McGraw-Hill, 1991); John M. Darley and C. Daniel Batson, "From Jerusalem to Jericho: A Story of Dispositional and Situational Variables," *Journal of Personality and Social Psychology* 27 (1973): 100–108; Douglas T. Kenrick and David C. Funder, "Profiting from Controversy: Lessons from the Person-Situation Debate," *American Psychologist* 43 (1988): 23–24.

21. See Rodolfo Mendoza-Denton et al., "Person x Situation Interactionism in Self-Coding (I am . . . when . . .): Implications and Affect Regulation and Social Information Processing," *Journal of Personality and Social Psychology* 80 (2001): 533–544.

22. A nice overview of the various positions as applied to questions of evidence is Susan M. Davies, "Evidence of Character to Prove Conduct: A Reassessment of Relevancy," *Criminal Law Bulletin* 27 (1991): 504–537.

23. Commonwealth v. Adjutant, 800 N.E.2d 346 (Mass. 2003).

24. Commonwealth v. Pring-Wilson, 863 N.E.2d 936 (Mass. 2007). Rule 404(a)(2)(B) explicitly allows a defendant in a criminal case to "offer evidence of an alleged victim's pertinent trait."

25. Under Federal Rule of Evidence 401, a piece of evidence is relevant "if it has any tendency to make a [material] fact more or less probable than it would be without the evidence."

26. Maggie Severns, "Burr's Alleged Conflicts Extend beyond His Coronavirus-Related Stock Trades," *Politico*, May 15, 2020, www.politico.com.

27. I say only a "good chance" because, depending on the exact nature of the charges and other evidence, the earlier acts might be admissible to show knowledge even if not to show propensity.

28. The example is controversial, and supporters of the kinds of pit bull restrictions found in, for example, Belgium, Canada, New Zealand, Norway, most German states, and some American cities have been accused of "breedism," "canine racism," and worse. But the statistics—the evidence—support the conclusion that a randomly selected pit bull (America Staffordshire Terrier, technically) is more likely to be dangerously aggressive than a randomly selected dog without regard to breed. See Frederick Schauer, *Profiles, Probabilities, and Stereotypes* (Cambridge, MA: Harvard University Press, 2003).

Chapter 13. Seeing What We Want to See

1. The question is not about whether *Salvator Mundi* is a forged Leonardo, a topic—forgery—touched on in Chapter 2 and discussed in more depth in Chapter 11. Rather, the question is whether the painting was painted not by Leonardo but instead by one of his followers, students, disciples, or contemporaries. For a taste of the controversy, see Margaret Dalivalle, Martin Kemp, and Robert B. Simon, *Leonardo's Salvator Mundi and the Collecting of Leonardo in the Stuart Courts* (Oxford: Oxford University Press, 2019); Ben Lewis, *The Last Leonardo: The Secret Lives of the World's Most Expensive Painting* (New York: Random House / Ballantine Books, 2019); Dalya Alberge, "Leonardo Scholar Challenges Attribution of $450m Painting," *The Guardian*, Aug. 6, 2018; Brook Mason, "What It Takes for a Leonardo da Vinci Painting to Be Deemed Universally Authentic," *Architectural Digest*, May 22, 2019; Matthew Shaer, "The Invention of the 'Salvator Mundi' or, How to Turn a $1,000 Art-Auction Pickup into a $450 Million Masterpicce," at www.vulture.com (Apr. 14,

2019); Kevin Shau, "On Leonardo da Vinci's Salvator Mundi—Is it Authentic?," at Art-Direct (Apr. 15, 2019), www.medium.com.

2. Brad Raffensperger, "I Have Fought to Uphold the Integrity of Elections in Georgia. It Doesn't Matter if the Attacks Come from the Guy I Voted for or Not," *USA Today*, Nov. 25, 2020.

3. Roberta Herzberg, "McCloskey versus McIntyre: Implications of Contested Elections in a Federal Democracy," *Publius* 16 (1986): 93–109.

4. Jeffery A. Jenkins, "Partisanship and Contested Election Cases in the Senate, 1789–2002," *Studies in American Political Development* 19 (2005): 53–74.

5. For discussion, with references, see Frederick Schauer, "Facts and the First Amendment," *UCLA Law Review* 57 (2010): 897–919.

6. Ziva Kunda, "The Case for Motivated Reasoning," *Psychological Bulletin* 108 (1990): 440–498; Kunda, "Motivation and Inference: Self-Serving Generation and Evaluation of Evidence," *Journal of Personality and Social Psychology* 53 (1987): 636–647. See also Peter H. Ditto, David A. Pizarro, and David Tannenbaum, "Motivated Moral Reasoning," *Psychology of Learning and Motivation* 50 (2009): 307–338; Ziva Kunda, *Social Cognition: Making Sense of People* (Cambridge, MA: MIT Press, 1999); William M. P. Klein and Ziva Kunda, "Motivated Person Perception: Constructing Justifications for Desired Beliefs," *Journal of Experimental Social Psychology* 28 (1992): 145–168; Matthew J. Hornsey, "Why Facts Are Not Enough: Understanding and Managing the Motivated Rejection of Science," *Current Directions in Psychological Science* 23 (2020): 583–591; Stephan Lewondowsky and Klaus Oberauer, "Motivated Rejection of Science," *Current Directions in Psychological Science* 25 (2016): 217–222; Daniel C. Molden and E. Tory Higgins, "Motivated Thinking," in *The Oxford Handbook of Thinking and Reasoning,* ed. Keith Holyoak and Robert Morrison (Oxford: Oxford University Press, 2012), 390–409.

7. On myside bias, see Keith E. Stanovich and Richard F. West, "Natural Myside Bias Is Independent of Cognitive Ability," *Thinking and Reasoning* 13 (2007): 225–247; Keith E. Stanovich and Richard F. West, "On the Failure to Predict Myside Bias and One-Side Bias," *Thinking and Reasoning* 14 (2008): 129–167; Keith E. Stanovich, Richard F. West, and E. Toplak, "Myside Bias, Rational Thinking, and Intelligence," *Current Directions in Psychological Science* 22 (2013): 259–264. See also Vladimira Cavojová, Jakub Srol, and Magdalena Adamus, "My Point Is Valid, Yours Is Not: Myside Bias in Reasoning about Abortion," *Journal of Cognitive Psychology* 30 (2018): 656–669.

8. See Martin Baekgaard et al., "The Role of Evidence in Politics: Motivated Reasoning and Persuasion among Politicians," *British Journal of Political Science* 49 (2017): 1117–1140; Oliver James and Gregg G. Van Ryzin, "Motivated Reasoning about Public Performance: An Experimental Study of How Citizens Judge the Affordable Care Act," *Journal of Public Administration Research and Theory* 27 (2017): 197–209; Dan M. Kahan, "Ideology, Motivated Reasoning, and Cognitive Reflection," *Judgment and Decision Making* 8 (2013): 407–424; Kahan, "Foreword: Neutral Principles, Motivated Cognition, and Some Problems for Constitutional Law," *Harvard Law Review* 126 (2011): 1–77.

9. Naomi Oreskes and Erik M. Conway, *Merchants of Doubt: How a Handful of Scientists Obscured the Truth on Issues from Tobacco Smoke to Global Warming* (New York: Bloomsbury Press, 2010).

10. Sheila Jasanoff, *Science at the Bar: Law, Science, and Technology in America* (Cambridge, MA: Harvard University Press, 1995).

11. See Stephen J. Ceci and Wendy M. Williams, "The Psychology of Fact-Checking," *Scientific American,* Oct. 25, 2020; Chares G. Lord, Lee Ross, and Mark R. Lepper, "Biased Assimilation and Attitude Polarization: The Effects of Prior Theories on Subsequently Considered Evidence," *Journal of Personality ad Social Psychology* 37 (1979): 2098–2109.

12. See Norwood Russell Hanson, *Patterns of Discovery: An Inquiry into the Conceptual Foundations of Science* (Cambridge: Cambridge University Press, 1958). Especially when it comes to science and scientists, the idea is not without controversy. See Jerry Fodor, "Observation Reconsidered," *Philosophy of Science* 51 (1984): 23–43.

13. See Zina B. Ward, "On Value-Laden Science," *Studies in the History and Philosophy of Science,* https://doi.org/10.1016/j.shpsa.2020.09.06 (Oct. 21, 2020).

14. Julian Reiss and Jan Sprenger, "Scientific Objectivity," in *Stanford Encyclopedia of Philosophy,* https://plato.stanford.edu/archives/win2020/entries/scientific-objectivity/ (2020); Isaac Levi, "Must the Scientist Make Value Judgments?," *Journal of Philosophy* 57 (1960): 345–357.

15. A good overview is Raymond S. Nickerson, "Confirmation Bias: A Ubiquitous Phenomenon in Many Guises," *Review of General Psychology* 2 (1998): 175–220. See also Jane Beattie and Jonathan Baron, "Confirmation and Matching Biases in Hypothesis Testing," *Quarterly Journal of Experimental Psychology, Section A* 40 (1988): 269–297; P. C. Wason, "On the Failure to Eliminate Hypotheses in a Conceptual Task," *Quarterly Journal of Experimental Psychology* 12 (1960): 129–140.

16. Cass R. Sunstein, "The Law of Group Polarization," *Journal of Political Philosophy* 10 (2002): 175–195. See also Caitlin Drummind and Baruch Fischhoff, "Individuals with Greater Science Literacy and Education Have More Polarized Beliefs on Controversial Science Topics," *Proceedings of the National Academy of Science, USA,* 114 (2017): 9587–9592; David Schkade, Cass R. Sunstein, and Reid Hastie, "When Deliberation Produces Extremism," *Critical Review* 22 (2010): 227–252.

17. Judges are fond of quoting the sportscaster Vin Scully, who observed that "statistics are used much like a drunk uses a lamppost: for support, not illumination." In re Wachovia Corp. "Pick a Payment" Mortgage Marketing and Sales Practices Litigation, 2013 WL 5424963 (N.D. Cal. Sept. 25, 2013). Sadly, this could be said about much of the use of evidence too.

18. See Man-pui Sally Chan, Christopher R. Jones, Kathleen Hall Jamieson, and Dolores Albarracin, "Debunking: A Meta-Analysis of the Psychological Efficacy of Messages Countering Misinformation," *Psychological Science* 28 (2017): 1531–1546, finding that a detailed debunking message correlated positively with the persistence of the misinformation that the debunking message was intended to debunk. And see also Thomas T. Hills, "The Dark Side of Information Proliferation,"

Perspectives on Psychological Science 14 (2019): 323–330; David N. Rapp, "The Consequences of Reading Inaccurate Information," *Current Directions in Psychological Science* 25 (2016): 281–295.

19. Lauren Giella, "Fact Check: Did Marjorie Taylor Greene Perpetuate Parkland Shooting Conspiracy Theory?," *Newsweek,* Jan. 27, 2021; Andrew Solender, "Trump-Backed Candidate Marjorie Taylor Greene Promotes 9 / 11 Conspiracy Theory," *Forbes,* Aug. 13, 2020.

20. On just this usage of "Panglossian," here in the context of a resistance to recognizing that that which is morally bad might be legally correct, and that that which is morally good might nevertheless be illegal, see Jeffrey Brand-Ballard, *Limits of Legality: The Ethics of Lawless Judging* (New York: Oxford University Press, 2010), 86–88, 311–312. For my own use of Brand-Ballard's sense of Panglossianism, see Frederick Schauer, "Rights, Constitutionalism, and the Perils of Panglossianism," *Oxford Journal of Legal Studies* 38 (2018): 635–652.

21. See Troy H. Campbell and Aaron C. Kay, "Solution Aversion: On the Relation between Ideology and Motivated Disbelief," *Journal of Personality and Social Psychology* 107 (2014): 809–814; Dan H. Kahan, Hank Jenkins-Smith, and Donald Braman, "Cultural Cognition of Scientific Consensus," *Journal of Risk Research* 14 (2011): 147–174.

22. Overviews include Gerrit Antonides, *Psychology in Economics and Business* (Dordrecht: Springer, 1991), 193–214; Bertram Gawronski and Fritz Strack, eds., *Cognitive Consistency: A Foundational Principle in Social Cognition* (New York: Guilford Press, 2012); Dan Simon, Chadwick J. Snow, and Stephen J. Read, "The Redux of Cognitive Constraint Theories: Evidence by Constraint Satisfaction," *Journal of Personality and Social Psychology* 86 (2004): 814–837.

23. Leon Festinger, *Conflict, Decision, and Dissonance* (Stanford, CA: Stanford University Press, 1964); Eddie Harmon-Jones, ed., *Cognitive Dissonance: Reexamining a Pivotal Theory in Psychology,* 2nd ed. (Washington, DC: American Psychological Association, 2019); Eddie Harmon-Jones and Cindy Harmon-Jones, "Cognitive Dissonance Theory after 50 Years of Development," *Zeitschrift für Sozialpsychologie* 38 (2007): 7–16.

24. Jordan R. Axt, Mark J. Lamdaum, and Aaron C. Kay, "The Psychological Appeal of Fake-News Attributions," *Psychological Science* 31 (2020): 848–857.

25. Marianne Levine, "Democrats' Big Shift in Trump's Second Impeachment," *Politico,* Feb. 7, 2021, at www.politico.com.

26. Charles S. Taber and Milton Lodge, "Motivated Skepticism and the Evaluation of Political Beliefs," *American Journal of Political Science* 50 (2006): 755–769. Even more depressing is the way in which evidence countering a false belief may increase rather than decrease the persistence of the false belief. See Chan et al., "Debunking."

Index

AIDS, false beliefs about sources and causes of, 228

art, evidence in authentication of, 26, 187–196, 248n25

astrology, as pseudo-science, 149

atomic bomb, 163–164

Austin, J. L., 90, 262n10

authority, of experts and expertise, 158

Ballantyne, Nathan, 162–163

ballistics evidence, 168–170, 177–178, 180

Barrett, Justice Amy Coney, 5, 9, 145, 242n7

base rates, neglect of, 70

Bayes, Thomas, 24

Bayesian approaches to evidence, 24–29, 31–33, 182, 247nn20, 21

Bentham, Jeremy, 244n16

Berman, Judge Richard, 218

big data, 92

biases, in selecting, transmitting, and using evidence, 232–233

Blackstone, William, 39, 179–180

Blue Bus problem, 63–64. *See also* statistical evidence

Bok, Sissela, 115

Boleyn, Anne, 198

Botticelli, Sandro, 187–193, 196

Brady, Matthew, 141

burden of proof: conjunction problem and, 251n7; decision theory and, 39–40; in criminal and civil trials, 35–43, 54; generally, 34–57; proof beyond a reasonable doubt, 35–36; proof by clear and convincing evidence, 38–39; proof by preponderance of the evidence, 36; qualifying adjectives as indicating, xi, 51–54, 56; quantifying, 35–36; and Scottish "not proven" verdict, 37; and Title IX university disciplinary proceedings, 37–42. *See also* sexual assaults, statistical significance

Burr, Richard, 219

Bush, George W., false beliefs about, 227

Capitol, United States, January 2021 assault on, 89, 93, 135, 137

causation, evidence of, 255n32; probabilistic, 49, 255n32

character, as evidence of behavior, 211–217

chicken sexing, as expertise, 186–187

circumstantial evidence. *See* evidence: circumstantial

295